WITHDRAWN FROM
KENT STATE UNIVERSITY LIBRARIES

What Can I Do Now?

Computers

Books in the
What Can I Do Now? Series

Art
Computers
Engineering, Second Edition
Fashion
Health Care
Music
Nursing, Second Edition
Radio and Television, Second Edition
Safety and Security, Second Edition
Sports, Second Edition

What Can I Do Now?

Computers

Ferguson
An imprint of Infobase Publishing

What Can I Do Now? Computers

Copyright ©2007 by Infobase Publishing

All rights reserved. No part of this book may be reproduced or utilized in any form or by any means, electronic or mechanical, including photocopying, recording, or by any information storage or retrieval systems, without permission in writing from the publisher. For information contact:

Ferguson
An imprint of Infobase Publishing
132 West 31st Street
New York NY 10001

ISBN-10: 0-8160-6027-4
ISBN-13: 978-0-8160-6027-6

Library of Congress Cataloging-in-Publication Data

What can I do now? Computers.
   p. cm.
  Includes index.
  ISBN 0-8160-6027-4 (hc : alk. paper)
 1. Computer science—Vocational guidance—uvenile literature. 2. Information technology—Vocational guidance—Juvenile literature. 3. Computer science—Vocational guidance. I. J.G. Ferguson Publishing Company. II. Title: Computers.
  QA76.25.W48 2007
  004.023—dc22   2006029871

Ferguson books are available at special discounts when purchased in bulk quantities for businesses, associations, institutions, or sales promotions. Please call our Special Sales Department in New York at (212) 967-8800 or (800) 322-8755.

You can find Ferguson on the World Wide Web at http://www.fergpubco.com

Text design by Kerry Casey
Cover design by Takeshi Takahashi

Printed in the United States of America

VB Hermitage 10 9 8 7 6 5 4 3 2 1

This book is printed on acid-free paper.

All links and Web addresses were checked and verified to be correct at the time of publication. Because of the dynamic nature of the Web, some addresses and links may have changed since publication and may no longer be valid.

Contents

Introduction	1
Section 1: What Do I Need to Know About the Computer Industry?	3
Section 2: Careers	17
Computer and Video Game Designers	18
Computer Engineers	28
Computer Network Administrators	36
Computer Programmers	47
Computer Service Technicians	57
Computer Systems Programmer/Analysts	66
Quality Assurance Testers	76
Software Designers	86
Technical Support Specialists	95
Webmasters	106
Section 3: Do It Yourself	115
Section 4: What Can I Do Right Now?	125
Get Involved	126
Read a Book	162
Surf the Web	171
Ask for Money	178
Look to the Pros	190
Index	197

Introduction

If you're considering a career in computer science—which presumably you are since you're reading this book—you must realize that the better informed you are from the start, the better your chances of having a successful, satisfying career.

There is absolutely no reason to wait until you get out of high school to "get serious" about a career. That doesn't mean you have to make a firm, undying commitment right now, however. One of the biggest fears most people face at some point (sometimes more than once) is choosing the right career. Frankly, many people don't "choose" at all. They take a job because they need one, and all of a sudden 10 years have gone by and they wonder why they're stuck doing something they hate. Don't be one of those people! You have the opportunity right now—while you're still in high school and still relatively unencumbered with major adult responsibilities—to explore, to experience, to try out a work path. Or several paths if you're one of those overachieving types. Wouldn't you really rather find out sooner than later that you're not as interested in Web design as you thought? That maybe you'd prefer to be a computer engineer, or a technical support specialist, or a computer and video game designer?

There are many ways to explore the computer industry. This book gives you an idea of some of your options. Section 1, "What Do I Need to Know About the Computer Industry?" will give you an overview of the field—a little history, where it's at today, and promises of the future—as well as a breakdown of its structure (how it's organized) and a glimpse of some of its many career options.

Section 2, "Careers," includes 10 chapters, each describing in detail a specific computer or technician specialty. The educational requirements for these specialties range from some postsecondary training to advanced degrees. These chapters rely heavily on firsthand accounts from real people on the job. They'll tell you the skills and personal qualities you need, and the ups and downs of the job. You'll also find out about educational requirements (including specific high school and college classes), advancement possibilities, related jobs, salary ranges, and the future outlook.

In keeping with the secondary theme of this book (the primary theme being "You can do something now"), Section 3, "Do It Yourself," urges you to take charge and start your own programs and activities where none exist—at your school, in your community, or nationally.

The real meat of the book is in Section 4, "What Can I Do Right Now?" This is where you get busy and DO SOMETHING. The chapter "Get Involved" talks about volunteer and intern positions, as well as summer camps and summer college study, high school computer programs, and student computer organizations.

"Read a Book" is an annotated bibliography of books (some new, some old) and periodicals. If you're even remotely considering a career in the computer industry, reading a few books and checking out a few magazines is the easiest thing you can do. Don't stop with our list. Ask your librarian to point you to more computer-related materials.

The best way to explore the computer field is to jump right in and start doing it, but there are plenty of other ways to get into the computer mind-set. "Surf the Web" offers a short annotated list of computer-related Web sites where you can explore everything from computer history, educational requirements, and on-the-job accounts to competitions and activities.

"Ask for Money" is a sampling of computer scholarships. You need to be familiar with these because you're going to need money for school. You have to actively pursue scholarships; no one is going to come up to you in the hall one day and present you with a check because you're such a wonderful student. Applying for scholarships is work. It takes effort. And it must be done right and usually one year in advance of when you need the money.

"Look to the Pros" is the final chapter. It's a list of professional organizations that you can turn to for more information about accredited schools, education requirements, career descriptions, salary information, job listings, scholarships, and much more. Once you become a computer science student, you'll be able to join many of these. Time after time, professionals say that membership and active participation in a professional organization is one of the best ways to network (make valuable contacts) and gain recognition in your field.

High school can be a lot of fun. You may be involved in a lot of social and extracurricular activities, or maybe you are just biding your time until you graduate. Whichever your approach, take a minute and try to imagine your life five years from now. Ten years from now. Where will you be? What will you be doing? Whether you realize it or not, how you choose to spend your time now—studying, playing, watching TV, working at a fast food restaurant, hanging out, whatever—will have an impact on your future. Take a look at how you're spending your time now and ask yourself, "Where is this getting me?" If you can't come up with an answer, it's probably "nowhere." The choice is yours. No one is going to take you by the hand and lead you in the "right" direction. It's up to you. It's your life. You can do something about it right now!

SECTION 1

What Do I Need to Know About the Computer Industry?

Computers are everywhere. From computer games, e-mail, and music downloads to travel reservations, term papers, and innumerable business uses, computers have come to play a key role in our daily existence. Just a few of their countless advantages include saving us time, allowing us to gather hard-to-find information, and letting us keep in touch via the Internet with our friends, family, and coworkers. Millions of workers are involved in the computer and Internet industries, and many millions more will be needed in coming years. Perhaps someone just like you may have a future in the computer industry. To learn more about this exciting industry, read on.

GENERAL INFORMATION

Computers can be divided into two broad categories: hardware and software. Hardware refers to the physical equipment of a computer, such as motherboards, memory chips, and microprocessors. Software includes the programs that tell the hardware exactly what to do and how to do it.

Developed in Asia and widely used during the Middle Ages, the abacus was perhaps the origin of modern computing devices. An abacus, composed of strings and beads representing numerical values, can be used for arithmetic.

French philosopher Blaise Pascal invented the world's first digital calculator in the 17th century. His machine was based on a system of rotating drums controlled with a ratchet linkage. He originally intended it for use in his father's tax office, but the principles behind it are still used in modern automobile odometers. In honor of his early contributions to computer technology, the programming language Pascal was named after him in the 1970s. A German, Gottfried Wilhelm von Leibnitz, later improved Pascal's design, making a handheld version similar to a handheld calculator. It never became available commercially, however.

The first significant automated data-processing techniques were applied to making fabric patterns, not calculating numbers. French weaver Joseph-Marie Jacquard introduced a punch-card weaving system at the 1801 World's Fair. His system was straightforward enough; the punched cards controlled the pattern applied to the cloth as it was woven. The introduction of these looms caused riots against the replacement of people by machines.

After proposing in 1822 that it might be possible to compute table entries using a steam engine, Charles Babbage had second thoughts about his idea and went on to design the analytical engine that had the basic components of the modern computer in 1833. This earned him the title of "father of the computer." He was aided greatly by the daughter of famous poet Lord Byron, Ada Augusta King, Countess of Lovelace, who is recognized as the world's first programmer. In 1890, U.S. inventor and statistician Herman Hollerith put the punched-card system to use for the 1890 census. He discovered that perforated cards could be read electrically by machines. Each

Lingo to Learn

Babbage, Charles Known as the father of computers.

browser User-friendly software that makes Internet searches quicker and more efficient.

bug An error, such as a design flaw, in software or hardware.

CAD (computer-aided design) The use of a computer in designing a product. Its principal application is in mechanical engineering.

debug To remove the bugs, or defects, from programs or equipment during the initial testing of products.

debugging The process of testing, making appropriate changes, and rechecking software before it is released.

DOS Disk operating system; the interface between the user, the programs stored on hardware, and the hardware itself.

E-commerce Electronic commerce; selling goods and/or services over the Internet.

GUI Graphical user interface.

hacker Person who breaks into the resources of corporate computer systems.

hardware The physical equipment of the computer, such as motherboards, memory chips, and microprocessors.

input devices Hardware such as keyboards, scanners, and video cameras.

Internet A worldwide system of computer networks connected to each other.

intranet A restricted Internet, available only to the members of a group, such as a club or business corporation.

IS Information services departments within corporations.

IT Information technology.

perforation could stand for some important piece of information that the machine could sort and manipulate. Hollerith founded the Calculating-Tabulating-Recording Company in 1914, which eventually was renamed International Business Machines (IBM) in 1924. IBM is still a computer industry leader today.

In the mid-1940s, punched cards were also used on the Electronic Numerical Integrator and Calculator (ENIAC) at the University of Pennsylvania. ENIAC's inventors developed the world's first all-electronic, general-purpose computer for the U.S. Army. This computer was enormous and relied on over 18,000 vacuum tubes. In 1949, they introduced the Binary

Automatic Computer (BINAC), which used magnetic tape, and then the Universal Automatic Computer (UNIVAC I) for the U.S. census. The latter was the first digital computer to handle both numerical data and alphabetical information quickly and efficiently. In 1954, IBM built the first commercial computer, the 650 EDPM, which was programmed by symbolic notation.

By the late 1950s, the transistor, invented 10 years earlier, had made the second generation of computers possible. Transistors replaced the bulky vacuum tubes and were lighter, smaller, sturdier, and more efficient.

The integrated circuits of the late 1960s introduced the solid-state technology that allowed transistors, diodes, and resistors to be carried on tiny silicon chips. These advances further reduced operating costs and increased speed, capacity, and accuracy. Minicomputers, much smaller than mainframes (large-scale computers) but of comparable power, were developed shortly afterward.

The next important advances included large-scale integration and microprocessing chips. Microchips made even smaller computers possible and reduced costs while increasing capacity. The speed with which a computer processed, calculated, retrieved, and stored data improved significantly. Decreased costs allowed manufacturers to explore new markets.

In the mid-1970s, Steve Wozniak and Steve Jobs started Apple Corporation out of their garage. Their vision was to bring computers into every home in America and even the world. Toward that end, they developed a user-friendly computer offered at a reasonable price. User-friendliness was essential, since many people without computer skills would have to adapt to the computer system. Their product, the Macintosh computer, was the first to give on-screen instructions in everyday language. In addition, Apple introduced the mouse, which allows users to point and click on screen icons to enter commands instead of typing them in one by one.

IBM and clone manufacturers were quick to enter the personal computer (PC) market once they recognized the tremendous sales potential. The result was a friendly debate among computer users over which are better—Macs or PCs? Regardless of personal preference, the two incompatible systems often led to problems when people tried to share information across formats. Software designers have since developed ways to make file conversions easier and software more interchangeable.

One major trend of the last decade has been the downsizing of computer systems, replacing big mainframe computers with client-server architecture, or networking. Networks allow users greater computing flexibility and increased access to different data.

The second major trend of the last decade has been the rapid growth of the Internet and World Wide Web. Initially developed for the U.S. Department of Defense, the Internet is composed of numerous networks connected to each other around the world. Not surprisingly, this massive network has revolutionized information sharing. It is used for real-time video conferencing, electronic mail services, online research, help lines, and long-distance telephone calls. The World Wide Web usually refers to the body of information that is available for retrieval online, while the Internet generally refers to the back-end network system plus its various services.

Hardware companies are continually striving to make faster and better microprocessors and memory chips. Intel and Motorola have been the innovators in microprocessor design, striving for faster and more efficient processors. Such innovations allow computer manufacturers to make smaller, lighter, and quicker computers, laptops, and hand-held models.

As processors get faster and memory increases, computers can process more sophisticated and complicated software programming. Advances in hardware technology have led directly to advances in software applications. As the developer of Windows, Microsoft has been the leader in the software industry. Windows is a user-friendly, visual-based operating system. (An operating system is the interface between the user, the programs stored on the hardware, and the hardware itself.) Disk operating system (DOS) is one of the early operating systems, and while still used, it requires more computer knowledge than other operating systems. The Windows and Mac systems allow users to point and click on icons and menus with a mouse to tell the computer what to do, instead of having to

> **More Lingo to Learn**
>
> **mainframe** A large, main computer that handles data, programs, and software required for extensive procedures.
>
> **motherboard or system board** The main, printed circuit board in a microcomputer. It contains various integrated circuits (including the microprocessor and RAM chips) and slots (receptacles) for expansion cards.
>
> **programming language** The form of instructions used to run computer programs; common languages include BASIC, COBOL, FORTRAN, and C++.
>
> **rollout** The release of a software package or upgrade.
>
> **search engine** Software located on large Web sites where the user enters keywords or phrases to search for specific information covered on the Internet.
>
> **software** A term commonly used to mean programs, as opposed to computer equipment. Originally, the term referred to the programs, programming aids, and the documentation associated with programs.
>
> **storage device** Device such as a CD-ROM, DVD-ROM, or floppy disk that stores computer files outside of the computer.
>
> **UNIVAC I** The first digital computer to handle both numerical and alphabetical information quickly and efficiently.
>
> **URL** Uniform Resource Locator; unique site address that points to a specific Internet site, including the Web, FTP, and other Internet resources. Usually begins with http://.
>
> **World Wide Web** The collection of information available for retrieval from the Internet.

type in specific commands by hand, as DOS requires.

STRUCTURE OF THE INDUSTRY

Hardware

Hardware firms produce every piece of equipment used to build a computer system. This includes the equipment inside a computer, such as memory chips, microprocessors, network cards, and motherboards. It also includes the equipment mostly found outside the computer, called peripheral hardware, such as keyboards, monitors, printers, fax modems, scanners, and CD-ROMs.

Internal hardware makes the difference between a slow, hard-to-use computer and cutting-edge technology. Memory chips store data and programs, while processors follow program instructions to manipulate the data in a desired manner. When a secretary uses a word processor to type letters, for example, the microprocessor transforms the keyboard input into electrical impulses that are stored on the memory chips. Many companies specialize in improving the speed, accuracy, and overall quality of these devices.

Secondary storage devices, such as floppy disks and recordable CD drives, are used to store information and transfer it physically to another computer location. Another type of storage is the hard drive, which is generally installed inside the computer. Hard drives hold a tremendous amount of information. External hard drives are also available to increase computer storage space.

Input devices are another type of hardware and include keyboards, scanners, and video cameras. Scanners read printed material (such as photographs) and convert it into electrical impulses to be stored in the computer. Systems operators can then change them in any way desired. They can also use them to prepare formal presentations in different media, including 35mm color slides, videotape, or computer presentations.

Output devices, such as monitors, allow users to access and change data and information. Some television manufacturers specialize in making monitors with higher resolution and better graphics capabilities, so that more complex applications can be run and displayed successfully on the systems. Another output device is a printer. Dot matrix printers of the early 1980s soon gave way to ink jet printers, bubble jet printers, and laser printers. Color printers have become as common as the black-and-white printers once were.

Communications devices, such as modems, enable computers to connect to other systems via cables or telephone lines. The modem allows the transfer of information between computers. Wireless broadband has recently been developed in response to the strong demand for fast access to data on the Internet. This technology allows connection to the Internet via a ground-based antenna system or via satellite signal. A modem or wireless broadband technology is necessary for users to access the World Wide Web and online services like America Online.

Research and Vocational Opportunities in Computing

artificial intelligence

computer architecture

computer design and engineering

computer theory

Information technology

operating systems and networks

software applications

software engineering

Source: IEEE Computer Society

Software

Programming is a vital part of the computer industry. Without detailed, precise programs, computers would be useless since they only do exactly what they are told to do. Several programs are necessary to make computers operate properly. *Systems programmers* write instructions for how hardware pieces should function with one another. This task includes configuring printers, hard drives, and memory chips. Programmers must be proficient in several programming languages and are greatly aided by commercial prepackaged programs.

The software industry is unique in the business world in that very little overhead (equipment, office space, or personnel) is needed to get started. When an individual or group of individuals comes up with a good idea for new software and can convince financial backers to invest in their idea, a start-up is born. Many start-ups have tried to make a name for themselves with innovative and creative software applications. Often, these companies are so small and have such limited resources that they operate out of garages or basements. Industry leaders such as Microsoft, Apple, and Netscape all came from such humble beginnings. Many start-ups, however, never make it and go bankrupt. It is a good idea for individuals interested in working in software to be flexible and keep their technical knowledge up to date. In this way, if a company folds, programmers and designers can more easily find other employment.

Most software companies approach software design in a similar fashion. First, they identify a client or consumer need, such as organizing home finances. This process can last many months, depending on the intended user and the company. If a mass-market product is being considered, companies must evaluate many different factors, including the specifications of average in-home computers, competitive products already on the market, costs of development and customer service, and potential market for the product.

When the decision is made to go ahead with the application, programmers write the code. (In the past, writing code for a major project could take months. Today, new technologies have eliminated the need for some routine programming work.) Each subsection of the program is tested and retested and then usually tested many times again. Just imagine the amount of coding required by a word processing program; features like the spell check, dictionary, and thesaurus alone could constitute millions of lines of commands.

There is much more to the computer business than research and development, however. Many people are employed by computer companies to market and advertise their products to the right people. Sales representatives must be trained, promotional brochures must be developed, and price schedules must be determined.

CAREERS

Within the hardware and software branches of the computer industry, there are a number of different types of jobs. Many positions overlap, and not every company hires people in each functional area. These basic areas are design, programming, administration, service, and sales. Many of these jobs also overlap with the Internet industry.

Design

For our purposes, *designers* include *researchers, computer scientists, computer engineers,* and *systems analysts* who evaluate the market or existing technology to find windows of opportunity for improvements or new product design. These professionals have considerable freedom to explore uncharted areas of computer technology. Often, their ideas are not implemented for years to come, until the market catches up to the theory.

Designers usually work on a project that has already been defined in some way. An accounting department, for example, might request a special system to improve its operations. A *software designer* is assigned to handle that problem. Generally, designers use their knowledge of hardware and software to design a computer system and set of applications that will solve a business or scientific problem. More specifically, designers can specialize in databases, networks, or software applications.

Computers, whatever their function, are based on the principles and processes of mathematics. The design process is similar regardless of position. The problem is defined, equipment is analyzed and upgraded if need be, software is customized, and new programming fills any gaps.

Programming

Programming is much more detail-oriented and less abstract than design analysis. It can involve hardware, software, or both. In any case, *programmers* write the coded instructions that make computers do what we want them to do. *Systems programmers* write the instructions that make different computers and peripherals perform well together. *Software programmers* write instructions for how computers should respond to various inputs and which on-screen displays should be generated. Programmers are required to know at least one, but usually more, computer-programming language, including BASIC, COBOL, FORTRAN, and C++.

Administration

Computer administrators are in charge of daily operations of different kinds of computer systems. The most common areas of specialization are database, network, systems, security, and quality assurance. Administrators are responsible for a variety of tasks. They help install new systems and train new users. They also address user problems as they arise; for example, a user might not be able to gain access to certain files on a network server. The administrator first verifies that the user is inputting the correct password and following the right procedure. If the problem is not due to user error, the administrator checks the security files, making sure the user is granted access. Administrators are also involved with backing up the system regularly. They also ensure good systems communications. If a network server goes down, for example, a network administrator attempts to isolate the cause of the problem and fix it. If it is too complicated, the administrator must call in higher-level systems people.

Service

Computer service is another broad category of careers in the computer industry. *Systems setup specialists, technical support specialists,* and *computer service technicians* are included in this group. Systems setup specialists install new hardware and software either at the client site or in a service center. Large installations at major corporations can take days or even weeks to properly install. Set-up work requires solid knowledge in the basics of computer technology as well as strong manual dexterity skills. Sometimes systems are so complicated that specialists are called to help plan the layout of the computer room, both of the multitude of wires and the physical equipment.

Technical support specialists, sometimes known as *computer support specialists* and *help desk technicians,* can also specialize in either hardware or software. They work in large corporations or for computer companies that offer technical support to end-users. A large bank, for example, probably has a technical support person on staff in the information systems department. This individual is responsible for helping users when they encounter problems, as well as fixing problems with the machines when they break down or crash. Technical support specialists who work for a computer

---

They Said That!

I think there is a world market for maybe five computers.
—*Thomas Watson, chairman of IBM, 1943*

There is no reason anyone would want a computer in their home.
—*Ken Olson, president, chairman/ founder of Digital Equipment Corporation, 1977*

Computers in the future may weigh no more than 1.5 tons.
—*Popular Mechanics, 1949*

> ## Computer Fun Facts
>
> The IEEE Computer Society has many interesting facts about computers on its Web site. Did you know that...
>
> - Grace Murray Hopper, while working on the Mark II computer at Harvard, found the first computer bug, which was a real insect that had been crushed in the jaws of a relay switch. She glued it to the logbook of the computer and thereafter when the machine stopped, told people they were debugging the computer. The very first bug still exists in the National Museum of American History of the Smithsonian Institution.
>
> - In the movie, *2001: A Space Odyssey*, Arthur C. Clark introduced HAL, the computer of the future and based it on the artificial intelligence proposals of I. J. Good and Marvin Minsky. Supposedly, HAL was the monosyllabic cipher of IBM.
>
> - Less than four months after IBM introduced the personal computer in 1982, *Time* magazine named the computer its "Man of the Year." Never before had an inanimate object been chosen for that honor.
>
> - Ada Augusta King, Countess of Lovelace and poet Lord Byron's daughter, translated a pamphlet on Charles Babbage's analytical engine. She added her own notes and worked closely with Babbage himself. She became recognized as the world's first computer programmer.

manufacturer may answer phone calls from frustrated users who cannot get their computers or applications to run properly. These specialists talk consumers through the problems and attempt to solve them over the phone.

Computer service technicians are called in when the hardware breaks down physically. Transistors can blow, for example, or motherboards or other internal hardware can be defective from the start. Computer repairers analyze the hardware, determine the cause of the problem, and fix it by repairing the equipment or replacing certain parts with new ones.

Sales

The computer industry would not exist without a sales force. *Computer sales representatives* work for computer manufacturers or retail stores. They are very knowledgeable about the wide range of products on the market and must be good at persuading consumers that their company's product is better. Their work requires technical expertise as well as strong interpersonal communication skills.

As an industry, the Internet is one of the most dynamic and evolving sectors of the U.S., and the world, economy. Job possibilities in cyberspace are practically endless. Naturally, crossover exists between the computer hardware and software fields and the Internet field, since the Internet developed from computer applications. Some traditional computer professionals (for example, computer engineers, software designers, computer programmers, and database specialists) continue to focus their work on supporting and enhancing the functioning of the Internet. Internet professionals as a group, however, include more than these computer workers: There are *Internet consultants* who build Web sites for clients; *Webmasters,* who maintain and update Web sites; *Internet quality assurance specialists,* who are responsible for testing and maintaining the quality of Web sites; *Internet transaction specialists,* who work on the programming that allows users to transfer their money to a business or organization to make a purchase or donation via a Web site; *Internet security specialists,* who are responsible for maintaining the security at a Web site; *Internet store managers,* who set up and run businesses on the Web; *Internet executives,* who are top-level management personnel responsible for conducting business over the Web; *game designers,* who create computer games that can be played on the Internet, computers, and other types of hardware; *online journalists,* professional writers or journalists whose writing appears in online publications; and *online researchers* or *information brokers,* who provide clients with survey results, government statistics, business reports, and other information on topics they have researched online.

As the Internet continues to grow in popularity, speed, strength, and uses, it is clear that more and more professionals will become involved in both the making of and the making use of the Internet.

EMPLOYMENT OPPORTUNITIES

Employment opportunities in the computer industry are numerous and varied. Three things are essential to aspiring computer professionals: determination to keep up with the latest technology; flexibility; and formal education. Of course, a solid understanding of computer basics is required as well. The technology of today, however, will be obsolete in months, if not weeks, and only those individuals who strive to be on the cutting edge will have long-term growth potential during their careers. Related to that, flexibility is also key because as the industry shifts into new, unexplored areas, computer professionals have to shift as well. In addition, many computer professionals use certain jobs as springboards to other higher-level jobs. Few professionals want to work in technical support long term, but many start there to get a foot in the company's door in order to be first in line for any internal positions that open up. If an individual is so specialized that such moving around was impossible, he or she might have difficulties in the future. Lastly, formal and continuing education is increasingly an important requirement because the job market is flooded with highly qualified, well-trained individuals.

Many different types of companies hire computer professionals. Computer manufacturers and software companies hire the whole range of professionals. Many of these employers are clustered in certain geographical areas like northern California, Seattle, and parts of the East Coast. Living in an area with many potential employers increases the likelihood of being hired (or rehired) by an employer relatively quickly.

Computer companies range from huge market leaders to small start-ups. In addition, there are thousands of small- to medium-sized companies that create specialized products, such as software to be used specifically to run corporate human resource departments.

Large corporations are major employers of computer professionals as well. Many maintain information systems (IS) departments, which hire people for the many different positions previously described. The number of in-house IS departments has grown with the increased usage of computers in the workplace. Almost all companies, including banks, insurance companies, consumer products firms, and government agencies, have IS departments.

Other employers of computer professionals are consulting firms, such as Deloitte and Ernst & Young. They hire college graduates with majors in computer science to help them integrate the latest technology into their clients' business. Most of these jobs are headquartered in large cities and require a lot of travel.

INDUSTRY OUTLOOK

Employment for many computer professionals, such as software engineers, systems administrators, computer systems analysts, and database administrators, is expected to increase much faster than average through 2014, as technology becomes more sophisticated and organizations continue to adopt and integrate these technologies, making job openings plentiful. Additionally, faster-than-average growth is predicted for technical support specialists and network administrators. Falling prices of computer hardware and software should continue to encourage more businesses to expand computerized operations and integrate new technologies. To maintain a competitive edge and operate more cost-effectively, firms will continue to demand computer professionals who are knowledgeable about the latest technologies and can apply them to the needs of businesses.

The outlook for computer professionals who are employed in computer and electronic product manufacturing is not very good. The U.S. Department of Labor predicts a decline in employment in this field due to improvements in productivity, the increasing import of electronic and computer products, and outsourcing of computer programming and engineering tasks by U.S. manufacturers to countries that pay lower wages to their workers. Despite this prediction, many employment opportunities should be available as new technology emerges and workers leave the field for other sectors of the industry.

As for the Internet, the expanding integration of Internet technologies has resulted in a rising demand for a variety of skilled professionals who can develop and support Internet, intranet, and World Wide Web applications. Growth in these areas is expected to create strong demand for computer scientists, engineers, and systems analysts who are knowledgeable about networks, data, and communications security.

According to the U.S. Department of Labor, employment of programmers should grow more slowly than the average for all occupations through 2014. Employment of computer equipment operators is expected to decline since advances in automation continue to increase, reducing the need for such workers.

SECTION 2

Careers

Computer and Video Game Designers

SUMMARY

Definition
Computer and video game designers create and document the ideas and interactivity for games played on various platforms, or media, such as video consoles and computers, and through online Internet subscriptions. They generate ideas for new game concepts, including sound effects, characters, story lines, and graphics.

Alternative Job Titles
None

Salary Range
$41,652 to $64,248 to $92,059

Educational Requirements
Bachelor's degree

Certification or Licensing
None available

Employment Outlook
About as fast as the average

High School Subjects
Art
Computer science
English (writing/literature)

Personal Interests
Art
Computers
Writing

At some point in each game's development, game designers run a series of what are called usability tests. "This involves putting players in front of the prototype game and watching them play," game designer Doug Kaufman explains, "without any prompting or explanation, to see which areas are difficult for them to understand—and in what way (if any) we can make the explanations clearer."

During a recent usability session, Doug and his colleagues were having trouble with people not getting out and exploring the various areas of the game. "Since this is a common activity in strategy games,"

Doug recalls, "we were a little baffled as to why in this particular game there seemed to be this mental block against leaving the starting position. What was different?

"We went through a list of possible causes: The art? Well, our art was similar to other games of this type, so it should have been clear to the players that this was 'unexplored territory.' Availability of assets? Well, we gave them assets that could be used for exploration, so it wasn't that they simply had no way to explore."

Finally, Doug decided that it was a simple matter of psychology. "None of the players' starting units was specifically designated as an 'explorer,' " he says. "I suggested renaming one of the starting assets 'Explorer.' I was so confident that this was the issue, I even bet one of the programmers $10 that the first player to have an 'Explorer' unit would use it to enter unexplored territory within the first few minutes of his usability session."

Doug and his colleagues waited with bated breath as the new player examined his starting assets. "These testers are asked to speak out loud as they play," Doug says, "so we can get an insight into their thought processes. This tester selected the Explorer unit and said 'Hmmm... an Explorer. Maybe I should use him to build things.' My heart sank. Then he said, 'Oh, no, what am I thinking? It's an Explorer. I should use him to explore.' He promptly moved that unit into the unexplored territory, and I won my bet and the problem was solved."

WHAT DOES A COMPUTER AND VIDEO GAME DESIGNER DO?

Designing games involves programming code as well as creating stories, graphics, and sound effects. It is a very creative process, requiring imagination and computer and communication skills to develop games that are interactive and entertaining. Some *computer and video game designers* work on their own and try to sell their designs to companies that produce and distribute games; others are employees of companies such as Electronic Arts and Broderbund, to name a few. Whether designers work alone or for a company, their aim is to create games that get players involved. Game players want to have fun, be challenged, and sometimes learn something along the way.

Each game must have a story line as well as graphics and sound that will entertain and engage the players. Story lines are situations that the players will find themselves in and make decisions about. Designers develop a plan for combining the story or concept, music or other sound effects, and graphics. They design rules to make it fun, challenging, or educational, and they create characters for the stories or circumstances, worlds in which these characters live, and problems or situations these characters will face.

One of the first steps is to identify the audience that will be playing the game. How old are the players? What kinds of things are they interested in? What kind of game will it be: action, adventure, "edutainment," role-playing, or sports? And which platform will the game use: video console (e.g., Nintendo), computer (e.g., Macintosh), or online (Internet via subscription)?

The next steps are to create a design proposal, a preliminary design, and a final game design. The proposal is a brief summary of what the game involves. The preliminary design goes much further, outlining in more detail what the concept is (the story of the game); how the players get involved; which sound effects, graphics, and other elements will be included (What will the screen look like? What kinds of sound effects should the player hear?); and the productivity tools (such as word processors, database programs, spreadsheet programs, flowcharting programs, and prototyping programs) the designer intends to use to create these elements. Independent designers submit a product idea and design proposal to a publisher along with a cover letter and resume. Employees work as part of a team to create the proposal and design. Teamwork might include brainstorming sessions to come up with ideas, as well as involvement in market research (surveying the players who will be interested in the game).

The final game design details the basic idea, the plot, and every section of the game, including the start-up process, all the scenes (such as innings for baseball games and maps for edutainment games), and all the universal elements (such as rules for scoring, names of characters, and a sound effect that occurs every time something specific happens). The story, characters, worlds, and maps are documented. The game design also includes details of the logic of the game, its algorithms (the step-by-step procedures for solving the problems the players will encounter), and its rules; the methods the player will use to load the game, start it up, score, win, lose, save, stop, and play again; the graphic design, including storyboards and sample art; and the audio design. The designer might also include marketing ideas and proposed follow-up games.

Designers interact with other workers and technologists involved in the game design project, including programmers, audio engineers, artists, and even *asset managers*, who coordinate the collecting, engineering, and distribution of physical assets to the *production team* (the people who will actually produce the physical product).

Designers need to understand games and their various forms, think up new ideas, and experiment with and evaluate new designs. They assemble the separate elements (text, art, sound, video) of a game into a complete, interactive form, following through with careful planning and preparation (such as sketching out scripts, storyboards, and design documents). They write an implementation plan and guidelines: How will designers manage the process? How much will it cost to design the game? How long will the guidelines be—5 pages? 300? Finally, they amend designs at every stage, solving problems and answering questions.

Computer and video game designers often keep scrapbooks, notes, and journals of interesting ideas and other bits of information. They collect potential game material and even catalog ideas, videos, movies, pictures, stories, character descriptions, music clips, sound effects, animation sequences, and interface techniques. The average time it takes to design a game, including all the elements and stages just described, can range from about 6 to 18 months.

WHAT IS IT LIKE TO BE A COMPUTER AND VIDEO GAME DESIGNER?

Doug Kaufman is a senior game designer at Big Huge Games, a developer of strategy-oriented games such as *Rise of Nations*.

A Brief History of Computer and Video Games

Computer and video game designers are a relatively new breed. The industry didn't begin to develop until the 1960s and 1970s, when computer programmers at some large universities, big companies, and government labs began designing games on mainframe computers. Steve Russell was perhaps the first video game designer. In 1962, when he was in college, he made up a simple game called *Spacewar*. Graphics of space ships flew through a starry sky on the video screen, the object of the game being to shoot down enemy ships. Nolan Bushnell, another early designer, played *Spacewar* in college. In 1972 he put the first video game in an arcade; it was a game very much like *Spacewar*, and he called it *Computer Space*. Many users found the game difficult to play, however, so it wasn't a success.

Bruce Artwick published the first of many versions of *Flight Simulator*, and Bushnell later created *Pong*, a game that required the players to paddle electronic ping-pong balls back and forth across the video screen. *Pong* was a big hit, and players spent thousands of quarters in arcade machines all over the country playing it. Bushnell's company, Atari, had to hire more and more designers every week, including Steve Jobs, Alan Kay, and Chris Crawford. These early designers made games with text-based descriptions (that is, no graphics) of scenes and actions with interactivity done through a computer keyboard. Games called *Adventure*, *Star Trek*, and *Flight Simulator* were among the first that designers created. They used simple commands like "look at building" and "move west." Most games were designed for video machines; not until the later 1970s did specially equipped TVs and early personal computers (PCs) begin appearing.

In the late 1970s and early 1980s, designers working for Atari and Intellivision made games for home video systems, PCs, and video arcades. Many of these new games had graphics, sound, text, and animation. Designers of games like *Pac-Man*, *Donkey Kong*, and *Space Invaders* were successful and popular. They also started to make role-playing games like the famous *Dungeons and Dragons*. Richard Garriott created *Ultima*, another major role-playing game. Games began to feature the names and photos of their programmers on the packaging, giving credit to individual designers.

Workers at Electronic Arts began to focus on making games for PCs to take advantage of technology that included the computer keyboard, more memory, and floppy disks. They created games like *Carmen Sandiego* and *M.U.L.E.* In the mid- to late-1980s, new technology included more compact floppies, sound cards, and larger memory. Designers also had to create games that would work on more than just one platform—PCs, Apple computers, and 64-bit video game machines.

In the 1990s, Electronic Arts started to hire teams of designers instead of "lone wolf" individuals (those who design games from start to finish independently). Larger teams were needed because games became more complex; design teams would include not only programmers but also artists, musicians, writers, and animators. Designers made

(continued on next page)

(continued from previous page)
such breakthroughs as using more entertaining graphics, creating more depth in role-playing games, using virtual reality in sports games, and using more visual realism in racing games and flight simulators. This new breed of designers created games using techniques like Assembly, C, and HyperCard. By 1994, designers began to use CD-ROM technology to its fullest. In only a few months, *Doom* was a hit. Designers of this game gave players the chance to alter it themselves at various levels, including choices of weapons and enemies. *Doom* still has fans worldwide.

The success of shareware (software that is given away to attract users to want to buy more complete software) has influenced the return of smaller groups of designers. Even the lone wolf is coming back, using shareware and better authoring tools such as sound libraries and complex multimedia development environments. Some designers are finding that they work best on their own or in small teams.

What's on the horizon for game designers? More multiplayer games; virtual reality; improved technology in coprocessors, chips, hardware, and sound fonts; and "persistent worlds," where online games are influenced by and evolve from players' actions. These new types of games require that designers know more and more complex code so that games can "react" to their multiple players.

He started his career as a designer of board games for West End Games in 1983 and made the transition to computer games in 1990. "West End was originally supposed to be a temporary job while I pursued a career in acting," Doug explains, "but it became full time, and since acting is such a difficult arena to break into, it just seemed natural to continue to pursue what I enjoyed, was good at, and was already doing professionally."

On any given day Doug may handle anywhere from three to a dozen different tasks. "Most of these tasks," he explains, "relate to fixing bugs or balance issues, adding help text, or conceiving of new ideas for the games that have been previously discussed but about which no conclusions have been reached. So I might start the day altering xml files in which all our data is stored, adding the proper values and flags to units to make them behave the way they're supposed to according to previous design. Then I might add or clarify help text on units and buildings in response to playtesting and feedback. Next, I might have to tackle the issue of making each side that can be played in the game stand out and be different, not just superficially but in some fundamental way that might (one would hope) alter the strategies you'd plan to use when taking that side. When I've got my ideas, I'll formalize them in a document and present them to a design group at our next scheduled meeting."

Doug typically ends his day playing the game in its current form, "taking notes," he says, "and making any alterations I can affect from the xml side, while drawing up tasks for programmers and artists to address issues that I've come across."

Computer and video game designers work in office settings, whether at a large company or a home studio. At some companies, artists and designers sometimes find themselves working 24 or 48 hours at a time, so the office areas are set up with sleeping couches and other areas where employees can relax. Because the game development industry is competitive, many designers find themselves under a lot of pressure from deadlines, design problems, and budget concerns.

DO I HAVE WHAT IT TAKES TO BE A COMPUTER AND VIDEO GAME DESIGNER?

One major requirement for game design is that you must love to play computer games. You need to continually keep up with technology, which changes fast. Although you might not always use them, you need to have a variety of skills, such as the ability to write stories, program, and design sound effects.

You must also have vision and the ability to identify your players and anticipate their every move in your game. You'll also have to be able to communicate well with programmers, writers, artists, musicians, electronics engineers, production workers, and others.

Computer and video game designers must have the endurance to see a proj-

> **To Be a Successful Computer and Video Game Designer, You Should . . .**
>
> - love playing computer games
> - be highly creative
> - have the ability to multitask and work well under pressure
> - be a good storyteller
> - have strong communication skills
> - be willing to accept constructive criticism about your ideas for games
> - be willing to constantly learn about new technology

ect through from beginning to end and also be able to recognize when a design should be scrapped. They must also have a thick skin to deal with occasional negative reactions to their creative ideas by coworkers and customers. "Game popularity is a capricious, subjective thing," says Doug. "Ideas may not work out the way you thought they would, or others may find your pet ideas completely un-fun and have ideas of their own that of course they think are much better. In any artistic endeavor that is relatively abstract in nature, the world is full of people who will be dubious about your talent and sure that they could do better. This can be quite frustrating at times."

HOW DO I BECOME A COMPUTER AND VIDEO GAME DESIGNER?

Education

High School

If you like to play *Madden NFL*, *Zelda*, or *The Sims*, you're already familiar with games. You will also need to learn a programming language like C++ or Java, and you'll need a good working knowledge of the hardware platform for which you plan to develop your games (video, computer, online). In high school, learn as much as you can about computers: how they work, what kinds there are, how to program them, and any languages you can learn. Since designers are creative, take courses such as art, literature, and music as well. "Don't forget typing," Doug advises. "Fast typing skills are extremely useful."

Doug also recommends that students participate in "any activity where a team is working together for a goal (preferably artistic but not necessarily), such as game clubs, yearbook, and student council. Play a variety of games, and ask yourself why you like and dislike various games. Don't limit your play to one type that you enjoy the most. Listen to your friends' opinions as well."

Postsecondary Training

Although strictly speaking you don't have to have a college degree to be a game designer, most companies are looking for creative people who also have a bachelor's degree. Having one represents that you've been actively involved in intense, creative work; that you can work with others and follow through on assignments; and, of course, that you've learned what there is to know about programming, computer architecture (including input devices, processing devices, memory and storage devices, and output devices), and software engineering. Employers want to know that you've had some practical experience in design.

A growing number of schools offer courses or degrees in game design. The University of North Texas, for example, has a Laboratory for Recreational Computing (LARC) that offers two senior elective courses, Game Programming and Advanced Game Programming. For more information, visit http://larc.csci.unt.edu. One of the best-known degree-granting schools is DigiPen Institute of Technology (http://www.digipen.edu) in Redmond, Washington, with programs both at the associate and bachelor's level. For a list of schools in the United States, visit http://www.igda.org/breakingin/resource_schools.php. The college courses you should take include programming (including assembly level), computer architecture, software engineering, computer graphics, data structures, algorithms, communication networks, artificial intelligence (AI) and expert systems, interface systems, mathematics, and physics.

Doug majored in dramatics in college. "Odd as it may seem," he says, "I find that acting and producing plays are actually a good preparation for working with a crew of brilliant people, all of whom have strong egos, to create a work of art such as a computer game."

Computer and Video Game Designers 25

> ### Industry Stats
>
> - Entertainment software sales were $7.3 billion in 2004—more than double the total sales in 1996.
> - More than 228 million computer and video games were sold in 2005.
> - Sixty-nine percent of American heads of households play computer or video games.
> - The average game player is 33 years old.
> - The average game purchaser is 40 years old.
> - Women make up 38 percent of computer and video game players.
> - The industry has a bright future, at least according to current game players. The average number of years adult gamers have been playing computer or video games is 12.
>
> Source: Entertainment Software Association, 2006 Essential Facts About the Computer and Video Game Industry

Internships and Volunteerships

If you live near a game company, try to land an after-school or summer internship as a game tester. "Listen and learn from the senior testers and designers," Doug advises. "Ask a lot of very simple questions, rather than, 'How do you design a game?' Ask, over the course of several weeks, questions such as, What's the first thing you usually do when designing? How closely does the finished product usually resemble the starting document? What special techniques do you have for getting started?, and other questions. When the opportunity comes for a more senior position or one with greater responsibility, step up to the plate."

WHO WILL HIRE ME?

There are a couple of ways to begin earning money as a game designer: independently or as an employee of a company. It is more realistic to get any creative job you can in the industry (for example, as an artist, a play tester, a programmer, or a writer) and learn as you go, developing your design skills as you work your way up to the level of designer.

Contact company Web sites and sites that advertise job openings, such as Game Jobs (http://www.gamejobs.com). In addition to a professional resume, it's a good idea to have your own Web site, where you can showcase your demos. Make sure you have designed at least one demo or have an impressive portfolio of design ideas and documents. Other ways to find a job in the industry include going to job fairs (such as the Game Developers Conference), where you find recruiters looking for creative people to work at their companies, and checking in with game developer forums and user groups, which often post jobs on the Internet.

Software publishers (such as Electronic Arts and Activision) are found throughout the country, though most are located in California, New York, Washington, and Illinois. Electronic Arts is the largest independent publisher of interactive entertainment, including several development studios; the company is known worldwide. Big media companies such as Disney have also opened interactive entertainment departments. Jobs should be available at these companies as well as with online services and interactive networks, which are growing rapidly.

Some companies are involved in producing games only for video; others produce only for computers; others make games for various platforms.

WHERE CAN I GO FROM HERE?

To advance their position and possibly earn more money, computer and video game designers have to keep up with technology. They must be willing to constantly learn more about design, the industry, and even financial and legal matters involved in development.

Becoming and remaining great at their job may be a career-long endeavor for computer and video game designers, or just a stepping-stone to another area of interactive entertainment. Some designers start out as artists, writers, or programmers, learning enough in these jobs to eventually design; for example, a person entering this career may begin as a 3-D animation modeler and work on enough game life cycles to understand what it takes to be a game designer. He or she may decide to specialize in another area, such as sound effects or even budgeting.

Some designers rise to management positions, such as president or vice president of a software publisher. Others write for magazines and books, teach, or establish their own game companies.

"In five years," Doug says, "I hope to be leading a team and working on a project of my own choosing that doesn't necessarily have to have obvious commercial appeal and follow the restrictions of 'the usual type of game.' In 10 years I'll be 56, and my children will be 13, so I may switch to some sort of educational field and/or teach courses in game design."

WHAT ARE THE SALARY RANGES?

Most development companies spend up to two years designing a game even before any of the mechanics (such as writing final code and drawing final graphics) begin; more complex games take even longer. Companies budget $1 million to $3 million for developing just one game. If the game is a success, designers are often rewarded with bonuses. In addition to bonuses or royalties (the percentage of profits designers receive from each game that is sold), designers' salaries are affected by their amount of professional experience, their location in the country, and the size of their employer. Gama Network, an organization serving electronic games developers, surveyed subscribers, members, and attendees of its three divisions (*Game Developer* magazine, Gamasutra.com, and Game Developers Conference) to find out what professionals in the game development industry were earning. The survey reveals that game designers with one to two years' experience had an average annual salary of approximately

Related Jobs

- animators
- art directors
- artists
- computer programmers
- game testers
- graphics programmers
- hardware engineers
- producers
- software designers
- sound workers
- toy and game designers
- writers

$41,652. Those with three to five years of experience averaged $53,031 annually, and those with more than six years of experience averaged $64,248 per year. Lead designers/creative directors earned higher salaries, ranging from $44,667 for those with less than two years of experience to $92,059 for workers with six or more years of experience in the field. It is important to note that these salaries are averages, and some designers (especially those at the beginning stages of their careers) earn less than these amounts. These figures, however, provide a useful guide for the range of earnings available.

Any major software publisher will likely provide benefits such as medical insurance, paid vacations, and retirement plans. Designers who are self-employed must provide their own benefits.

WHAT IS THE JOB OUTLOOK?

Computer and video games are a fast-growing segment of the U.S. entertainment industry. In fact, the NPD Group, a market information provider, reports that sales of computer and video games reached $7.3 billion in 2004. As the demand for new games, more sophisticated games, and games to be played on new systems grows, more and more companies will hire skilled people to create and perfect these products. Opportunities for game designers, therefore, should be good.

In any case, game development is popular; the Interactive Digital Software Association estimates that about 60 percent of the U.S. population (approximately 145 million people) play computer and video games. People in the industry expect more and more integration of interactive entertainment into mainstream society. Online development tools such as engines, graphic and sound libraries, and programming languages such as Java will probably create opportunities for new types of products that can feature game components.

Computer Engineers

SUMMARY

Definition
There are two main types of computer engineers: hardware engineers and software engineers. Hardware engineers design, build, and test computer hardware, such as computer chips and circuit boards, as well as computer systems and software. They also work with peripheral devices, such as printers, scanners, modems, and monitors. Software engineers maintain existing code, develop new enhancements to older products, and write custom interfaces with other projects. These professionals also possess strong programming skills, but are more concerned with analyzing and solving programming problems than simply with code.

Alternative Job Titles
Applications software engineers
Directors of network services
Hardware engineers
Network engineers
Software engineers
Systems software engineers

Salary Range
$46,520 to $74,980 to $123,560+

Educational Requirements
Bachelor's degree

Certification or Licensing
Voluntary

Employment Outlook
About as fast as the average (hardware engineers)
Much faster than the average (software engineers)

High School Subjects
Computer science
Mathematics
English (writing/literature)
Speech

Personal Interests
Building things
Computers
Figuring out how things work
Writing

Mapping, designing, and redesigning networks; configuring routers and order lines; meeting with existing and potential clients; reporting bad data lines to telephone companies; investigating new technology that will save the company and clients time and money; talking a client about to give a trade show presentation through a quick fix of malfunctioning equipment. This is just a typical morning for network engineer Nick Asvos. "Work as a network engineer is generally challenging," Nick says, "and people with good troubleshooting skills will get to apply them regularly. The field generally pays well, and it is still expanding."

WHAT DOES A COMPUTER ENGINEER DO?

There are two main types of computer engineers: *hardware engineers* and *software engineers*. Hardware engineers work with the physical parts of computers, such as CPUs (central processing units), motherboards, chipsets, video cards, cooling units, magnetic tape, disk drives, storage devices, network cards, and all the components that connect them, down to wires, nuts, and bolts.

Hardware engineers design parts and create prototypes to test, using CAD/CAM technology to make schematic drawings. They assemble the parts using fine hand tools, soldering irons, and microscopes. Parts are reworked and developed through multiple testing procedures. Once a final design is completed, hardware engineers oversee the manufacture and installation of parts.

Computer hardware engineers also work on peripherals, such as keyboards, printers, monitors, mice, track balls, modems, scanners, external storage devices, speaker systems, and digital cameras. Some hardware engineers are involved in maintenance and repair of computers, networks, and peripherals. They troubleshoot problems, order or make new parts, and install them.

Software engineers are responsible for customizing existing software programs to meet the needs and desires of a particular business or industry. First, they spend considerable time researching, defining, and analyzing the problem at hand. Then, they develop software programs to resolve the problem on the computer.

Software engineers fall into two basic categories. *Systems software engineers* build and maintain entire computer systems for a company. *Applications software engineers* design, create, and modify general computer applications software or specialized utility programs.

Engineers who work on computer systems research how a company's departments and its respective computer systems are organized; for example, there might be customer service, ordering, inventory, billing, shipping, and payroll record-keeping departments. Systems software engineers suggest ways to coordinate all these parts. Systems software engineers known as *network engineers* might set up intranets or networks that link computers within the organization and ease communication. These professionals deal with LAN and WAN support and PC/LAN connectivity. They have lots

---

FYI

The information technology industry has suffered from a critical shortage of skilled workers. One solution to this employment problem may lie in the hiring of people with mental disabilities. Those with neurological disorders such as autism have been excelling at IT work in data entry, programming, and Web design. IT projects require the talents possessed by many workers with mental disabilities: creativity, problem-solving abilities, and great concentration.

of interaction with users, and troubleshoot network conditions. This job also includes designing networks and analyzing products. *Directors of network services* handle all of the network communications responsibilities.

WHAT IS IT LIKE TO BE A COMPUTER ENGINEER?

Nick Asvos has been a network engineer for more than eight years. He currently works at Audio Visual Services Corporation, a company that provides audiovisual equipment (lights, cameras, microphones, projectors, plasma displays, etc.) rental and services for trade shows, conferences, and other sorts of productions, and high-speed Internet access for hotels and conference centers.

Nick works from 7:00 a.m. to 4:00 p.m. He normally starts each day by addressing problems that occurred after he left work the previous day. "Generally, it's smaller things that break," he explains. "A client's data line (DSL, T1, T3, etc.) will go down, and we have to open 'trouble tickets' with the telephone companies to get the lines fixed. Sometimes equipment dies overnight, and we have to configure and ship replacement equipment. Additionally, our clients may change something or unplug equipment, and we have to walk them through fixing it."

Nick spends most of his day working on projects and attending meetings. "Projects that I work on," Nick says, "include things such as mapping networks, designing new networks, and redesigning existing networks in such a way as to minimize downtime; exploring and evaluating new technologies; and meeting with vendors to explore new technologies and with clients/potential clients to figure out and address their needs. Additionally, I configure routers and order lines for clients, and send the help desk information on how to assist them in getting their connections up and running." Nick also works with the systems administration team at his company to bring servers online, get them connected to the network, and assist with testing.

Computer engineers usually work in comfortable office environments. Contrary to popular perceptions, they do not spend their entire workdays cooped up in their offices. Instead, they spend the majority of their time meeting, planning, and working with various staff members from different levels of management and technical expertise. Since it takes numerous workers to move a project from start to finish, team players are in high demand.

Overall, computer engineers usually work 40- to 50-hour weeks, but this depends on the nature of the employer and expertise of the engineer. In consulting firms, for example, it is typical for engineers to work long hours and frequently travel to out-of-town assignments. Weekend work is common with some positions. "Putting in changes sometimes requires working evening and/or weekends so as not to interrupt normal business with network downtime," Nick says. "When emergencies occur, they generally need to be fixed as soon as possible, so long nights are also sometimes a part of the job. Going in to work at midnight after a full day at the office can be trying sometimes. On the upside, a decent amount of the late-night work can be preformed remotely."

Computer engineers generally receive an assignment and a time frame within which to accomplish it; daily work details are often left up to the individuals. Some engineers work relatively lightly at the beginning of a project, but work a lot of overtime at the end in order to catch up. Most engineers are not compensated for overtime.

To Be a Successful Computer Engineer, You Should . . .

- have a broad knowledge of and experience with computer systems and technologies
- be a good problem-solver and have strong analytical skills
- be patient, self-motivated, and flexible
- have the ability to multitask and work well under pressure
- be willing to pursue continuing education throughout your career
- have strong communication skills

DO I HAVE WHAT IT TAKES TO BE A COMPUTER ENGINEER?

Computer engineers need a broad knowledge of and experience with computer systems and technologies. You need strong problem-solving and analysis skills and good interpersonal skills. Patience, self-motivation, and flexibility are important. Often, a number of projects are worked on simultaneously, so the ability to multitask and work well under pressure is important. Because of rapid technological advances in the computer field, continuing education is a necessity.

HOW DO I BECOME A COMPUTER ENGINEER?

Education

High School

If you are interested in pursuing this career, take as many computer, math, and science courses as possible, because they provide fundamental math and computer knowledge and teach analytical thinking skills. Classes that rely on schematic drawing and flowcharts are also very valuable. English and speech courses will help you improve your communication skills, which are very important for computer engineers.

Postsecondary Training

Computer engineers need at least a bachelor's degree in computer engineering or electrical engineering. Employment in research laboratories or academic institutions might require a master's or Ph.D. in computer science or engineering. For a list of accredited four-year computer engineering programs, visit the Accreditation Board for Engineering and Technology's Web site, http://www.abet.org.

Obtaining a postsecondary degree in computer engineering is usually considered challenging and even difficult. In addition to natural ability, you should be hard working and determined to succeed. If you plan to work in a specific technical field, such as medicine, law, or business, you should receive some formal training in that particular discipline.

Certification and Licensing

Not all computer professionals are certified. The deciding factor seems to be if their employer requires it. Many companies offer tuition reimbursement, or incentives, to those who earn certification. Certification is available in a variety of specialties. The Institute for Certification of Computing Professionals offers the Associate Computing Professional designation for those new to the field, and the Certified Computing Professional designation for those with at least 48 months of full-time professional-level work in computer-based information systems. Certification is considered by many to be a measure of industry knowledge as well as a means of leverage when negotiating salary.

Another option is to pursue commercial certification. These programs are usually run by computer companies that wish to train professionals to work with their products. Classes are challenging and examinations can be rigorous. New programs are introduced every year.

The Institute of Electrical and Electronics Engineers Computer Society offers the designation Certified Software Development Professional to individuals who have a bachelor's degree, a minimum of 9,000 hours of software engineering experience within at least 6 of 11 knowledge areas, and pass an examination.

Top Computer Engineering Programs in the United States*

1. Rose-Hulman Institute of Technology (http://www.cs.rose-hulman.edu)
2. Rochester Institute of Technology (http://www.rit.edu/~932www/ugrad_bulletin/colleges/coe/compeng.html and http://www.rit.edu/~625www/programs_comp_eng.html)
3. California Polytechnic State University, San Luis Obispo (http://www.cpe.calpoly.edu)
4. Harvey Mudd College (http://www.eng.hmc.edu)
5. Cooper Union for the Advancement of Science and Art, Albert Nerken School of Engineering (http://www.cooper.edu/engineering/departments.html#electric)

Source: *U.S. News & World Report*
*Schools whose terminal degree is the bachelor's or master's in computer engineering

Internships and Volunteerships

Most postsecondary institutions offer internship programs that provide practical hands-on experience to students. Students do not usually receive pay for their work, but gain valuable experience and the opportunity to network with other students and potential employers.

WHO WILL HIRE ME?

As a technical, vocational, or university student of computer engineering, you should work closely with the career services office at your school, as many professionals find their first position through on-campus recruiting. Career services staff are well trained to provide tips on resume writing, interviewing techniques, and locating job leads.

Individuals not working with a career services office can check the classified ads for job openings. They can also work with a local employment agency that places computer professionals in appropriate jobs. Many openings in the computer industry are publicized by word of mouth, so you should stay in touch with working computer professionals to learn who is hiring. In addition, these people may be willing to refer you directly to the person in charge of recruiting. The Internet offers a wealth of employment information plus several sites for browsing job openings, or to post your resume. Most companies maintain a Web page where they post employment opportunities or solicit resumes.

Nick Asvos landed his first job through a recruiting firm, and was initially hired as a Unix administrator by ABN AMRO, an international financial services company. "I began doing network engineering when the network engineer who was there at the time left," Nick says. "I took over his position, attended one class on Cisco switching, and learned the rest from online resources (such as the Cisco Web site) and books."

Small and large corporations alike employ approximately 77,000 computer hardware engineers in nearly every industry. According to the *Occupational Outlook Quarterly,* 43.2 percent of hardware engineers are employed in computer and electronic product manufacturing.

More than 800,000 computer software engineers are employed in the United States. Approximately 460,000 work with applications and 340,000 work with systems software. Software engineering is done in many fields, including medical, industrial, military, communications, aerospace, scientific, and other commercial businesses. The majority of software engineers, though, are employed by computer and data processing companies and by consulting firms.

WHERE CAN I GO FROM HERE?

Computer engineers who demonstrate leadership qualities and thorough technical know-how may become *project team leaders* who are responsible for full-scale development projects. Project team leaders oversee the work of technicians and engineers. They determine the overall parameters of a project, calculate time schedules and financial budgets, divide the project into smaller tasks, and assign these tasks to engineers. Overall, they do both managerial and technical work.

Computer engineers with experience as project team leaders may be promoted to a position as *computer* or *hardware manager,* running a large research and development department. Managers oversee software projects with a more encompassing perspective; they help choose projects to be undertaken, select project team leaders and engineering teams, and assign individual projects. In some cases, they may be required to travel, solicit new business, and contribute to the general marketing strategy of the company. Nick sees himself eventually moving into a management position as either an information technology manager or network operations center manager.

Some computer professionals working on the technical side of the industry opt to switch over to the marketing side of the business. Advancement opportunities here may include positions in product management or sales.

Many computer professionals find that their interests change over time. As long as individuals are well qualified and keep up to date with the latest technology, they are usually able to find positions in other areas of the computer industry.

WHAT ARE THE SALARY RANGES?

Starting salary offers in 2005 for bachelor's degree candidates in computer engineering averaged $52,464, according to the National Association of Colleges and Employers. Master's degree candidates averaged $60,354.

The U.S. Department of Labor reports that median annual earnings of computer hardware engineers were $81,150 in 2004. Salaries ranged from less than $50,490 to more than $123,560.

Computer engineers specializing in applications earned median annual salaries of $74,980 in 2004, according to the U.S. Department of Labor's *National Occupational Employment and Wage*

> ### Related Jobs
>
> - computer network administrators
> - computer programmers
> - computer systems/programmer analysts
> - computer trainers
> - computer-aided design drafters and technicians
> - database specialists
> - graphics programmers
> - Internet developers
> - Internet security specialists
> - microelectronics technicians
> - quality assurance testers
> - semiconductor technicians
> - software designers
> - systems setup specialists
> - technical support specialists
> - technical writers and editors
> - webmasters

Estimates. The lowest 10 percent averaged less than $46,520; the highest 10 percent earned $113,830 or more annually. Software engineers specializing in systems software earned median salaries of $79,740 in 2004. The lowest-paid 10 percent averaged $50,420 annually, and the highest-paid engineers made more than $118,350 per year.

When computer engineers are promoted to project team leader or hardware or software manager, they earn even more. Computer engineers generally earn more in geographical areas where there are clusters of computer companies, such as the Silicon Valley in northern California.

Most computer engineers work for companies that offer extensive benefits, including health insurance, sick leave, and paid vacation. In some smaller computer companies, however, benefits may be limited.

WHAT IS THE JOB OUTLOOK?

Employment in computer hardware engineering will grow about as fast as the average for all occupations through 2014, according to the *Occupational Outlook Handbook*. The number of people earning computer hardware engineering or related degrees has increased rapidly over the past several years, reducing shortages of hardware engineers. Additionally, foreign competition and increased productivity at U.S. companies will limit opportunities for hardware engineers. In addition to new jobs openings, other positions will be available as current computer professionals leave the industry due to retirement or other reasons.

The field of software engineering is expected to be one of the fastest growing occupations through 2014, according to the U.S. Department of Labor. Demands made on computers increase every day and from all industries. The development of one kind of software sparks ideas for many others. In addition, users rely on software programs that are increasingly user-friendly. Nick feels that network engineers will also enjoy strong employment prospects over the next several years. "Corporate networks continue to grow in both size and complexity," he says, "and while network engineering and management does get outsourced from time to time, these jobs tend to stay within the United States and are not sent overseas."

Since technology changes so rapidly, software engineers are advised to keep up with the latest developments. While the need for software engineers will remain high, computer languages will probably change every few years and software engineers will need to attend seminars and workshops to learn new computer languages and software design. They should also read trade magazines, surf the Internet, and talk with colleagues about the field. These kinds of continuing education techniques help ensure that software engineers are best equipped to meet the needs of the workplace.

Computer Network Administrators

SUMMARY

Definition
Computer network administrators manage computer networks so that they operate smoothly and consistently for high efficiency and productivity.

Alternative Job Titles
Computer network security administrators
Computer network specialists
Data communications analysts

Data recovery operators
Network control operators
Network programmers
Network security specialists
System administrators

Salary Range
$37,100 to $58,190 to $91,300+

Educational Requirements
Bachelor's degree

Certification or Licensing
Voluntary

Employment Outlook
Much faster than the average

High School Subjects
Computer science
Mathematics

Personal Interests
Computers
Figuring out how things work
Fixing things

What's the key to being a successful computer network administrator? According to Stella Camacho, a computer network administrator for more than six years, good troubleshooting skills, which, in the event of disaster, can help you save your company time and money. Such skills came in handy when a file server with 300 users at Stella's company could no longer be accessed by anyone on the network. "The first thing I did," she recalls, "was to look for errors on the event logs. The log did show an error that was new to me. (I routinely check event logs on critical servers to make sure the server is healthy).

A search on the Internet for that error showed that it was a known bug. I simply followed the fix described in the article and within 15 minutes from the time the server first went down, it was accessible to all of its users."

WHAT DOES A COMPUTER NETWORK ADMINISTRATOR DO?

Businesses and organizations choose to network, or connect, their computers for many different reasons. One important reason is so that numerous computer users can simultaneously access the same hardware, software, and other computer equipment like printers, fax machines, and Internet connections. By networking such equipment, the business avoids having to purchase individual products for each user. If a small business, for example, has four different computer terminals, all terminals might be able to share a single printer instead of having four of them. In addition, if the company maintains a database that is accessed by multiple users, it has to set up the system in such a way as to make the database, with its constant changes, available to everyone.

These networks can range in size from two computer terminals to hundreds, and can operate with one or more of several different network servers or none at all. Each network is different and tailored to the needs of the business or large corporate department. And each network is invariably messy—problems come up often, employees have difficulties learning the system, passwords and file names are regularly changed, software is updated, backup files must be made, communications lines are broken and must be reestablished—the list can go on and on. *Computer network administrators* must know the network well enough to be able to handle all of these situations.

The specific job duties of a computer network specialist vary greatly depending on the size and structure of the company or department and on the kinds of network systems used. For example, in larger companies the positions may be extremely well defined; they may employ one person for computer security, one for network administration, and one for data recovery. In smaller companies or those departments in which networks are just being introduced, however, employers may hire one or two people to do everything.

Computer network administrators are responsible for adding files to and deleting files from the network server. The

---

Lingo to Learn

application A software program that allows users to perform certain tasks like word processing and record keeping.

backup Copies of computer files stored in a place other than the main work site. Used in case of an emergency.

hardware The physical equipment inside a computer that makes it operate.

LAN (local area network) A network that exists at one location, typically an office.

network Collection of computers connected by wires, radio waves, or optical fibers so that they can communicate to share hardware, software, and files.

operating system Software designed to mediate between hardware and user applications.

server The centralized computer in a network that stores all programs and other information required to make networks function properly.

software Programs that tell the hardware what to do and how to do it.

WAN (wide area network) A network that includes remote sites in different buildings, cities, states, or countries.

server is a centralized computer that stores, among other things, software applications used on a daily or regular basis by the network users. The files updated might include those for database, electronic mail, or word processing applications. Network administrators also handle printing jobs. They must tell the server where the printer is located and establish a printing queue, or line, designating which print jobs have priority. They might also tell the server to hold or change certain files once they reach the printing queue.

Network administrators might also be responsible for setting up user access. Since highly confidential and personal information can be stored on the network server, employees generally have access to only certain applications and files; the network administrator assigns each user or group of users access to the appropriate files and often makes up passwords to be used by each employee. The passwords protect the system from both internal and external computer spying.

Network security specialists often work in companies that make extensive use of computer networks. They are responsible for regulating user access to various computer files, monitoring file use, updating security files, preventing internal/external security breaches and threats, and eliminating virus/worm-related activity. If an employee forgets his or her password, the network security specialist changes it to grant access. Network security specialists ensure that security measures are running accurately by tracking nonauthorized entries, reporting unauthorized users to management, and modifying files to correct the errors. They maintain employee information in the security files. They add new employees to the list, delete former employees, and make official name changes. They look for massive external attacks to a corporate network, such as denial of service where so much improper data traffic is trying to enter the network from the Internet that internal network activity becomes exceedingly slow, and excessive e-mails going out, which could signal an infection from an e-mail-based virus or worm.

Data recovery operators are responsible for developing, implementing, and testing off-site systems that will continue to work in case of emergencies at the main office, such as terrorist attacks, power outages, fires, earthquakes, or floods. Their work is encompassed within the larger framework of disaster recovery planning and business continuity, meaning the actions you should take when a disaster happens and how you can ensure that business operations continue. These tasks are very important because many businesses cannot operate at all without their computer networks. Some businesses, like insurance companies and banks, depend even more on their computer systems during emergencies.

Data recovery operators must determine which hardware and software should be stored at the emergency site, which applications receive operating priority in case of an emergency, where to locate the emergency site, and which employees would be needed to run emergency operations. After testing the system they develop, they report the results to supervisors and management. Data recovery operators work primarily in larger companies.

Network control operators are in charge of all network communications, which usually operate over telephone lines, fiber optic cables, or wireless applications. If a user cannot get the computer to send his or her file to the appropriate place, he or she calls the network control operator for help. The control operator then explains to the employee the step-by-step procedure he or she should have followed to send the file. If the error is not an employee mistake, the network control operator attempts to diagnose the problem by making sure information stored in computer files is accurate, verifying that modems are functioning properly, or running tests on the phone lines or wireless equipment with special equipment. Sometimes, the control operator must ask for outside help from the company who sold or manufactured the malfunctioning system.

Network control operators also keep records of the daily number of communications transactions made, the number and type of problems arising, and the actions taken to solve them. They might also train staff to use the communications systems efficiently and help coordinate or install communication lines.

WHAT IS IT LIKE TO BE A COMPUTER NETWORK ADMINISTRATOR?

"Computer-related problems never end," says Stella Camacho. "To be an effective network administrator I have to prioritize my time so that the most critical issues get addressed first. My job includes second-level support, so I support both servers and desktops." Most of Stella's calls are logged by a help desk and sent to her queue when they can't be resolved. "I spend the first few hours in the morning taking care of these, as well as any other open calls (unresolved from the previous day)," she says. "They range from simple things, like the user not typing in the correct URL to go to a Web site or not having the latest drivers on the print server, to more serious problems, like servers running out of disk space or experiencing hardware failures. The rest of the day I try to spend time on projects like upgrading hardware; patching desktops and servers so they are protected from viruses, worms, spyware, and adware; and evaluating administration tools to make my job more organized." Stella says, however, that she is constantly interrupted by pages from the help desk about more critical problems or requests via phone, e-mail, or "hallway-hijacks." "It is a very busy, fast-paced job," she says, "and the day goes by quickly."

Computer network administrators work indoors in a comfortable office environment. Their work is generally fast paced and can be frustrating. Some tasks, however, are routine and might get a little boring after a while. But many times, network administrators are required to work under a lot of pressure. If the network goes down, for example, the company is losing money, and it is the network administrator's job to get it up and running as fast as possible. The administrator must be able to remember complicated relationships and many details accurately and quickly. Administrators are also called on to deal effectively with the many complaints from network users.

When working on the installation of a new system, many network administrators are required to work overtime until it is fully operational. This usually includes long and frequent meetings. During initial operations of the system, some network administrators may be on call during other shifts for when problems arise, or they may have to train network users during off hours. Stella regularly works nights and

A Short History of Computer Networks

The first major advances in modern computer technology were made during World War II. After the war, it was thought that the enormous size of computers, which easily took up the space of entire warehouses, would limit their use to huge government projects. Accordingly, the 1950 census was computer-processed.

The introduction of semiconductors to computer technology made possible smaller and less expensive computers. Businesses began adapting computers to their operations as early as 1954. Within 30 years, computers had revolutionized the way people work, play, and shop. Today, computers are everywhere, from businesses of all kinds, to government agencies, charitable organizations, and private homes. Over the years, technology has continued to shrink computer size and increase speed at an unprecedented rate.

The first computers commercially used consisted of a big mainframe computer, located in a special computer room, and several independent terminals around the office. Though efficient and effective, the mainframe had several problems. One problem was the update delay, or the time lapse, between when an employee input information and when that information became available to other employees. Though advances in hardware technology have begun addressing this and other problems, many computer companies and businesses have turned to networking instead.

Computer networks do not rely on a mainframe system, but rather use a network server to centralize the processing capacity of several different computers and peripherals. In a network, terminals and other computers are linked directly to the server. This link provides other computer users access to the information instantaneously. The need for computer network administrators that are qualified to oversee network operations has increased in parallel to the growth of computer networking.

The use of networks has grown rapidly, as more companies move from mainframe computers to client-server networks or from paper-based systems to automated record keeping using networked databases. The explosion of Internet technology has created a new area that is also in need of networking professionals.

weekends to ensure that systems are working correctly. "Because we have international divisions, our systems require 24/7 support," she says. "Even without the international connection, maintenance/upgrades to the system are usually done during off-hours to reduce downtime." As a salaried employee, Stella doesn't receive overtime pay, but she gets to take a day off during the week if she works on a Saturday or a Sunday. "Currently, I average about three hours a week for off-hour support," she says. "This is a relatively low number of hours compared to a typical smaller division because we have several network people in our corporate division, and we share the workload."

One other potential source of frustration is communications with other employees. Network administrators deal every day with people who usually don't understand the system as well as they do. They must be able to communicate at different levels of understanding.

DO I HAVE WHAT IT TAKES TO BE A COMPUTER NETWORK ADMINISTRATOR?

Computer network administrators work with a lot of detail; every type of computer, every software application, every network system has a particular set of codes that must be used to get things done. Since users contact them when they have problems, network administrators must have a running knowledge of all the codes, plus an understanding of how they all link together. This also requires strong logical thinking skills. To succeed as a network specialist, you must be very good at organizing and analyzing large amounts of detail at both the micro and macro levels. Often, network technicians are called on to solve multiple problems at once.

Working as a network specialist also involves a certain amount of pressure. When a system is down, you must be able to think things through thoroughly without panicking.

Effective communication skills are also important for network administrators, who must explain complex information to both technical experts and people who have little understanding of computers. Since the computer industry has generated a lot of jargon, it can be difficult to simplify explanations.

Stephen Ibaraki, board director of the Network Professional Association, believes that "successful computer network administrators should have good problem-solving aptitude, perseverance, the ability to work long hours without complaint, a good, positive approach to work and life, a willingness for continual learning, good communications and writing skills, and the ability to work alone, collaborate with others, and lead by sharing."

HOW DO I BECOME A COMPUTER NETWORK ADMINISTRATOR?

Education

High School

High school courses in computer science provide a solid understanding of basic computing principles. Math courses such as algebra and geometry help develop logical and analytical thinking skills, while those in psychology and English improve verbal and written communication skills. Any business courses will increase knowledge about the ways in which management decisions are made, often important for network administration and engineering choices.

Stephen Ibaraki encourages students to keep up with recent updates in the field by subscribing to newsletters such as those offered by *Network Computing* magazine. These weekly e-newsletters include *Network Computing Report, Network Computing Online, Network Computing's Mobile Observer,* and *Network Computing's IT Pro Downloads.* He also recommends that they participate in IT-based blogs and forums, as well as become student members of computer associations and professional groups. "Usually," he says, "students can join for a modest fee, attend regular special lectures/events/Webcasts, receive access to expensive resources, build future professional networks, often receive bursaries and scholarships, obtain mentoring, and receive valuable tips from working and experienced professionals. Every major group has student programs containing one or more of these elements."

Postsecondary Training

Many network jobs require at least a bachelor's degree in network technology, network security, computer science, or computer engineering. "A background and education in business is also becoming important," according to Stephen, "as network activities are closely aligned with business goals—especially if you are on a management path." More specialized positions require an advanced degree. Workers with a college education are more likely to deal with the theoretical aspects of computer networking and are more likely to be promoted to management positions. Opportunities in computer design, systems analysis, and computer programming, for example, are open only to college graduates. In addition to college training, you will also need to pursue continuing education to stay up to date with this ever-changing field. "To stay current," Stella Camacho says, "I

To Be a Successful Computer Network Specialist, You Should . . .

- be organized and possess logic skills
- understand basic computer principles and be willing to learn more complex skills as technology advances
- enjoy challenges and solving problems
- be able to patiently communicate complicated material in simple terms
- be able to work well under pressure
- have the ability to work with people of different computer skill levels
- be willing to continue to learn throughout your career

attend seminars, 'webinars,' read books and publications, and discuss various topics with my peers."

Certification and Licensing

There are a number of certification programs, and Microsoft, Novell, Cisco, CompTIA, LPI (Linux Professional Institute—the largest in the Linux community), and Red Hat are the most popular. If you are already employed, it is wise to become certified by a program designed to complement the system your company is already using, unless the goal is to branch out into a different career field.

While certification may provide you with a competitive advantage over fellow job seekers, not all companies require it. In fact, experience means more than certification today. This is due in large part to the rapidly changing world of networking. You may receive certification one day and discover a new version of the operating system is being released the next. In addition, more and more systems will combine features from different companies and sources, so being strictly a Microsoft Windows 2000 specialist won't necessarily get you very far.

Internships and Volunteerships

Since many people complete commercial certifications while working full time, there are not many internship opportunities available. Those who would like to put their knowledge to work on a volunteer basis should contact local or national charities of interest. Most charity offices run on computers, and such valuable help is often very sought after and appreciated.

College students should contact their career services office for help identifying and applying to internship programs. Large companies may be persuaded to take on a student, you just need to convince them of your value.

WHO WILL HIRE ME?

Computer network administrators work in companies that rely on computer networks to do business. As insurance companies, banks, and other financial institutions automate more and more of their services, they will count more heavily on computer networking, creating many job opportunities for individuals trained in these areas.

Since most companies are moving toward networking, positions are multiplying, and demand for network administrators is currently very high. Some companies might decide to promote and train administrators from within, so employees wishing to work in networking should keep up with in-house job-opening lists. For these positions, individuals already certified are likely to be hired rather quickly, especially if they have experience and knowledge of multiple systems.

Federal and state governments are also good places to look for jobs in computer networking. Since many governmental offices manage huge amounts of information on many different networks, their overall need for network administrators is high. In addition, these positions are often on the top of the list to be filled, even during hiring slowdowns or freezes.

Several professional newsletters and magazines offer job listings in the area of computer networking, most of which can be found on the Internet—another indispensable job search tool. Job openings are also listed in all major newspapers' classified sections and in computer trade magazines like *PC World* and *Macworld*.

In addition, many professional associations, including the Association for Computing Machinery, the Network Professional Association, the IEEE Computer Society, and the Association of Information Technology Professionals, provide job lists.

Network administrators might also find out about good job openings from their colleagues in the industry. As individuals work their way through the education requirements for network certification, they can ask instructors and other education center personnel about where to apply.

College students should work through their college career services office, which typically sets up recruiting programs with many employers. Other than companies specializing in the service industries like insurance companies and banks, graduates might look at Hewlett-Packard Co., Microsoft Corporation, and Novell. Competition for jobs at these companies is very stiff, however.

Advancement Possibilities

Computer network engineers set up computer networks, often from scratch. They interview employers and employees to determine their needs, analyze and prioritize those needs, select appropriate hardware and software, make any necessary changes, supervise installation and initial operations of the system, and sometimes provide training to network users.

Enterprise computer network engineers perform many of the same duties as computer network engineers but at a higher level. They may work, for example, on company-wide networks or systems instead of networks serving only one department or several departments in a large company.

Multimedia administrators design ways to make graphics, audio, and video work well together, producing multimedia games, presentations, and other types of programs.

WHERE CAN I GO FROM HERE?

Advancement for computer network administrators varies greatly, depending on education, experience, and personal interest. If you begin as a network administrator, you might next work toward becoming a network engineer. Then, you might progress to the level of *enterprise network engineer*, a position that includes responsibility for all computer systems within a single, medium- or large-sized company.

But a network administrator might wish to become more specialized and train as a network security specialist (something Stella Camacho is interested in doing in the future), data recovery planner, or data communications operator.

Another possible career path to take is to become an *information systems manager*. Larger companies need someone in charge of all their computer systems and services. Administrators who have strong, effective communication skills, the ability to motivate teams and organize team projects, as well as technical expertise of the computer systems involved in their work, make exceptional candidates for such management positions. Increasingly, a business background and education is important for management positions, and many senior network administrators receive a master's in business administration while working.

WHAT ARE THE SALARY RANGES?

Factors such as the size and type of employer, the administrator's experience, and specific job duties influence the earnings of network administrators. According to the U.S. Department of Labor, the median annual income for computer network and systems administrators was $58,190 in 2004. The lowest paid 10 percent made less than $37,100 per year, and the highest paid 10 percent earned more than $91,300 annually that same year.

Many companies that employ computer network administrators offer a full range of benefits, including health insurance, paid vacation, and sick leave. In addition, many companies have tuition reimbursement programs for employees seeking to pursue education or professional certification.

Related Jobs

- computer network engineers
- computer programmers
- computer scientists
- computer security coordinators
- computer systems analysts
- computer systems hardware analysts
- computer systems software analysts
- computer systems/programmer analysts
- computer trainers
- data communications analysts
- database specialists
- graphics programmers
- Internet security specialists
- network control operators
- software designers
- software engineers
- systems setup specialists
- technical support specialists
- technical writers and editors

WHAT IS THE JOB OUTLOOK?

Stephen Ibaraki feels that the employment outlook for computer network administrators is good. "Key areas of growth," he says, "include wireless, security, identity management, Web services, high-end storage management, supply-chain management, server virtualization, database administration, business intelligence, software engineering, open source environments, enterprise information integration, anything Internet-related, and enterprise services such as VOIP (Voice-Over IP—enabling voice communications over a network including the Internet)."

Job opportunities for computer network administrators are expected to grow much faster than average through 2014, according to the U.S. Department of Labor. There are several reasons for this. Many companies that used to rely on very large-sized computers (mainframes) are now finding it better to develop a series of networks comprised of smaller computers that can communicate with each other and achieve the same results. The companies are already beginning and will continue to search for well-qualified people to help administer and engineer networking projects.

In addition, many service industries that relied more heavily on paperwork for record keeping now prefer to automate and keep records on computer databases. Insurance companies, for example, are looking to eliminate all paper forms from the insurance process. Instead, they want to have online forms that can be filled out by the client on the computer. This would allow them to avoid delays and expenses caused by the post office and paper processing. Computerized form procedures would be handled through a network that, in turn, would need administrators and engineers to run it. The economic and productive advantages of networking currently make it such that companies will continue to invest in network development, even in times of economic difficulty. This means that computer network jobs should be relatively easy to find for the next several years.

The growing trend toward networking is occurring particularly in insurance companies, banks, and other financial institutions, although any business with more than one computer may be heading toward networking. As you begin to prepare for careers in computer networking, you should pay attention to the current economic climate to ascertain which industries may be more financially stable.

The federal government is also very involved in the process of setting up networks among different offices and departments. This, combined with the fact that the government is handling ever-growing amounts of information and pays competitively in mid-level jobs, makes it a prime target in future job hunting.

If you develop expertise in a specific area, like computer security, you can look to larger companies and computer companies for jobs that best match your qualifications. It is important to remain well trained in several areas, however, because companies may choose to hire one or two people to do everything instead of numerous administrators when business is down.

Many computer companies are shifting to a service-based paradigm, offering comprehensive service to clients. This means that big computer companies will be hiring more and more technical support staff who can help clients install their networks, train client staff, and answer client questions. Computer network administrators might be well qualified for some of these positions.

Computer Programmers

SUMMARY

Definition
Computer programmers write instructions that tell computers what to do in a computer language, or code, that the computers understand.

Alternative Job Titles
Applications programmers
Business and commercial applications programmers
Computer and video game programmers
Engineering and scientific applications programmers
Systems programmers

Salary Range
$36,470 to $62,890 to $99,610+

Educational Requirements
Bachelor's degree

Certification or Licensing
Voluntary

Employment Outlook
More slowly than the average

High School Subjects
Computer science
Mathematics
Physics

Personal Interests
Computers
Writing

Computer programming has evolved in leaps and bounds from the 1970s, when Michael Wido started in the industry. "I used to write up my COBOL code and Job Control Language on coding forms," he recalls, "put it in a basket, and the next day, punched cards were delivered to me, which I put into a card reader. A year or two later, my company brought in the 'Tubes,' which were 3278 terminals, and we typed in our own code, using Interactive System Productivity Facility (ISPF). When PCs first came out, we would have to enter our code into an editor, similar to ISPF, and run it through a batch compiler. In the early to mid-90s and through today, much of the code is generated by tools that utilize a graphic user interface. Less and sometimes no actual programming is needed to build simple applications."

WHAT DOES A COMPUTER PROGRAMMER DO?

Computer programmers work in a variety of business, industrial, professional, and governmental settings to create the detailed instructions that tell a computer what to do. These instructions are called *programs*, or software.

Because computers cannot think, computer programmers must know how to arrange instructions in an order and language that the computer can follow. The programmer's first step is to think about the task and how to instruct the computer to perform it. At this stage, programmers usually create a flowchart to illustrate each step the computer will have to follow to get the desired results. Programmers must then translate this flowchart into a coded language that computers can follow. There are many programming languages, including traditional languages such as COBOL, FORTRAN, and C; object-oriented languages such as Java, C/C++, and Visual Basic; fourth- and fifth-generation languages; graphic user interface (GUI); and more. Programmers put the coded steps of the language into the computer, thereby creating a program.

After the programmers have saved the program on disk, CD-ROM, or on the main computer, they must test it using sample data to see if it runs correctly. If the task is not being performed as intended, the programmers must examine the program and make changes in it until it provides the desired outcome. This process is called *debugging*.

Once a program is debugged and running as expected, the programmers may help write an instruction manual explaining how to operate the program. Because the end user may have limited technical knowledge, the programmer must be able to communicate in simple, clear language.

There are two main types of computer programmers: *applications programmers* and *systems programmers*. Applications programmers create or revise software for specific jobs or tasks, such as software to help a business office process payments or to help the navy monitor the course of submarines. As new tasks arise at an organization, applications programmers are asked to develop software that will perform the desired job. Applications programmers often specialize in one of two fields: business and commercial applications programming or engineering and scientific applications programming. *Business and commercial applications programmers* write software to help a business run more smoothly. Often, their programs will involve accounting, billing, payroll, inventory, and database procedures. *Engineering and scientific applications programmers* create programs that are used for scientific or mathematical purposes. For example, their programs may instruct computers to analyze medical data or assist in air traffic control.

Systems programmers control and maintain the overall operation of the organization's computer system, including the central processing unit and peripheral equipment, such as printers, terminals, and disk drives. They instruct the computers on how to accept and store information and how to communicate with other equipment via cables, known as a network. Systems programmers often assist applications programmers with troubleshooting and problem solving because of their in-depth knowledge of the entire system.

Whether working in systems or applications, a computer programmer is the link between the computer needs of an organization and the capabilities of the machines.

> **Lingo to Learn**
>
> **debug** To search for and correct errors in a program.
>
> **documentation** Written instructions explaining how to operate the program.
>
> **flowchart** A diagram that shows step-by-step progression through a procedure or system.
>
> **hardware** The physical components of a computer.
>
> **port** To adapt a program written for one type of hardware to another type of hardware.
>
> **run book** Instructions written by programmers to explain to computer operators how to use a program.
>
> **software** Programs, procedures, and related documentation associated with a computer system.

One popular specialty that has emerged over the last two decades is that of *computer and video game programmer*. These programmers write code for computer and video games played on various platforms, such as video game consoles, arcade machines, handheld devices, and computers, and through online Internet subscriptions.

WHAT IS IT LIKE TO BE A COMPUTER PROGRAMMER?

Michael Wido began working as a computer programmer in 1978—back in the days of computer punched cards and COBOL (a very early computer programming language). But even before that, he was experimenting with programming. "My high school had a Hewlett Packard computer that had 4K of RAM, an optical card reader, and one line display," he recalls. "The first program I created was a blackjack game, quickly followed by roulette and horse racing."

Over the years, Michael has worked in a variety of programming jobs, as well as in supervisory and managerial positions in software help desk support, mainframe programming, and microcomputer software engineering. He has been a freelance contract programmer since 1990.

Michael begins his day around 7:00 or 7:30 a.m. by checking and responding to e-mails and voicemail. He then takes care of daily backup and maintenance tasks that are required for some of his customers' Web sites. "From about 9:30 a.m. to about 3:00 p.m.," he says, "I design, code, or document, depending on what's in the queue. This can be broken up by calls, meetings, or e-mails. What I do depends on priorities, timelines, milestones, and deadlines. If I'm tight with a deadline, I let the phone bounce to voicemail and check e-mail less often."

Around 3:00 p.m., Michael takes a break to spend time with his kids and have dinner. (He has two teenage sons who are involved heavily in sports, and he spends quite a bit of time supporting them.) "I start up again at about 7:30 p.m. and work until 10 or 11," he says. "If I'm on track with the deadlines for the current projects, I'll handle some of the administrative duties. These range from responding to RFPs [requests for proposals], invoicing, marketing, bookkeeping, and tax and payroll deposits."

Most programmers work in pleasant office conditions, since computers require an air-conditioned, dust-free environment. Programmers perform most of their duties in one primary location but may be asked to travel to other computing sites on occasion. Michael works in a home office in his basement. "Early on, I did some on-site work," he says. "Now, I go on site just for meetings. I have a summer home in the north woods and sometimes go up there to work. I can work anywhere."

The average programmer works between 35 and 40 hours weekly. In some job situations, the programmer may have to work nights or weekends on short notice. This might happen when a program is going through its trial runs, for example, or when there are many demands for additional services.

work before proceeding to the next steps. Programmers must have the patience and problem-solving skills to debug a program, going through the codes and carefully examining them for error, entering test data, and running the program again. For someone with little patience, this type of work might quickly become frustrating.

Being accurate and detail oriented is also essential to computer programming. Because computers only understand specific instruction codes, even the smallest error will make an entire program unusable. Finally, since computer programmers act as the link between the capabilities of the computers and the needs of the computer operators, programmers have to be able to communicate with both people and machines. They need to be able to listen well and to communicate succinctly what they mean.

DO I HAVE WHAT IT TAKES TO BE A COMPUTER PROGRAMMER?

Computer programmers need to have a can-do attitude and a willingness to keep trying, to be able to handle setbacks and failures, and to keep going forward.

Computer programming requires a great deal of patience, persistence, and concentration. When creating software, programmers must focus on determining the correct steps and instructions for the computer to follow. This takes thought, planning, and immense creativity. Programmers must test and retest steps of the program, making sure they

To Be a Successful Computer Programmer, You Should . . .

- be able to think logically
- have a long attention span
- be creative
- be well organized, precise, and detail oriented
- like to work independently
- enjoy solving problems

HOW DO I BECOME A COMPUTER PROGRAMMER?

Michael trained for the field by taking programming classes at a junior college. "At the same time," he says, "I had a job in the mailroom at International Harvester. I was promoted to a mainframe operator and, a year or two later, got the opportunity to go through their extensive programming training. I continued with some junior college classes, seminars, and did a lot of self-study when new technologies came out. I also had an 8080 at home, about three years before the IBM PC came out. I taught myself Basic, CP/M, and assembler."

Education

High School

If you are interested in becoming a computer programmer, you must complete high school. You should take college-preparatory courses in mathematics, which is the basis for computer programming and will help you develop the logical sequencing abilities necessary in the field. High-level courses in physics will also help you.

If your high school offers courses in computers and has computer laboratories on campus, you should take as many of these courses as possible. In this way, you can become well acquainted with the functions of computers before entering college and the job market. High school courses in business are especially important if you are interested in becoming a business and commercial applications programmer or systems programmer for a business or corporation.

Postsecondary Training

Most employers prefer their programmers to be college graduates. In the past, as the field was first taking shape, employers were known to hire people with some formal education and little or no experience but determination and the ability to learn quickly. As the market becomes saturated with individuals wishing to break into this field, however, a college degree is becoming increasingly important. The U.S. Department of Labor reports that about 67 percent of computer programmers held a bachelor's degree or higher in 2004.

Most four-year colleges and universities have computer science departments with a variety of computer-related majors, any of which can prepare a student for a career in programming. Employers who require a college degree often do not express a preference as to major field of study, although mathematics or computer science is highly favored. For a list of accredited four-year computer science programs, visit the Accreditation Board for Engineering and Technology's Web site, http://www.abet.org. Other acceptable majors may be business administration, accounting, engineering, or physics. Entrance requirements for jobs with the government are much the same as those in private industry.

Many employers also send new programmers to special training courses before the programmer is allowed to begin working with company computers. In this situation, expenses are usually paid by the employer, and training time can take anywhere from two weeks to two months. Some computer programming jobs do require graduate degrees.

Certification and Licensing

Criteria and qualifications for being hired as a computer programmer vary between employers. Some employers may require work experience, others may require degrees from two- or four-year colleges, and still others may look for a combination of the two. Most people who work as computer programmers are not certified in this field. It is possible, however, to become certified as a computer programmer, and certification could help in attracting the attention of potential employers. The Institute for Certification of Computing Professionals (ICCP) offers a series of exams that, once passed, will provide the programmer with certification at one of two levels: Associate Computing Professional or Certified Computing Professional. The level at which programmers are certified depends upon the programmers' work and educational backgrounds and the exams taken. While ICCP certification is not required for most programming jobs, it may provide you with a competitive advantage over other job seekers.

Internships and Volunteerships

Today, most homes and even the smallest businesses have computers, providing ample opportunity for you to gain hands-on experience with computers and programming. At home, surf the Internet for information about computer-related careers, education, and scholarships. You may want to join a local or school computer club, and you should pick up books or magazines about programming. You might be able to find summer or after-school jobs or internships working with a computer company, helping to input or process data and becoming familiar with the ways a computer is used in a business setting. You may be able to work at small shops, such as book and pet stores, helping to maintain inventory records on a computer, in a library using computerized library catalogs and loan information, or on a school or local newspaper that uses computers for writing, graphics, and production. Some young people's business organizations such as Junior Achievement may also offer high school

---

Unlimited Possibilities

Computer programmers may find work in a wide variety of settings, including:

- medical laboratories
- software companies
- colleges and universities
- banks
- small businesses
- large corporations
- nonprofit organizations
- research companies
- robotics manufacturers
- commercial aviation companies
- the military

students an opportunity to work with computers. While computer-oriented jobs for most high school students will not involve programming, these jobs will help you gain exposure to and experience with a variety of computer capabilities.

WHO WILL HIRE ME?

Many programmers are hired right out of college, and most two-year colleges offer job placement services. These services help you set up interviews with local businesses, even before you've finished the program. In most cases, programmers will have jobs, or at least job offers, by the time they graduate.

The first step in finding a job in computer programming is to isolate the type of work you are interested in doing. Because computers are such a large part of today's world, programmers can find work at small or large businesses, in science, health, or the military, or even at a company that creates software to sell to other companies. You should think about whether you are interested in systems or applications programming and whether you are more interested in the business and commercial applications of computers or the engineering and scientific aspects of the field.

Once you have selected an area of interest, you can take numerous approaches to job hunting. Often, the newspaper classified section advertises job fairs and openings for computer programmers, but many employers now turn to the Internet to post jobs. Thousands of companies and organizations advertise job

> **Advancement Possibilities**
>
> *Chief computer programmers* plan, schedule, and direct preparation of programs to process data and solve problems by use of computers, often consulting with managerial and systems analysis personnel.
>
> *Systems analysts* analyze user requirements, procedures, and problems to automate processing or to improve existing computer systems. They confer with personnel of organizational units involved to analyze current operational procedures and identify problems.
>
> *Programmer analysts* plan, develop, test, and document computer programs, applying knowledge of programming techniques and computer systems.

opportunities on their Web sites, and there are many Web sites devoted specifically to helping you land a job. It is even possible to post a resume or apply for open positions directly online. If you have a specific interest, such as flight simulation or medical technology, you might want to find companies in this field and contact them directly with a resume and cover letter. Systems programmers usually work for larger corporations or companies with extensive computer systems, and job-hunting efforts should be directed toward these companies. In addition, some agencies specialize in placing computer professionals in both temporary and permanent positions. These agencies work to match programmers to companies needing computer assistance. Computer consulting and independent contracting is also a growing field. Rather than hiring computer programmers as permanent employees, many companies are turning to computer contractors who are hired to come into the company and perform computer work on an as-needed basis. These consulting firms are usually found on the Internet or in the Yellow Pages under "Computers-Consultants."

WHERE CAN I GO FROM HERE?

Some companies offer a programmer with extensive programming background the job of *chief programmer*. This job entails overseeing the work of the programming staff, assigning projects, and consulting with management to determine deadlines and special needs and concerns. Programmers can also advance into the position of *systems analyst*, computer specialists who are employed by many large companies to examine the computer needs of the company and then create methods to improve the system.

Computer programmers may get involved in software or hardware sales, helping clients to select appropriate computer equipment and providing them with instructions on its proper use. They may open their own businesses to sell computer equipment or to offer consulting services to companies needing computer help. Computer programmers also work as computer science instructors at high school, community college, and university levels. With the prevalence of computers in today's society, skilled computer programmers have a wide variety of opportunities for advancement in their field.

Michael Wido plans to continue to do contract programming as much as he can, "but as things are becoming more and more positive with my new business venture [an Internet-based business]," he says, "my work may shift to that entirely. I'm just trying to survive now."

WHAT ARE THE SALARY RANGES?

According to the National Association of Colleges and Employers, the starting annual salary for college graduates with bachelor's degrees in computer programming averaged $50,820 in 2005. The U.S. Department of Labor reports the median annual salary for computer programmers was $62,890 in 2004. The lowest-paid 10 percent of programmers earned less than $36,470 annually, and at the other end of the pay scale, the highest-paid 10 percent earned more than $99,610 that same year. Programmers in the West and the Northeast are generally paid more than those in the South and Midwest. This is because most big computer companies are located in the Silicon Valley in California or in the state of Washington, where Microsoft, a major employer of programmers, has its headquarters. Also, some industries, such as public utilities and data processing service firms, tend to pay their programmers higher wages than do other types of employers, such as banks and schools.

Most staff programmers receive the customary paid vacation and sick leave and are included in such company benefits as group insurance and retirement benefit plans.

Related Jobs

- computer network administrators
- computer support service owners
- computer systems programmer/analysts
- computer trainers
- database specialists
- detail programmers
- electronic data processing managers
- engineering analysts
- graphics programmers
- hardware engineers
- information scientists
- Internet developers
- Internet security specialists
- mathematical technicians
- operations research analysts
- software designers
- software engineers
- software technicians
- systems analysts
- technical support specialists

WHAT IS THE JOB OUTLOOK?

"The market for computer programmers is shrinking," Michael says. "Too many cheap offshore options are available. It's hard to be competitive when someone is willing to do your job for one-fifth to one-quarter of your rate and has tax advantages. I used to be able to get many projects that lasted months. Now I have to fight to get the small ones. Additionally, large software companies are building more and more features into the packages they sell, so less and less custom programming is required. For Web sites, there are more and more low-cost options available (template based) which are limited, but the small business owner doesn't understand that. They just want the Web presence at the lowest cost."

The employment rate for computer programmers is expected to grow more slowly than the average through 2014, according to the U.S. Department of Labor. Factors that make job growth for this profession slower than job growth for other computer industry professions include the outsourcing of these jobs to other countries, new technologies that eliminate the need for some routine programming work of the past, the increased availability of packaged software programs, and the increased sophistication of computer users who are able to write and implement their own programs.

Job applicants with the best chances of employment will be college graduates who know several programming languages, especially newer ones used for computer networking and database management. In addition, the best applicants will have some training or experience in an applied field such as accounting, science, engineering, or management. Competition for jobs will be heavier among graduates of two-year data processing programs and among people with equivalent experience or with less training. Since this field is constantly changing, programmers should stay abreast of the latest technology to remain competitive.

Computer Service Technicians

SUMMARY

Definition
Computer service technicians install, maintain, troubleshoot, and repair computers and related equipment.

Alternative Job Titles
Bench servicers
Computer servicers
Field service representatives

Salary Range
$24,190 to $40,430 to $69,110+

Educational Requirements
Associate degree

Certification or Licensing
Voluntary

Employment Outlook
Faster than the average

High School Subjects
Computer science
Shop (trade/vo-tech education)

Personal Interests
Building things
Computers
Figuring out how things work
Fixing things

One of Richard Strand's favorite aspects of work as a computer service technician is the feeling of reward he gets when he's able to get a PC back into action. "There's a great deal of satisfaction," he says, "when someone brings in a computer they've been working on for four days, and you put it on a bench and an hour later, you've got it working perfectly."

WHAT DOES A COMPUTER SERVICE TECHNICIAN DO?

Computer service technicians are employed by computer companies to fulfill the obligations of the service contract (which is often provided to a customer when he or she purchases a product). They install and set up computer equipment when it first arrives at the client's business. They follow up installation with regular preventive maintenance visits, adjusting and cleaning mechanical parts. In addition, one technician is always on call in case equipment fails. They know how to run diagnostic tests with specialized equipment in order to determine the nature and extent of the problem. They are usually trained in replacing semiconductor chips, circuit boards, and other hardware components. If they cannot fix the computer on site, they bring it back to their employer's service area.

Some technicians are employed in the maintenance department of large companies. They generally have a good working knowledge of mechanics and electronics and then are trained further by the company to work with the specific equipment the business uses most. In-house training is often provided by industrial and manufacturing companies as well as those corporations that depend on big machinery, like mail sorters and check processors.

Employed either by a specialty repair shop, machine manufacturer, or product-specific service company, *field service representatives* are computer service technicians who travel to the client's workplace to do maintenance and repairs. Their duties include following a predetermined schedule of routine maintenance. They might, for example, change the toner, clean the optic parts, and make mechanical adjustments in photocopiers and printers. They must also make time each day to respond to incoming requests for emergency service. Supervisors are usually responsible for prioritizing maintenance and repair requests, but juggling the variety and number of responsibilities can be hectic. In addition, technicians are required to keep detailed written explanations of all service provided so that future problems can be dealt with more effectively.

Sometimes computers need major repairs that are too complicated and messy to be handled in the office or workplace. These computers are taken to a repair shop or company service area to be worked on by *bench servicers*, that is, technicians who work at their employer's location.

Some very experienced computer servicers open their own repair shops. Often, these entrepreneurs find it necessary to offer service for a wide range of equipment in order to be successful, particularly in areas where competition is tight. To further supplement their income, they might start selling certain products and offering service contracts on them. Business owners have the added responsibility of normal business duties, such as bookkeeping and advertising.

WHAT IS IT LIKE TO BE A COMPUTER SERVICE TECHNICIAN?

Richard Strand is the owner/primary technician of Contact A+ Plus Comput-

---

Lingo to Learn

bench servicer A repairer who works exclusively in his or her company's shop area and does not make house calls.

calibrate To adjust precisely according to specifications.

computer peripherals Any equipment linked to a computer hard drive, such as disk drives, terminals or screens, printers, and modems.

diagnostic tests Tests run on various mechanical and electronic machines to determine the nature and extent of a particular problem.

field service representative A repairer who makes service calls at the client's business.

troubleshoot To problem solve in a step-by-step fashion, checking first for the simplest causes and moving up to the more complex.

ers, a family-owned computer repair and sales business in Paw Paw, Michigan. A service technician for more than 15 years, Richard started his career in a slightly nontraditional way. In the early 1990s, he ran a privately owned computer bulletin board service. "What happened," he explains, "was that people using the boards started asking questions about computers, and I provided the answers. I started a home-based business finding computer parts for people. They wanted me to do the work because they were afraid to take their computer apart, and it kind of snowballed. About four years ago, we opened a store in downtown Paw Paw."

Richard works from 7:30 a.m. to 6:00 p.m. Monday through Friday and from 9:00 a.m. to 1:00 p.m. on Saturday. "I do service calls after the shop closes," he says, "and it can get late into the night. But whenever someone needs a service call, we have to do it."

Richard begins each day by balancing his books, checking phone messages (and making notes as to whom to call back and what they need), and taking a quick inventory of products or supplies that he may need to reorder. After that, he checks the notes on the computers that are on the benches so he knows where he left off the day before and then gets to work.

"The most common problems we deal with are viruses, which create a lot of problems with a computer," Richard says. "Music download sites (such as Kazaa) and online gaming sites are notorious for creating a lot of problems in a computer. Most of the hardware problems we fix are pretty straightforward, like power supplies or modems, but I also will change the capacitors on motherboards if they are bad. The harder problems to diagnose are things like bad RAM or a bad video card, and sometimes I get computers where everything seems okay but they still don't work, and the only way to solve it is to swap parts until you find the bad one. Some of the machines that come in really aren't worth fixing, and I try to let the customer know that without sounding like my goal is to sell them a new computer."

To fix computers, Richard uses tools like pliers, electric and manual screwdrivers, dental picks, soldering irons, jeweler's tool kits (a variety of small tools used to repair laptops), and vacuums and paintbrushes (for cleaning computers). "I also have power supply testers to check power supplies," he says, "and LAN testers to check cables. For those hard-to-find problems, I use parts from other computers to test them. I don't save a lot of parts, but I do keep enough to use for testing in other computers to find a problem."

Amidst his repair work, Richard must also answer phone calls from people who are having computer problems and wait on customers who are interested in purchasing computers and related equipment. "We sell computers, software, cables, keyboards, mice, printers, hard drives, flash cards, toner, modems… just about anything for a computer," he says.

DO I HAVE WHAT IT TAKES TO BE A COMPUTER SERVICE TECHNICIAN?

Computer service technicians should have a solid grasp of the basics of computers, electronics, mechanics, and photography. This knowledge is important for several reasons. First of all, it allows the technician to handle simple repairs easily. Second, it provides the background necessary for further training on more complicated machinery.

Third, such knowledge adds to an individual's willingness to learn about new equipment and allows the individual to be flexible about the kinds of computers and peripherals he or she can work on.

Technicians are often those who have long been interested in figuring out how things work and who have the manual dexterity to tinker around with gadgets, tools, and household machines. Computers and peripherals often need repairs in spots that are hard to get to, where the parts and tools used are small, even tiny.

As is the case in most jobs, technicians should have solid communication skills. They should be able to explain technical problems to a wide variety of people, from people who have no understanding of how something works, to people who actually design certain machines. It can be a delicate issue and actually more important than one might think; companies who specialize in service lose customers if technicians make them feel stupid or do not take the time to carefully explain what is going on. "I think that any customer service worker needs to be aware that the bosses, their peers, and their subordinates are included in a group called 'internal customers,'" says Dan Haeder, a telecommunications/supervisory controls and data acquisition instructor at Mitchell Technical Institute in Mitchell, South Dakota. "It is very important to be courteous, compassionate, and cooperative with the end user or 'external customer,' and that group of internal customers as well. Get to work on time, do more than 'just enough' on each and every job, and remember that you may be the only individual that your clients associate with from your company. You need to maintain a professional profile at all times. You are company XYZ in the external customer's eyes!"

Richard Strand feels that a good, friendly personality is key to success as a computer service technician. "The most

To Be a Successful Computer Service Technician, You Should . . .

- have superior manual dexterity
- be able to follow complex written instructions and diagrams
- enjoy learning about new computers and technology
- work well alone, without direct supervision
- be able to communicate difficult technical ideas effectively to people with different levels of experience

important personal skill for a computer technician is to be friendly to everyone at all times. Working on computer problems all day can be frustrating, and technicians must have the ability to separate themselves from the problem—especially when dealing with customers. If, for example, the phone rings during one of these frustrating moments, you can't let yourself get upset and not be as polite as you should to the potential customer. I would rather hire a technician who is polite and caring and not a great technician than a person who is a brilliant technician but who has a bad personality."

HOW DO I BECOME A COMPUTER SERVICE TECHNICIAN?

Education

High School

Traditional high school courses like mathematics, physics, and other laboratory-based sciences can provide a strong foundation for understanding basic electronic and mechanical principles. English and speech classes can help boost your written and verbal communication skills.

More specialized courses offered at the high school level, such as electronics, electricity, automotive/engine repair, or computer applications, are a very good source of practice in manual aptitude. Any other courses focusing on the use of flowcharts and schematic reading are also beneficial. In addition, any experience with audiovisual equipment is a plus; opportunities for such experience might be found in school theatrical productions or any other kind of multimedia presentation.

Postsecondary Training

For those individuals interested in specializing in computer and peripheral repair, courses designed around computer technology, like microelectronics and computer design, should be selected. Some technical schools already offer specialized degrees in computer technology. Computer repair positions usually require the completion of at least an associate's degree.

Even with a degree in hand, new employees will receive a heavy dose of on-the-job training. From the employer's point of view, the degree proves that the new employee has the ability to do the work, but he or she still needs to be trained specifically on the computers and peripherals most often used by the company. Training programs vary greatly in duration and intensity, depending on the employer and the nature of the position. Training courses may be self-study or held in organized classrooms. Generally, they will include some degree of hands-on instruction.

Keeping up with technology is extremely important for technicians. Anyone who is considering this career should be prepared for the stress involved in working with such rapidly changing technology. Technicians are expected to participate in seminars and workshops offered at regular intervals by the employer, a computer manufacturer, or outside service companies.

Another way technicians keep up is by reading detailed brochures and service manuals on new equipment. They also read a variety of magazines and newsletters on electronics and mechanical devices.

Certification and Licensing

Certification as a computer service technician is not mandatory, but several associations offer voluntary certification to computer service technicians. Technicians with less than four years' experience who pass an examination administered by the International Society of Certified Electronics Technicians can earn the designation Associate Level Certified Electronics Technician. Those with more than four years of experience who pass an examination can become journeymen-level certified electronics technicians.

Computer service technicians with the equivalent of 500 hours of hands-on experience who pass an examination can earn the CompTIA A+ certification—which is offered by the Computing Technology Industry Association. The Electronics Technicians Association International also offers voluntary certification in several specialties.

Other voluntary certification exists for individuals who are specialized computer technicians. The Institute for Certification of Computer Professionals offers certification to computer professionals under the titles of certified computing professional and associate computing professional.

Internships and Volunteerships

As is true for someone trying to break into any field, initial entry may be difficult. If you are still in high school, you may wish to get a summer or weekend job in a local repair shop. This experience will give you a feel for the variety of activities that go on there. Technical schools often have internship programs for students, offering off-quarter employment in various companies. Many of these internships turn into full-time jobs after graduation.

One way you can practice your skills is to offer repair services to people in your neighborhood, by repairing their computers, VCRs, DVD players, or TVs. In this way, you can begin to develop expertise at the skills that will later make you an excellent computer service technician.

WHO WILL HIRE ME?

Most vocational and technical schools offer career services offices. These offices work very closely with local companies that regularly recruit computer service technicians. To get an idea of how successful a school's graduates are at getting jobs, ask an admissions counselor for the school's placement statistics.

Approximately one of every three computer service technicians work for wholesalers of computers and/or office machines and for independent repair shops. This includes service divisions of large computer companies that offer maintenance to the client with the purchase of a computer system; it also includes service companies that sell maintenance contracts to new equipment buyers or leasers.

Others work for large companies that have enough equipment to justify employing a full-time maintenance and repair staff. Corporations that typically have in-house repair departments are insurance companies, financial institutions (particularly those involved in any aspect of credit card processing), and banks. Large factories, whose production depends on large machinery, also have in-house technicians. Still other technicians work for retail companies. Different branches of the military, as well as federal, state, and local governments, provide opportunities for employment as well.

Most computer technicians work for computer manufacturers that are usually located in geographical clusters, like California's Silicon Valley or Washington State (where the headquarters of Microsoft, Inc. is located). Some computer repair specialists work for maintenance firms, and others work for corporations whose complex network of computers requires a full-time computer technician.

Individuals may look in the classified ads of major metropolitan newspapers and related magazines for job opportunities. In addition, many professional organizations publish newsletters and magazines that include job lists.

WHERE CAN I GO FROM HERE?

Most computer service technicians start working on relatively simple computers and peripherals and gradually become familiar with more and more complex equipment as their experience increases. When they are trained in most of the equipment, they may be promoted to maintenance supervisor. Then, with demonstrated leadership and business skills, technicians may be promoted to managerial positions. Promotion to management

Advancement Possibilities

Maintenance supervisors assign service technicians to handle specific jobs when repair requests come into the office. They are in charge of a group of employees, fulfilling such administrative duties as verifying that repair records are kept in good order by each repairer and keeping track of hours spent on different equipment. They help other technicians troubleshoot problems and might also have expertise in working on more technologically complicated and expensive computers and peripherals.

Maintenance managers perform many of the same duties as supervisors but are usually in charge of a greater number of employees. They might also be responsible for deciding when a computer should be replaced, what type of new computer should be purchased, and how the office should be laid out in order to ensure ease of repair. In addition, they perform normal managerial functions, such as preparing departmental budgets, interviewing, and hiring.

Computer sales representatives may get their start in computer repair because such experience provides them with a very solid understanding of particular machines. Their knowledge, as well as experience in explaining technical problems in easy-to-understand terms, gives them a head start in the active "selling" of a product that salespeople must develop.

often requires further education in business or engineering, and the job often entails more office work than repair work.

Another advancement route a technician can take is to become a *sales representative* for the company with which he or she has had the most experience. Technicians develop expert hands-on knowledge of particular computers and peripherals and are thus often in a better position than anyone else to advise potential buyers about important purchasing decisions.

Some technicians might aspire to owning their own businesses, which is also an option for advancement. Entrepreneurship is always risky and the responsibilities are great, but so are the potential rewards. Unless they have already determined a market niche, technicians usually find it necessary to branch out when they open their own repair shop in order to service a wide range of computers and office machines.

WHAT ARE THE SALARY RANGES?

The U.S. Department of Labor reports that computer support specialists earned median annual salaries of $40,430 in 2004. The middle 50 percent earned between $30,980 and $53,010, the lowest 10 percent earned less than $24,190, and the highest 10 percent earned more than $69,110. Those with certification are typically paid more than those without.

Standard work benefits for full-time technicians include health and life insurance and paid vacation and sick time, as well as a retirement plan. Most technicians are given travel stipends; some receive company cars.

WHAT IS THE JOB OUTLOOK?

Dan Haeder predicts good employment opportunities for computer service technicians. "With the advent of programmable logic controllers and smart home technology," he says, "I am confident that the job market will remain strong. Everything has been computerized in society today, which in turn creates very good

> ### Related Jobs
>
> - aircraft mechanics
> - appliance and power tool technicians
> - automatic teller machine servicers
> - automobile, motorcycle, and bicycle mechanics
> - biomedical equipment technicians
> - communications equipment technicians
> - computer programmers
> - electrical technicians
> - electronics engineering technicians
> - farm equipment mechanics
> - industrial machinery mechanics
> - photographic equipment technicians
> - service sales representatives
> - vending machine technicians

job security for the hard-working computer guru. The medical field uses computerized equipment that must be meticulously maintained. There will always be a need for service technicians working in these and other areas that are yet to be developed. It is exciting to see the advancements being made and to think about what wonders are yet to come."

According to the U.S. Department of Labor, employment of computer service technicians is expected to grow faster than the average for all occupations through 2014. Technology is improving at a rapid pace. With the development of more complex computers and software, more and more customers and users will need technical assistance. The key for individuals interested in this career: keep up with technology and be flexible.

There will be demand in large corporations with in-house repair departments for well-rounded technicians, those who can maintain and repair both computers and office machines. Computer companies and service contractors will look for people with strong computer backgrounds, whether in education or professional experience. Interested individuals should make a habit of keeping up to date with technological advances.

Many opportunities in computer repair will continue to open up as long as computer sales remain steady or increase. Many computer companies offer service contracts with new purchases, and they need technicians to fulfill these contractual obligations. Businesses are relying much more on computers and the Internet in order to conduct daily business. These systems need to be installed and properly maintained.

Computer Systems Programmer/Analysts

SUMMARY

Definition
Computer systems programmer/analysts plan and develop new computer systems or update existing systems to meet changing business needs.

Alternative Job Titles
Programmer analysts
Systems analysts

Salary Range
$41,730 to $66,460 to $99,180+

Educational Requirements
Associate degree

Certification or Licensing
Voluntary

Employment Outlook
Much faster than the average

High School Subjects
Computer science
Mathematics
Physics

Personal Interests
Computers
Reading/Books
Writing

Imad Makdah, a programmer/analyst for more than 20 years, believes that the number-one problem of most businesses is communication.

"I learned that at my first client meeting, when I joined a consulting company," he recalls. "The technical people were speaking a language that the client did not understand, and the client could not get the techies to understand his company's business problems. I heard more four-letter words that day than in all my work career before or since.

"Having a unique insight into that client's business (wholesale distribution) helped me understand their needs while providing a suitable solution. In my following interactions with this client, I listened a lot more than I spoke, and I mostly spoke through actions. When the customer saw results that met his expectations, I gained his trust. At the same time I salvaged a system implementation that was going nowhere fast and costing a lot more than expected.

"When communicating with clients, be honest, because even if you can lie with words, you can't lie with your actions. This career is result-driven. The end result is a function of your abilities and communication skills."

WHAT DOES A COMPUTER SYSTEMS PROGRAMMER/ANALYST DO?

Businesses invest hundreds of thousands of dollars in computer systems to make their operations more efficient and thus more profitable. As older systems become obsolete, businesses are also faced with the task of replacing them or upgrading them with new technology. *Computer systems programmer/analysts* plan and develop new computer systems or upgrade existing systems to meet changing business needs. They also install, modify, and maintain functioning computer systems. The process of choosing and implementing a computer system is similar for programmer analysts who work for very different employers; however, specific decisions in terms of hardware and software differ depending on the industry.

The first stage of the process involves meeting with management and users to discuss the problem at hand. A company's accounting system, for example, might be slow, unreliable, and generally outdated. During many hours of meetings, systems programmer/analysts and management discuss various options, including commercial software, hardware upgrades, and customizing possibilities that may solve the problems. At the end of the discussions, which may last as long as several weeks or months, the programmer/analyst defines the specific system goals as agreed upon by participants.

Next, systems programmer/analysts engage in highly analytic and logical activities. They use tools such as structural analysis, data modeling, mathematics, and cost accounting to determine which computers, including hardware and software and peripherals, will be required to meet the goals of the project. They must consider the trade-offs between extra efficiency and speed and increased costs. Weighing the pros and cons of each additional system feature is an important factor in system planning. Whatever preliminary decisions are made must be supported by mathematical and financial evidence.

As the final stage of the planning process, systems programmer/analysts prepare reports and formal presentations to be delivered to management. Reports must be written in clear, concise language that business professionals, who are not necessarily technical experts, can understand thoroughly. Formal presentations in front of groups of various sizes are often required as part of the system proposal.

If the system or the system upgrades are approved, equipment is purchased and installed. Then, the programmer/analysts get down to the real technical work so that all the different computers and peripherals function well together. They prepare specifications, diagrams, and other programming structures and, often using computer-aided systems engineering technology, they write the new or upgraded programming code. If they work solely as systems analysts, it is at this point that they hand over all of their information to the systems programmer so that he or she can begin to write the programming code.

Systems design and programming involves defining the files and records to be accessed by the system, outlining the processing steps, and suggesting formats for output that meet the needs of the company. User-friendliness of the front-end applications is extremely important for user productivity. Therefore, programmer/analysts must be able to envision how nontechnical system users view their on-screen work. Systems programmer/analysts might also specify security programs that allow only authorized personnel access to certain files or groups of files.

As the programming is written, programmer/analysts set up test runs of various parts of the system, making sure that major goals are reached each step of the way. Once the system is up and running, problems, or "bugs," begin to pop up. Programmer analysts are responsible for fixing these last-minute problems. They must isolate the problem and review the hundreds of lines of programming commands to determine where the mistake is located. They then must enter the correct command or code and recheck the program.

Depending on the employer, some systems programmer/analysts might be involved with computer networking. Network communication programs tell two or more computers or peripherals how to work with each other. When a system is composed of equipment from various manufacturers, networking is essential for smooth system functioning; for example, shared printers have to know how to order print jobs as they come in from various terminals. Some programmer/analysts write the code that establishes printing queues. Others might be involved in user training, since they know the software applications well. They might also customize commercial software programs to meet the needs of their company.

Many programmer/analysts become specialized in an area of business, science, or engineering. They seek education and further on-the-job training in these areas

---

Lingo to Learn

ASCII (American Standard Code for Information Exchange) Numerical code used by personal computers.

database A collection of information stored on the computer.

GUI (goo-ey; Graphical User Interface) A system that uses symbols (icons) seen on screen to represent available functions.

network Several computers that are electronically connected to share data and programs.

LAN (local area network) A network that exists at one location, typically an office.

spreadsheet A program that performs mathematical operations; used mainly for accounting and other record keeping.

WAN (wide area network) A network that includes remote sites in different buildings, cities, states, or countries.

to develop expertise. They may therefore attend special seminars, workshops, and classes designed for their needs. This extra knowledge allows them to develop a deeper understanding of the computing problems specific to the business or industry.

WHAT IS IT LIKE TO BE A COMPUTER SYSTEMS PROGRAMMER/ANALYST?

"As a programmer/analyst, I wear many hats," says Imad Makdah, a self-employed computer systems programmer/analyst in Chicago. "Each day can be different, depending on the project at hand and the stage of the project," he explains. "There are days when I am on site troubleshooting programming bugs, rebuilding corrupted data files, or just making minor enhancements to existing programs. Other days involve meeting with clients for requirements analysis, project design, proposal/solution presentation, and program implementation and user training."

Imad says that the best days for him are the ones he spends doing actual programming/analysis work—or, as he calls it, the 'fun' work. "On days when I am designing and programming a system (most of the time I can do this work on my home-office computer and copy the programs to the client's systems)," he explains, "I start early because I do my best thinking in the morning." I begin by analyzing the requirements for the project, and then I design the file/table structures, the menu options, the data entry screens, and the reports layout." Imad then decides what programs are needed and writes the specs for them. After he completes this task, he begins writing each program. "I test each program as I finish it and do comprehensive testing when the system is completed," he says. "Once I am satisfied with the results, I install a test system for the client to beta test. I then do any changes and fixes as needed. If I did my system design and programming right, then implementation and training is very smooth and pleasant."

Computer systems programmer/analysts work in comfortable office environments. If they work as consultants, they may travel frequently. Otherwise, travel is limited to trade shows, seminars, and visitations to vendors for demonstrations. They might also visit other businesses to observe their systems in action. Imad spends about 25 percent of his time working in his home office, and the rest of the time working at client sites, which are located throughout Chicago and its suburbs.

Programmer/analysts usually work 40-hour weeks and enjoy the regular holiday schedule of days off. As deadlines for system installation, upgrades, and spot-checking approach, however, they are often required to work overtime. Extra compensation for overtime hours may come in the form of time-and-a-half pay or compensatory time off, depending on the precise nature of the employee's duties, company policy, and state law. If the employer operates off-shifts, programmer analysts may be on call to address any problems that might arise at any time of the day or night. This is relatively rare in the service sector but more common in manufacturing, heavy industry, and data processing firms.

> **To Be a Successful Computer Systems Programmer/Analyst, You Should . . .**
>
> - have good communication skills
> - enjoy working with both people and ideas
> - be detail oriented
> - be able to juggle many tasks at once
> - have good writing skills
> - be willing to continue to learn throughout your career

DO I HAVE WHAT IT TAKES TO BE A COMPUTER SYSTEMS PROGRAMMER/ANALYST?

Analysts often work long hours and deal with a wide variety of people. They work both alone and in groups. Patience and attention to detail are important qualities, as well as logical thinking and an ability to translate highly technical and complex concepts into simple language.

If you prefer to sit at a computer by yourself all day, every day, computer systems programmer/analyst isn't the job for you. An outgoing personality, good communication and listening skills, and being able to work well with others are as much a part of the job as computer knowledge. An analyst must be able to talk easily to both technical personnel, such as programmers and management, as well as to staff who might not have any knowledge of computers.

Self-motivation and being able to juggle many different tasks at once are critical to the job. It is important that you have problem-solving abilities and the ability to pay attention to even the smallest details.

HOW DO I BECOME A COMPUTER SYSTEMS PROGRAMMER/ANALYST?

Imad majored in accounting in college and also took elective classes in programming and systems analysis. "It was a natural fit to design and program systems for business and accounting solutions," he says. "I also trained on the job and by reading books. Throughout my career, the end-user has been an important trainer. I always try and make their work life easier and simpler, and a well-designed new system does not confuse the user, but fits naturally into their daily workflow. A happy user is a result of good analysis and good programming."

Education

High School

A high school diploma is necessary for a future as a computer systems programmer/analyst. Knowledge of IBM-compatible computer programs as well as Macintosh systems is very important. If possible, enroll in computer classes and labs to gain hands-on experience. Also join user groups or computer clubs to share information and make contacts.

High school courses in the sciences are necessary, since many computer systems programmer/analysts work in industries directly involved in the scientific fields. Math classes are good for understanding the programming languages taught in college. Mathematical ability is also useful when writing and developing computer programs, and a good math background helps develop skills in logical thinking.

Also useful for developing analytical thinking skills are strategy games such as chess.

Imad encourages students to start designing and programming systems early, even if it is just for fun. "Find a small business and ask to program and/or set up a system for them without charging for your time," he advises. "Also, read books about communicating and dealing with people; a good part of this job is trying to understand people's needs and intentions and trying to tell them how a system works. Classes or books that teach proper database design and programming techniques are also essential."

Postsecondary Training

A bachelor's degree in computer science is a minimum requirement for systems programmer/analysts. Course work in preparation for this field includes math, computer programming, science, and logic. Several years of related work experience, including knowledge of programming languages, are

---

The Pros and Cons of Being a Computer Systems Programmer/Analyst

The following is what Imad enjoys the most, and least, in his work, in his own words:

Pros

- I enjoy the challenge of the field, and it is a perfect fit for my analytical skills and my personality.
- You are free to design and create the solutions for your customers with little or no interference from other parties.
- You usually get to see your creation from concept, through design, programming, and implementation.
- With most jobs, you either work alone or work with other people; with this job, you get to do both!

Cons

- The small amount of contact with customers is intense. You are either trying to understand the impossible or trying to explain the impossible, and at the same avoid feeling stupid and avoid making people feel stupid.
- The field is always changing, it is a 'do-or-die' career. If you don't adapt to today's technology, you will not get the project tomorrow and your career will be over.
- Competition for jobs is intense; sometimes the person who gets the contract is the one with the best marketing, not the best solution.

often necessary as well. For some very high-level positions, an advanced degree in a specific computer subfield may be required. Also, depending on the employer, proficiency in business, science, or engineering may be necessary.

In addition to college-level classes and training sessions, Imad advises aspiring analysts to read books, magazines, and product manuals to stay up to date about the industry. "This is a dynamic field," he says, "and any person pursuing this career must have a love affair with change. Half of what you learn today will serve you 5 to 10 years, at the most. I stay up to date by forcing myself to take on assignments using newer technologies that I am not familiar with and then dedicating the extra time to learn them."

Certification and Licensing

Getting certified as a computer professional is not a requirement for a job as a computer systems programmer/analyst, but might give you a competitive edge over other applicants. When Imad started his career, little certification, if any, was available. "Currently," he says, "certification is offered by all companies with systems you are specializing in, or with programming languages you are using. Someone starting out should seek as much certification as possible from the companies with which they plan to work."

The Institute for Certification of Computing Professionals also offers a series of exams that, once passed, will provide the programmer/analyst with certification at one of two levels: Associate Computing Professional or Certified Computing Professional.

Internships and Volunteerships

An important, but not mandatory, part of preparing for a career as a computer systems programmer/analyst is participating in an internship program. Internships provide practical hands-on experience for students. Universities and technical institutes usually have programs that help arrange internships for their students.

Employers look for practical experience in job applicants. Most internships offer little or no pay for long hours and hard work, but the experience gained is

Advancement Possibilities

- *Senior systems programmer/analysts,* also known as *lead programmer/analysts,* are in charge of an entire project, coordinating and overseeing the work efforts of all the analysts working on a team.
- *Managers of information systems,* also known as *project managers,* supervise all the projects in which analysts are involved.
- *Database design analysts* work as liaisons between the computer systems programmer/analysts and the company. They evaluate project requests, their costs, and time limitations. They review and restructure the database to work with programs developed by the computer systems programmer/analyst.

priceless. Many students make valuable contacts this way, and some are hired as regular employees when the internship is finished.

WHO WILL HIRE ME?
As more businesses, organizations, and federal agencies expand their computer systems, jobs for computer systems programmer/analysts open up in a variety of areas. The largest number of analysts is found in computer and data processing firms, but opportunities in many other fields exist as well. Government agencies, manufacturers of computer-related equipment, insurance agencies, universities, banks, and private businesses all require the skills of computer systems programmer/analysts.

Most analyst jobs are concentrated in or near larger cities. Many employers actively recruit applicants on college campuses, interviewing students while they're still in school. Most simply advertise in the want ads of big city newspapers.

Following a trend in the overall workforce, growing numbers of computer systems programmer/analysts are employed on a temporary basis as short-term consultants. A company that needs the services of an analyst to install or create a new computer program may not be able to justify hiring a full-time analyst but will turn to a computer consulting agency or contract a computer systems programmer/analyst to do the work. These contracts usually last for several months and sometimes up to two years.

Trade magazines often have job listings and are good sources for job seekers. They are also a great place to learn about changing technologies and trends in the industry. Reading several different publications may help to identify where the jobs are.

The Internet is an excellent tool for finding job opportunities. Most major companies post job openings, and many Web sites are dedicated solely to helping you land a position.

A computer systems programmer/analyst is not an entry-level job. Many analysts start in programming or data processing. Occasionally, some are promoted from another area altogether. An auditor in an accounting department, for example, might become a systems analyst specializing in accounting systems development.

WHERE CAN I GO FROM HERE?
"I enjoy what I do," Imad says, "and I see myself doing this for another five or 10 years. However, the technology I utilize will be different. The integration of computers into all aspects of businesses has forced the newer business applications to contain functionality that accommodates a larger 'business' audience. And the continuous expansion of the Internet has forced systems to be mobile and interconnected. I cannot implement a system nowadays without making sure that it will serve everybody in the company and that they can equally use it from the office, home, or the Bahamas if they choose or need to. These aspects were of no concern to us 10 years ago; future technology will force us to think and work differently. When I tire of 'living on

the edge,' I can become a manager of other programmer/analysts who are at the start of their careers."

As a greater diversity of businesses become dependent on computers, the need for consultants in the field grows; for example, a small bookstore chain may not have the need for a full-time systems analyst but will hire one as specific projects arise, such as creating an automated inventory and purchasing system.

The career path of a company computer systems programmer/analyst usually leads to management. After a few years' experience, those who show leadership ability, good communication skills, and diverse business and technical knowledge are promoted along these lines.

WHAT ARE THE SALARY RANGES?

According to the U.S. Department of Labor, the median annual salary for computer systems analysts was $66,460 in 2004. At the low end of the pay range, 10 percent of systems analysts earned less than $41,730. The top 10 percent earned more than $99,180. Salaries are slightly higher in geographic areas where many computer companies are clustered, such as Silicon Valley in California and Seattle, Washington.

Level of education also affects analysts' earnings. The National Association of Colleges and Employers reports that starting salaries for those with master's degrees in computer science averaged $62,727 in 2004. Those with bachelor's degrees in computer science, however, had starting salaries averaging $50,820, and those with bachelor's degrees in computer systems analysis averaged $46,189, also in 2004.

Working for a large company or the federal government brings other nonsalaried benefits as well, such as health insurance, retirement plans, and paid vacations. Private consultants do not get these benefits and must provide their own; they also have the extra work of running their consulting business.

Related Jobs

- business programmers
- computer network administrators
- computer programmers
- computer trainers
- database specialists
- engineering analysts
- engineering and scientific programmers
- graphics programmers
- information scientists
- information system programmers
- mathematical statisticians
- operations-research analysts
- process control programmers
- software designers
- systems setup specialists
- technical support specialists
- technical writers and editors

WHAT IS THE JOB OUTLOOK?

The U.S. Department of Labor predicts that the job of computer systems programmer/analyst will grow much faster than the average for all occupations through 2014. As smaller businesses utilize the efficiency of computers in the workplace, and technology becomes more affordable to private users, an even greater demand for systems and programmer/analysts will arise.

There is an ever-increasing emphasis on personal computers. Businesses are moving away from the larger and extremely expensive mainframes that have traditionally been used by large companies. They are going toward a network of many smaller yet powerful computers that share the workload. As this trend continues, programmer/analysts will be indispensable in an office environment. Someone must program, organize, and link all these individual systems together.

As these intricate computer systems improve and grow, the programmer/analyst will be needed to continually upgrade and weed out errors in the programs. Maintenance and debugging will provide steady work as long as computers are part of our daily lives.

The role of computer systems programmer/analyst is an upwardly mobile one. Tens of thousands of jobs will open up as analysts move into managerial positions. Those who go into business for themselves or to private consulting firms will keep this field open for new analysts.

Quality Assurance Testers

SUMMARY

Definition
Quality assurance testers evaluate a wide range of new or modified computer-related products to verify that they perform in accordance with company and legal specifications.

Alternative Job Titles
Quality assurance analysts
Quality control testers or analysts

Salary Range
$17,160 to $55,909 to $67,034+

Educational Requirements
Associate or bachelor's degree in computer-related field required for most advancement

Certification or Licensing
Voluntary

Outlook
Faster than the average

High School Subjects
Computer science
English
Speech

Personal Interests
Computers
Figuring out how things work
Writing

Stu Smeglane played the same downhill ski computer game for several hours. He had become quite skilled at it, not "falling" at all. He was so good, in fact, that he was getting bored. But he couldn't quit, because he was actually at work in the quality assurance laboratory of a software company. Just then, a man walked into the lab and asked Stu what he thought about the game he was testing.

"I don't know why a company like ours would waste its time on such a boring game. This game first came out five years ago; who's going to buy it now? Look—the skier just goes from the left to the right, up and down, over and over again."

The man looked at Stu a moment and left, thanking him for the comments.

When he was gone, a colleague leaned over to Stu. "Do you know who that was?" he asked abruptly. "That was the president of the company," he continued, "and probably the person who decided to sell that game you dislike so much."

Stu was initially embarrassed, but later, when he found out his company had discontinued work on the game, he remembered the unique privilege quality assurance testers have in software companies. They are there, in part, to play, talk, and act like consumers.

WHAT DOES A QUALITY ASSURANCE TESTER DO?

Before being released in consumer markets, most products, especially computer products, are put through a series of quality assurance tests designed to anticipate and help solve problems that the user might encounter. *Quality assurance testers* evaluate and test new or modified software programs to determine whether or not they perform according to designer specifications and user requirements. They also "test the tests," that is, they evaluate automated procedures used to verify that software programs function properly.

Some quality assurance testers, like Stu Smeglane, spend most of their time actually using the software applications, attempting to simulate the way in which the average consumer would use it. If it is a computer game, they play it over and over and over for hours, trying to make it crash. When the program crashes, or stops working, they fill out special forms explaining the combination of moves or commands that apparently made the program crash.

Each program or product arrives in the lab with a request for testing during a specified number of hours. After the quality assurance testers have logged in those hours and have completed detailed performance reports and documentation, the program or software product is sent back to the programmer for revisions and corrections. Some testers have direct contact with the programmers in order to describe the problems more accurately and advise about the ways in which they might go about solving the glitches. They might also make suggestions about how to make the program more user-friendly, efficient, exciting, or fun.

The trend in the computer industry is toward the development of automated quality assurance tests. Oftentimes, even the automated tests require a "live" tester to administer and supervise them, as well as to interpret results and write reports explaining conclusions. Testers in this area tell the computer which tests to run and verify that tests run properly by watching the computer monitor for interruption codes and breakdown signals. They run the results through special testing programs that verify their accuracy and reliability.

Some quality assurance testers work with consumers who are experiencing specific problems with already-purchased software. They usually listen to the customer's complaint and try to identify exactly what sequence of commands led to the problem. Then they attempt to duplicate the problem in the lab in order to perform more in-depth tests on the program and eventually contact the programmers about correcting it.

Quality assurance testers with solid work experience in the industry and some formal education in computer programming may work as *quality assurance analysts.* Analysts write and revise the quality standards or specifications for each software program. They also create the quality assurance tests that testers use to verify that the program operates well, a task that involves computer programming. They evaluate proposals for future software developments, deciding whether or not the proposed project is capable of doing what it aims to do. As individuals most familiar with the performance of certain programs, they might become involved in training software users.

WHAT IS IT LIKE TO BE A QUALITY ASSURANCE TESTER?

Stu Smeglane works for a major software developer that creates a variety of products ranging from graphics/publishing packages and home and landscape design software to specialty games and educational software. As a high school student, he worked there full time during the summers, earning $11 an hour as an independent contractor. "Independent contractor translates as very good hourly wage, no benefits," says Stu. But, he explains, working a couple months as a "QA" [quality assurance] person gives an individual a good taste of what it's like in the field. "My mom always yelled at me when I was young for playing too many video games. Then, there I was, still in high school, making more money than anyone else in my family for doing just that!"

Some entry-level quality assurance work can be boring, according to Stu. Just before the holidays one year, for example, his company wanted to release a graphic software package that printed out holiday decorations like wreaths and candy canes. "For eight hours a day, I would stare at these things, trying to find even just the slightest imperfections."

The important thing to keep in mind, however, is that despite the boring tasks that a quality assurance tester may have to endure, this position is generally a gateway to bigger and better computer-related jobs. And this is especially helpful for individuals with little or no experience or formal education in computers. "Unless you have an ingenious idea that will make you a million dollars, you break into the industry any way you can," says Stu.

Stu's desk is one of several in a large, well-lit computer laboratory. When he arrives in the morning, he checks in with

---

Lingo to Learn

alpha testing The first formal testing of new hardware or software. Alpha testing is typically done by and within the company that is developing the product.

application A software program that allows users to perform certain tasks, such as word processing, database record keeping, or spreadsheets.

beta testing Hardware or software testing performed by a limited number of users under normal conditions. Beta testing occurs after in-house (alpha) testing.

glitch A bug or problem with a computer program, hardware design, or software application.

hardware The physical equipment inside a computer that makes it operate.

software development tools Special programs used to develop, analyze, debug, and perfect software.

his supervisor to see what program he is assigned for the day. Then he takes it to his desk and starts playing. "We look for glitches," says Stu, "and pretty soon you get good at finding them." He tries all kinds of things, like typing very fast or clicking the mouse on the border of an icon instead of squarely on it. "It can be really fun to see how quickly you can make a program crash."

When Stu successfully crashes a program, he reboots the system to see if he can reenact the crisis. "The idea is to isolate those moves or commands that were too much for the program to handle," he explains. "I have to be able to write down in my report exactly what went wrong so that the programmer can locate the problem quickly and accurately." The bug sheets—forms testers fill out when they find problems—must be clear, concise, neat, and detailed.

Sometimes, instead of testing programs that will definitely be sold by the company, the testers test a whole group of games the company is considering buying for resale on the mass market. "I love playing games and imagining ways to make them better. Some games people come up with are downright stupid," Stu says. This aspect of his job is very satisfying to Stu because his opinions and ideas have a lot to do with determining which products his company sells.

Like most areas of business and industry, quality assurance is relying more and more on technological advancements. It is becoming a science and branch of engineering in its own right.

> **To Be a Successful Quality Assurance Tester, You Should . . .**
>
> - like to play with computers
> - have strong short-term memory skills
> - pay attention to detail
> - communicate effectively, both verbally and in writing
> - not be overwhelmingly frustrated or bored by repetitive job duties

Individuals with experience in it as well as formal education in computer science will have many opportunities in the years to come.

DO I HAVE WHAT IT TAKES TO BE A QUALITY ASSURANCE TESTER?

In the computer industry, most quality assurance tasks involve playing around on the computer, so individuals who dislike computers should stay away from this field. Although most labs set up quality assurance tests so that a tester need not have prior computer experience, it is helpful to have a basic understanding of how computers work. This foundational knowledge enables a tester to move swiftly through computer setups and program procedures. It also helps the tester identify more accurately the potential source of a particular problem as well as more clearly explain the problem in the report to the programmer.

Quality assurance testers should also have strong short-term memory skills. "You can be playing along and then all of a sudden crash the game, and you have to be able to remember what you just did, even if you were in 'auto-pilot,'" explains Stu. The ability to pay close attention to detail is important for the same reason. Computer programming is a very precise science; a tester must be just as precise and detailed in his or her explanations of problems. "You can't say to a programmer, 'It kind of messes up when I do something like this.' You have to explain exactly what happens and what precipitates it, down to the last keystroke."

Since testers have a lot of indirect and direct contact with programmers and marketing representatives, they should be able to communicate effectively, both verbally and in writing. And, given the amount of repetitive work, quality assurance testers should not allow themselves to become overwhelmed, stressed, or frustrated by a certain degree of monotony in their job duties. "Even video games can get boring," cautions Stu.

In addition, good testers are generally not the kind of people who get upset when things break. "After all, that's our job—to make these things break down!" says Stu. Individuals who succeed in this field generally have their eye on professional advancement, keeping up with technological advances and pursuing formal education in a computer-related discipline.

Are You Good with Words?

If you're good with words and computer programs, you may be able to combine these skills as a freelance writer. Computer magazines, such as *PC Magazine, PC World,* and *Macworld,* regularly feature articles on software development and columns on fixing bugs.

HOW DO I BECOME A QUALITY ASSURANCE TESTER?

Education

Stu found out about the opening at his current company through a friend. "A lot of jobs in the computer industry are made known by word of mouth," says Stu. Initially hired as an independent contractor, Stu maintained contact with his supervisor even during periods in which he did not work. He was called back for several summers and various special projects throughout the year and was offered a full-time job upon graduation.

High School

For most temporary or independent contracting jobs as quality assurance testers, a high school diploma is not required. In fact, some testers, like Stu, were still in high school when they obtained their first job in this field. However, a minimum of an associate degree is usually required for most full-time tester positions.

Any high school course in computers, whether programming, operating, or fundamentals, provides a solid background in computer basics that is valuable for quality assurance testers. An academic background in computers is not necessary for all quality assurance tester jobs, however. A company may want to hire people with computer skills comparable to those held by their customers, who may have no prior experience at all.

Math and science classes, especially those that incorporate the use of flowcharts, are also good preparation. English and speech courses give students multiple opportunities to improve both written and verbal communication skills.

Postsecondary Training

Many technical and vocational schools offer a wide range of courses in computer-related technologies leading to a two-year associate degree in computer engineering technology, for example. The curricula often include courses in hardware construction and design, software programming basics, network administration, single and multi-board microcomputing, and other basics in computer science.

FYI

Quality assurance is considered a good point of entry into the computer industry and is often used as a springboard to the harder-to-get jobs.

Since the thrust of the industry is toward the automation of quality assurance tests, individuals interested in this field should pursue at least an associate degree in order to distinguish themselves from colleagues in case staffing cuts are made due to automation. As testers learn the processes by which programs are written, tested, and revised, they tend quite naturally to become interested in increasing their involvement with projects. Some formal education is a helpful stepping-stone in this pursuit.

It is debatable whether or not a bachelor's degree is necessary to become a quality assurance tester. Some companies require a bachelor's degree in computer science, while others prefer people from the business sector who have a small amount of computer experience because they best match the technical level of the software's typical users. If testers are interested in advancement, however, a bachelor's degree is almost a mandate.

Another option for a quality assurance tester is to complete a bachelor's or advanced degree in computer science or computer-related discipline. The field of quality assurance engineering is an up-and-coming field. Who better to work on test design and product development than those testers most familiar with how quality assurance tests perform in the lab? College classes in computer science can be rigorous and competitive, but they definitely pay off in the professional long run. As the industry becomes more competitive, a strong postsecondary education becomes more and more important during job hunting.

Certification and Licensing

As the information technology industry becomes more competitive, the necessity for management to be able to distinguish professional and skilled individuals in the field becomes mandatory, according to the Quality Assurance Institute Worldwide. Certification demonstrates a level of understanding in carrying out relevant principles and practices, and provides a common ground for communication among professionals in the field of software quality. The organization offers the designations Certified Software Tester, Certified Software Quality Analyst, and Certified Software Project Manager.

Internships and Volunteerships

Since quality assurance testing is an entry-level position, and since many people are hired on an independent contractor basis, there are very few internships in this area. An independent contractor is an individual who is hired for a specific amount of time or to complete a specific job or set of tasks within a time limit agreed to by the employer and the contractor. Independent contractors are usually paid relatively well, but they do not receive any benefits and are responsible for paying their own taxes since no taxes are withheld from their earnings. Many computer companies offer summer jobs to students or other individuals as independent contractors. School placement offices usually maintain information about these kinds of opportunities. Local newspapers, computer trade magazines, and computer professionals are also good job-hunting sources.

Advancement Possibilities

Quality assurance supervisors assign testing projects to the quality assurance testers. They also do quality assurance testing themselves, but may tend to work with more complicated procedures or interesting products. They have more report-writing responsibilities and work more closely with computer programmers, who try to correct product glitches by revising the programs.

Quality assurance engineers are members of a growing field. Currently, the computer industry is pushing for automated quality assurance tests that would not necessarily require a tester to run them. Quality assurance engineers are working in part on such large-scale projects. These engineers work on quality assurance test design, methods of interpreting test results and correcting diagnosed problems, and on writing specification manuals and technical sheets.

Software engineers analyze industrial, business, and scientific problems and conceive software programs that can provide solutions to them. They meet with clients to determine the specific nature of the problem, give presentations of software proposals and demonstrations of finished products, and consult with other engineers in the regular course of their work.

WHO WILL HIRE ME?

Many quality assurance testers work for hardware or software development companies that have numerous permanent, full-time positions in quality assurance.

Computer companies tend to be clustered in the same geographical area, like the Silicon Valley between San Francisco and San Jose in Northern California, for example. There, computer companies open and close seemingly overnight; it is not at all uncommon for a company to be created in order to develop just one product. If the product fails on the market or even before it gets to market, the company folds. For the period of time the "start-ups" stay open, however, they may hire quality assurance testers to evaluate and test their products on an independent contracting basis.

Some of these jobs are advertised in computer trade magazines, such as *PC Magazine, PC World,* and *Macworld.* But they might also be publicized by word of mouth. A friend who worked at the company told Stu about the job in quality assurance, the job he eventually obtained. Professional networking in the computer industry is very important; an interested individual should stay in contact with as many computer professionals as he or she can. Otherwise, close attention must be paid to newspaper and magazine advertisements.

As quality assurance grows in stature, service companies designed only to provide quality assurance evaluation to product manufacturers and developers are also increasing in number. Currently, these firms are mostly found in those areas where computer companies are clustered. Interested individuals should consult a local telephone directory to determine if such companies exist in their area.

General consulting companies, particularly those specializing in computer system integration or analysis, might also hire quality assurance testers. Many large corporations like insurance companies and banks are beginning to investigate ways to automate forms and other kinds of paperwork. Much of this development work is being subcontracted to outside computer programmers, but some is being performed in-house. People interested in quality assurance should check with any major employers in the area to see if they are hiring quality assurance testers. The farther away an individual goes from a full-fledged computer company, however, the harder it will be for him or her to move up the ranks of the computer industry's hierarchy.

WHERE CAN I GO FROM HERE?

If a quality assurance tester wants to stay deeply involved in the technical side of operations, he or she will eventually have to decide what area of computer technology is the most appealing—quality assurance, software or hardware engineering, networks, systems—the list could go on and on.

After some experience and maybe even some formal education, a tester is a good candidate for promotion to a supervisory position. Such a position would involve a few administrative duties, such as schedule writing and assignment distribution. But supervisory positions also involve more complex and interesting technical duties. Supervisors also have greater responsibility than testers in terms of report and technical writing and meetings with the programmers.

Positions above those in quality assurance supervision require more education (probably at least a bachelor's degree), more experience, and more definite goals. In the technical track, supervisors can be promoted to quality assurance or software engineering positions. They may also be promoted to programming positions.

Those who wish to focus mainly on the managerial side of operations might go into product sales. Testers are particularly well suited for sales since they are extremely familiar with the products they have tested. They might also go into marketing or low-level and middle management. Many of these positions require formal education after a certain point. Education requirements vary with the company and the potential, expertise, and experience of the individual.

WHAT ARE THE SALARY RANGES?

The exact hourly range for a quality assurance tester working as an independent contractor is generally dependent on the individual's work history, the proposed length of employment, and the level of technical difficulty incorporated into the specific tests to be run.

Software quality assurance testers had median annual earnings of $55,909 in 2005, according to Salary.com. Salaries ranged from less than $48,318 to $67,034 or more annually. Workers with many years of technical and management experience can earn higher salaries. Testers in all industries had earnings that ranged from less than $17,264 to $50,856 or more annually in 2004, according to the U.S. Department of Labor. Testers generally receive a full benefits package as well, including health insurance, paid vacation, and sick leave.

Testers promoted to supervisory positions can expect to make several thousand dollars more annually. Salaries also increase dramatically as a tester completes higher levels of education.

Related Jobs

- computer hardware technicians and engineers
- computer network engineers
- computer programmers
- computer programming technicians
- computer scientists
- computer security coordinator and specialists
- computer systems hardware analysts
- data recovery planners
- database technicians
- quality control engineers and technicians
- software designers
- software engineering technicians
- software engineers
- systems setup specialists
- technical support specialists

WHAT IS THE JOB OUTLOOK?

The number of positions in quality assurance is expected to grow at a rate that is faster than the average over the next decade. One reason for this is somewhat complicated but important to understand. Many computer products on the market are basically replicas of one another; they perform the same function but under a different brand name. Thus, there are many accounting software programs available, all of which work reasonably well. Where before a computer company could distinguish itself by introducing a one-of-a-kind product, like spreadsheet software, it no longer can.

Many computer companies are taking a different approach in order to set their products apart from the competition. Simply put, they aim to offer higher performance levels and better technical support, including user training, than anyone else. This market trend translates into a boom for quality assurance. It is now crucial that products be near perfect before they are put on the market, and quality assurance is responsible for just that.

This situation also helps explain why quality assurance is being treated more and more as a science. Companies want the most accurate, most efficient, and most financially feasible ways to test their products. This means, of course, increased automation; so quality assurance testers should prepare themselves for the future by becoming educated and experienced in software design and programming. In this way, they can be the ones creating the tests that, as testers, they only run.

Software Designers

SUMMARY

Definition
Software designers devise applications, such as word processors, front-end database programs, and spreadsheets that make it possible for computers to complete given tasks and solve problems.

Alternative Job Titles
None

Salary Range
$48,930 to $85,190 to $118,500+

Educational Requirements
Bachelor's degree plus one year of experience with a programming language

Certification or Licensing
Voluntary

Employment Outlook
Much faster than the average

High School Subjects
Computer science
Mathematics
Physics

Personal Interests
Building things
Computers
Reading/Books
Writing

George Oliver's first job in software design was to develop a Web site for his high school. Knowing what he knows today, he now realizes he would have tackled the project in a different manner:

I should have started out by creating a methodology that would address how the content would be organized—the constructs of the database, client and backend connectivity with the database, and specifications of constraints for the overall Web site. Instead, I went straight to creating the Web pages and incorporating links to images and database content with no real regard to a structure.

The Web site was completed, with minor problems, and was successfully deployed. However, as time went on, I was charged to make changes to the Web site and add new content. As the site grew in size, I began to realize the importance of organization and proper software design. The site at one point had more than 30 separate content folders containing more than 2,000 links and 500 images, with no real documentation of how it all fit together.

It was then that I decided to redesign the site. It took a good two weeks for a final design and documentation, followed by six months of organizing the content to fit the new design. The site didn't grow too much after the redesign, but the documentation assisted greatly in training my successor in maintaining the site.

WHAT DOES A SOFTWARE DESIGNER DO?

Without software, computer hardware would have nothing to do. Computers need to be told exactly what to do. Software is the set of codes that gives the computer those instructions. It comes in the form of the familiar prepackaged software that you find in a computer store, such as games, word processing programs, spreadsheets, and desktop publishing programs, and in a customized application designed to fit the specific need of a particular business. *Software designers* are the initiators of these complex programs. *Computer programmers* then create the software by writing the code that carries out the directives of the designer.

Software designers must envision every detail of what an application will do, how it will do it, and how it will look (the user interface). A simple example is how a home accounting program is created. The software designer first lays out the overall

---

Web Sites for Aspiring Software Designers

CNET Software Reviews
http://reviews.cnet.com/Software/2001-3513_7-0.html

Designer-info.com
http://www.designer-info.com

The Freeware Network
http://www.fwnetwork.com

The History of Shareware
http://www.asp-shareware.org/users/history-of-shareware.asp

The Kleper Report on Digital Publishing
http://www.printerport.com/kdp

Nerd's Heaven: The Software Directory Directory
http://boole.stanford.edu/nerdsheaven.html

***PC World:* Freeware, Shareware, and Trialware Downloads**
http://www.pcworld.com/downloads

Software History Center
http://www.softwarehistory.org

The Software View
http://www.softwareview.com

Yahoo: Computers and Internet: Software
http://dir.yahoo.com/computers_and_internet/software

ZDNet: Product Reviews
http://reviews-zdnet.com.com

ZDNet Software Library
http://downloads-zdnet.com.com/2001-20-0.html?legacy=cnet

functionality of the program, specifying what it should be able to do, such as balancing a checkbook, keeping track of incoming and outgoing bills, and maintaining records of expenses. For each of these tasks, the software designer will outline the design detail for the specific functions that he or she has mandated, such as which menus and icons will be used, what each screen will look like, and whether there will be help or dialog boxes to assist the user. The designer may, for example, specify that the expense record part of the program produce a pie chart that shows the percentage of each household expense in the overall household budget. The designer can specify that the program automatically display the pie chart each time a budget assessment is completed or only after the user clicks on the appropriate icon on the toolbar.

Some software companies specialize in building custom-designed software. This software is highly specialized for specific needs or problems of particular businesses. Some businesses are large enough that they employ in-house software designers who create software applications for their computer systems. A related field is software engineering, which involves writing customized complex software to solve a specific engineering or technical problem of a business or industry.

Whether the designer is working on a mass-market or a custom application, the first step is to define the overall goals for the application. This is typically done in consultation with management if working at a software supply company, or with the client if working on a custom-designed project. Then, the software designer studies the goals and problems of the project. If working on custom-designed software, the designer must also take into consideration the existing computer system of the client. Next, the software designer works on the program strategy and specific design detail that he or she has envisioned. At this point, the designer may need to write a proposal outlining the design and estimating time and cost allocations. Based on this report, management or the client decides if the project should proceed.

Once approval is given, the software designer and the programmers begin working on writing the software program. Typically, the software designer writes the specifications for the program, and the *applications programmers* write the programming codes.

In addition to the design detail duties, a software designer may be responsible for writing a user's manual or at least writing a report for what should be included in the user's manual. After testing and debugging the program, the software designer will present it to management or to the client.

WHAT IS IT LIKE TO BE A SOFTWARE DESIGNER?

George Oliver has been a software designer for more than 10 years. He works for a company that specializes in printing, graphic design, and advanced technology development. George enjoys the field not only because of the opportunity to create software solutions that save his company time and money, but also the opportunity it gives him to learn more about other occupations totally unrelated to the computer industry. "Software designers have the opportunity, as one person once told me, to stay at their desks and become pipe fitters," George explains. "The projects that I've worked on have increased my knowledge of business processes in other fields, and allowed me to experience, to a very good degree, work in these areas. It has helped me continue to become a well-rounded person, with familiarity in many different areas of human involvement."

George begins each workday by looking at customer support issues that have been flagged as feature requests and problems (bugs) with existing software. "I determine which of the requests are doable," he says, "and create a rough design. Most feature requests are minor changes (report changes, aesthetics, etc.) to the software that can be done in very little time. On occasion, I have to consult with other departments, mostly management, on feature changes that are broad in scope or controversial."

He continues his day by doing design work on existing software projects, which entail matters such as optimizing code execution, user interface layouts, component integration, and creation of SOWs (scopes of work). "Design work that is completed is passed on to project managers (PMs) for review," George explains, "who then, upon approval, pass on to developers. More often that not, PMs and developers will rebut a design specification. Reasons for this can vary from conflicts with existing software to limitations in current technology—and in those cases the specification is modified and resubmitted."

George also attends afternoon research and development sessions with members of his company's advanced technology department to see if a proposed software design is feasible. He also meets with customers to gather information on potential software projects and to showcase design specifications for existing projects.

Software designers work in comfortable environments. Many computer companies are known for their casual work atmosphere; employees generally do not have to wear suits, except during client meetings. Overall, software designers work standard weeks, but they may be required to work overtime to meet a deadline. George works Monday through Friday 8:00 a.m. to 5:00 p.m., but also works two to three hours of overtime several days a week, and two to five additional hours each weekend.

It is common in software design to share office or cubicle space with two or three coworkers, which is typical of the team approach to working. As a software designer or applications programmer, much of the day is spent in front of the computer, although a software designer will have occasional team meetings or meetings with clients.

Software design can be stressful work for several reasons. First, the market for software is very competitive, and companies are pushing to develop more innovative software and to get it on the market

> **To Be a Successful Software Designer, You Should . . .**
>
> - have superior technical skills and knowledge
> - be detail-oriented
> - enjoy solving problems
> - be able to work under deadline pressure
> - have strong communication skills
> - be able to work both independently and collaboratively
> - be willing to continue to learn throughout your career

before competitors do. For this same reason, software design is also very exciting and creative work. Second, software designers are given a project and a deadline. It is up to the designer and team members to budget their time to finish in the allocated time. Finally, working with programming languages and so many details can be very frustrating, especially when the tiniest glitch means the program will not run.

DO I HAVE WHAT IT TAKES TO BE A SOFTWARE DESIGNER?

Software design is project- and detail-oriented, and therefore, you must be patient and diligent. You must also enjoy problem-solving challenges and be able to work under a deadline with minimal supervision. As a software designer, you should also possess good communication skills for consulting both with management and with clients who will have varying levels of technical expertise.

Software companies are looking for individuals with vision and imagination to help them create new and exciting programs to sell in the ever-competitive software market. Superior technical skills and knowledge combined with motivation, imagination, and exuberance will make you an attractive candidate.

HOW DO I BECOME A SOFTWARE DESIGNER?
Education
High School

If you are interested in computer science, you should take as many computer, math, and science courses as possible; they provide fundamental math and computer knowledge and teach analytical thinking skills. According to George, the courses that you choose to take in high school and college should be based on the aspect of software design you want to pursue. "These days," he explains, "software design falls generally into two areas, user interface and backend coding (as I like to call it). Students with an eye for graphics and visual-layout work will want to take drafting, art, desktop publishing, and computer-assisted graphic design courses. Backend coding is mostly suited for students who have a knack for engineering; classes in this area include, but are not limited to, advanced math and engineering (really any class that improves the dynamics of one's thinking in solving a problem). All students interested in software design, however, should enroll in at least one programming and, if available, application development class."

In addition to computer science, take as many math and science courses as possible; they provide fundamental knowledge and teach analytical thinking skills. Classes that focus on schematic drawing and flowcharts are also very valuable. English and speech courses will help you improve your communication skills, which are very important to software designers who must make formal presentations to management and clients.

Postsecondary Training

A bachelor's degree in computer science plus one year of experience with a programming language is required for most software designers. For a list of accredited four-year computer science programs, visit the Accreditation Board for Engineering and Technology's Web site, http://www.abet.org.

In the past, the computer industry was pretty flexible about official credentials; demonstrated computer proficiency and work experience have often been enough to obtain a good position. As more people enter the field, however, competition has increased, and job requirements have become more stringent. Technical knowledge alone does not suffice in the field of software design anymore. In order to be a successful software designer, you should have at least a peripheral knowledge of the field for which you intend to design software, such as business, education, or science. Individuals with degrees in education and subsequent teaching experience are much sought after as designers for educational software. Those with bachelor's degrees in computer science with a minor in business or accounting have an excellent chance for employment in designing business or accounting software.

Certification and Licensing

Certification in software development is offered by companies such as Sun Microsystems, Hewlett-Packard, IBM, Novell, and Oracle. While not required, certification tells employers that your skills meet industry education and training standards.

Additionally, the Institute of Electrical and Electronics Engineers Computer Society offers the designation Certified Software Development Professional to individuals who have a bachelor's degree, a minimum of 9,000 hours of software engineering experience within at least 6 of 11 knowledge areas, and pass an examination.

Internships and Volunteerships

Students in technical schools or universities should take advantage of the career services office on campus. They should check regularly for internship postings, job listings, and notices of on-campus recruitment. Placement offices are also valuable resources for resume tips and interviewing techniques. Internships and summer jobs with such corporations are always beneficial and provide experience that will give you the edge over the competition.

WHO WILL HIRE ME?

Software design positions are regarded as some of the most interesting, and therefore the most competitive, in the computer industry. Some software designers are promoted from entry-level programming positions. Software design positions in software supply companies and large custom software companies will be difficult to secure straight out of college or technical/vocational school.

Entry-level programming and design jobs may be listed in the help-wanted sections of newspapers. Employment agencies and online job banks are other good sources.

General computer job fairs are also held throughout the year in larger cities.

There are many online career sites listed on the World Wide Web that post job openings, salary surveys, and current employment trends. The Web also has online publications that deal specifically with computer jobs. You can also obtain information from computer organizations such as the IEEE Computer Society. Because this is such a competitive field, you will need to show initiative and creativity that will set you apart from other applicants.

Software designers are employed throughout the United States. Opportunities are best in large cities and suburbs where business and industry are active. Programmers who develop software systems work for software manufacturers, many of which are in Silicon Valley in northern California. There is also a concentration of software manufacturers in Boston, Chicago, and Atlanta, among other places.

WHERE CAN I GO FROM HERE?

In general, programmers work between one and five years before being promoted to software designer. A programmer can move up by demonstrating an ability to create new software ideas that translate well into marketable applications. Individuals with a knack for spotting trends in the software market are also likely to advance.

Those software designers who demonstrate leadership may be promoted to *project team leader.* Project team leaders are responsible for developing new software projects and overseeing the work done by software designers and applications programmers. With experience as a project team leader, a motivated software designer may be promoted to *software manager,* running projects from an even higher level.

In 5 or 10 years, George sees himself as a senior officer, probably managing several units of software developers. "In any case," he says, "I'd like to be in a position, such as I'm in now, where I have the ability to experience other walks of life, whether it's through software design or something else."

WHAT ARE THE SALARY RANGES?

Salaries for software designers vary with the size of the company and with location. Salaries may be slightly higher in areas where there is a large concentration of computer companies, such as the Silicon Valley in northern California and parts of Washington, Oregon, and the East Coast.

The National Association of Colleges and Employers reports that average starting salaries for graduates with a bachelor's degree in computer science were $50,820 in 2005. Graduates with a doctoral degree in computer science averaged $93,050.

Median salaries for computer and information scientists (which include software designers) were $85,190 in 2004, according to the U.S. Department of Labor's National Occupational Employment and Wage Estimates. Salaries ranged from less than $48,930 to $132,700 or more annually. At the managerial level, salaries can reach $118,500 or more.

Most designers work for large companies, which offer a full benefits package that includes health insurance, vacation and sick time, and a profit-sharing or retirement plan.

WHAT IS THE JOB OUTLOOK?

Jobs in software design are expected to grow much faster than the average through 2014, according to the *Occupational Outlook Handbook*. Employment

> **Related Jobs**
>
> - computer programmers
> - computer support service owners
> - computer systems programmer/analysts
> - computer trainers
> - database specialists
> - graphic designers
> - graphics programmers
> - hardware engineers
> - microelectronics technicians
> - quality assurance testers
> - semiconductor technicians
> - software engineers
> - systems setup specialists
> - technical support specialists
> - technical writers and editors

will increase as technology becomes more sophisticated and organizations continue to adopt and integrate these technologies, making for plentiful job openings. Hardware designers and systems programmers are constantly developing faster, more powerful, and more user-friendly hardware and operating systems. As long as these advancements continue, the industry will need software designers to create software to use these improvements.

Business may have less need to contract for custom software as more prepackaged software arrives on the market that allows users with minimal computer skills to "build" their own software using components that they customize. Growth in the retail software market, however, is expected to make up for this loss in customized services.

The expanding integration of Internet technologies by businesses has resulted in a rising demand for a variety of skilled professionals who can develop and support a variety of Internet applications.

In the next five years, George predicts an influx of software designers with complementary degrees in medicine/medical systems, mechanical engineering, electronic/radio technologies, and financial services. "Eventually," he says, "specialties in software design will vary, just as they do in engineering today. They are currently few in number, but some of these specialists already exist."

Technical Support Specialists

SUMMARY

Definition
Technical support specialists investigate and resolve problems with the hardware, software, and peripherals of computer systems. They also answer phone calls from users experiencing problems and walk them through appropriate procedures.

Alternative Job Titles
End-user consultants

Help-desk representatives
Information center specialists
Microcomputer support specialists
Support engineers
User support analysts

Salary Range
$24,190 to $40,430 to $69,110+

Educational Requirements
Some postsecondary training

Certification or Licensing
Voluntary

Outlook
Faster than the average

High School Subjects
Computer science
Mathematics
Speech

Personal Interests
Computers
Figuring out how things work
Fixing things

Michael Canty was once assigned the task of recovering data from a laptop that had quite literally been run over by a car.

"I tackled this issue with a chisel and a hammer," he recalls, "because the hard drive couldn't be removed through the typical easy slide out, due to bending and cracking of other pieces in and around the drive.

"We had a second laptop available that was the same model as the one that was damaged. Once we removed the hard drive from the damaged laptop, we installed it in the working laptop and were able to copy all the data files that were pertinent for restoration. I was shocked that the drive didn't go bad from all the physical trauma that happened around it."

WHAT DOES A TECHNICAL SUPPORT SPECIALIST DO?

Businesses and individuals rely on computers for everything from basic word processing to complex databases. People who use computers on a daily basis recognize how lost they would be without them. When computer users, consumers, and business colleagues run into problems, they contact a *technical support specialist* for help. Technical support specialists investigate and resolve problems in computer functioning. "If you like working with customers, this is a great job," says Mark Ellis, director of emerging technologies for Kronos, Inc., a Chelmsford, Massachusetts-based company that specializes in front-end labor management systems. "There is a tremendous satisfaction in being able to help a customer solve a problem so that they can do their jobs."

The professional area known as technical support can officially be broken down into several categories: user support, technical support, and microcomputer support, among others. Positions in the computer industry differ among companies; the duties of a technical support specialist in one company might be the responsibility of the user support specialist in another. Job titles and descriptions vary depending on the nature, size, and needs of the company. Almost all technical support specialists, however, perform some combination of the tasks described below.

Technical support specialists fall into several categories, according to what they fix and whom they assist. *User support specialists* direct much of their efforts at the users themselves, training them in proper procedures and explaining how to resolve recurrent problems. They answer phone calls, taking notes on the precise nature of the user's problem and the commands he or she entered that led to that problem. In some companies, they might enter a description of the problem into a special computer program that tells them how to help the user or "take over" a customer's system using the Web and other technology.

Their goal is to locate the source of the problem. If it is the user, specialists explain procedures related to the program in question, maybe a statistical, graphics, database, printing, word processing, or e-mail program. If the source of the problem is located in the program or hardware, the user support specialists consult with technical support specialists, programmers, and other computer professionals to work out a solution if they are not able to resolve the issue on their own, which they usually are able to do up to 80 percent of the time.

Technical support specialists employed by computer companies are mainly involved with solving problems caused by the computer system's operating system, other software, or hardware. They consult manuals, meet with programmers, and inspect peripheral equipment in order to isolate the problem. Then, they try to solve the problems through a variety of methods, including program modifications and the replacement of certain hardware or software.

Technical support specialists employed by the information processing departments of large corporations do this kind of troubleshooting as well, but they also oversee the daily performance of their office's computer systems. They compare their department's projected workload on a computer system with its specified capacity to determine whether a given system is sufficient or if it should be upgraded and how. They might also test and modify commercial programs to customize them to their particular needs.

Microcomputer support specialists specialize in preparing a computer for delivery to a client, including loading the appropriate operating system and other software, installing the unit at the client's location, answering the client's immediate questions, and fielding later questions over the telephone. They also diagnose problems, repairing minor ones themselves and referring major ones to other support specialists.

All technical support specialists evaluate software programs in some capacity. They write technical reports of their findings and offer suggestions to designers and programmers about how to improve the program. They may be involved with the writing of training manuals and with the training of users. Most specialists read trade magazines and current books to keep up with changes in the field.

WHAT IS IT LIKE TO BE A TECHNICAL SUPPORT SPECIALIST?

Michael Canty is a technical support specialist at a manufacturing company in Tinley Park, Illinois. "I specialize in the support of our sales staff," he says, "which I believe is the most unique and challenging environment to support throughout our infrastructure.

> **Lingo to Learn**
>
> **application** A software program that helps you do word processing, build databases, or create spreadsheets.
>
> **back-up** Copies of computer files on tape or diskette stored in a place other than the main work site, to be used in case of an emergency.
>
> **crash** When a computer freezes up and must be rebooted in order to operate; a "hard drive crash" means the computer can't be repaired.
>
> **data dictionary** Information about data, including name, description, source of data item, and key words for categorizing and searching for data items.
>
> **glitch** A "bug" or error in programming that causes interruptions or problems in computer operations.
>
> **hardware** The physical equipment inside a computer that makes it work.
>
> **peripheral** Any machine connected to a computer, such as a printer or an external modem or CD-ROM.
>
> **user** A person who uses a computer.
>
> **user support** Online or live telephone assistance offered by a support specialist to a system user.

Michael works from 8:30 a.m. till 4:30 p.m., but often stays until 6:00 p.m. to handle ongoing support issues. "I field approximately 50 issues per day," he says. "I handle these issues through phone calls, voice mails, e-mails, and informal meetings. I resolve approximately 20 issues per day. These might include Internet access problems, e-mail failures and concerns, and application failures and questions regarding application uses. I also coordinate the information necessary for users of systems to best make use of our technologies."

Technical support specialists work in comfortable business environments. They generally work regular, 40-hour weeks. For certain products, however, they may be asked to work evenings or weekends or at least be on call during those times in case of emergencies. If they work for service companies, they may be required to travel to clients' sites and log overtime hours.

Technical support work can be stressful, since specialists often deal with frustrated users who may be difficult to work with. Communication problems with people who are less technically qualified may also be a source of frustration. Patience and understanding are essential for handling these issues.

Technical support specialists are expected to work quickly and efficiently and be able to perform under pressure. The ability to do this requires thorough technical expertise and keen analytical ability. "You must be able to react quickly to develop the best processes for handling continually unique issues at the spur of the moment, oftentimes in very high volume over short amounts of time," Michael says. "This can be positive if you can rise to meet this difficult challenge, and you will be viewed as an 'ace in the hole' if you are the best at representing resolution to your company's business needs."

To Be a Successful Technical Support Specialist, You Should . . .

- have a thorough understanding of computer basics
- like challenges and problem solving
- have strong written and verbal communication skills
- perform well in stressful situations
- be a logical, analytical, and quick thinker

DO I HAVE WHAT IT TAKES TO BE A TECHNICAL SUPPORT SPECIALIST?

Good interpersonal skills are important in this career because you will have a lot of interaction with users and coworkers. "There is a great deal of collaboration with your peers in this career," Mark Ellis says. "If you need help to solve a problem the first place you will look to is one of your peer group members. All of our Level 1 [or Help Desk] support engineers sit in what we call 'quadrants'. This is basically one very large cube, and each support engineer has his or her own desk in the corner with no walls in between. This allows them to turn and face the others in their group of four to ask questions and seek help as necessary. So, very often you may be supporting not only customers but also your peers in your quadrant."

Good stress management techniques can help specialists keep a clear mind. Strong logical and analytical thinking skills enable them to understand on the spot how a user complaint is linked to software programming.

Quick analysis of this kind also requires thorough knowledge of computer basics. Specialists are not expected to know everything about a particular program before they begin work, of course, but rather they should have a broad understanding of computer principles that allows them to learn specifics relatively easily.

Technical support specialists like challenges and finding creative ways to deal with them.

Solid written and verbal communications skills are a must for a prospective technical support specialist. To write technical materials, it's especially important to be clear and concise.

Technical support specialists must be prepared to continue to learn throughout their careers. "Most people in this business are constantly learning both in the classroom as well as on their own," Mark says. "Like any technical business, the products, as well as the supporting technology platforms, are constantly changing. You need to stay abreast of these changes."

Michael Canty says that technical support specialists need to constantly test the information and processes that are being deployed to the users whom they support. "You must have knowledge of not only the internal systems to your company, but also the external technologies that users will need assistance with," he says. "These can be obtained through Internet searching, newsgroups related to specific topics, and technical magazines."

HOW DO I BECOME A TECHNICAL SUPPORT SPECIALIST?
Education
High School

You need at least a high school diploma to become a technical support specialist. Courses in mathematics, such as algebra and geometry, can give you the opportunity to develop strong logical and analytical thinking skills. Science classes are equally important, as they teach you to analyze and investigate the world around you. In physics and chemistry, for instance, you will use analytical methods similar to those used by technical support specialists when they are solving a problem.

English and speech classes are important because they teach you the basic communication skills vital to being a good technical support specialist. Computer classes, such as basic principles, business applications, programming, or computer science, can give you excellent background information about computers. Business classes like accounting or statistics might help you down the line when you're involved in making administrative decisions. Drafting and mechanical drawing classes let you practice skills that carry over to the proper use of flow charts.

Michael Canty recommends that students take computer programming in classes in basic languages/structures, "which," he says, "could be of use to understand scripting and some of the backbone involved in the applications that run on networks."

Postsecondary Training

In deciding whether to pursue formal postsecondary training, you need to think about which area of technical support interests you the most. If you would like to work in the computer information service department of a large corporation, an associate degree in PC support and administration can be a strong asset. These companies often hire technical support specialists who can double as system administrators, and they take the educational background of an applicant into consideration. Technical schools offer many majors in business-related computer technologies, such as computer communications or PC support and administration. A two-year associate degree in PC support and administration, for instance, emphasizes hardware and software support, PC DOS data communications, and networking, along with general business classes. In addition to the associate degree, some companies prefer applicants with training or vendor-certification in a specific area like networking.

An associate degree is by no means a requisite for employment as a technical support specialist. Most major computer companies who hire people to field user calls and do other minor technical or microcomputer support look for someone with general computer proficiency and demonstrated potential to learn their systems quickly through in-house training programs. One good way to prepare for this field—and to get promoted from within a company—is through self-study.

Once a company hires you, you can also participate in vendor-sponsored in-house workshops to expand your knowledge. At these workshops, the manufacturer of a program sends its best employees to train new users on the product.

While vast computer experience and talent may be enough for success in the field, many computer professionals eventually feel the need to earn a bachelor's degree to stay competitive in the job market. Not only can a four-year degree give you an edge when looking for a job, but it can lead to better pay. Universities offer a wide spectrum of majors in computer science, from computer software engineering to computer-generated graphic design. "Most of our employees have a degree in computer science or have prior experience with other companies or in the military or both," Mark Ellis says. "There are two levels of training at our company. Basic computer skills are a prerequisite of the job. You must have these to even be considered for this type of position at Kronos. Once hired as a support engineer, new employees will complete about three to six months of formal training, depending on the product. This training is done mostly by Kronos instructors. Some training, however, is self-paced online training. After the

> ### Advancement Possibilities
>
> *Technical support supervisors* are generally responsible for solving the more complicated problems and for implementing the more complex solutions and programming changes. They have some administrative duties as well.
>
> *Computer network engineers* design, install, maintain, modify, and repair computer networks for business applications.
>
> *Software engineers* analyze industrial, business, and scientific problems and conceive software programs that can provide solutions to them.

formal training period ends, the new support engineers will usually work with a 'mentor' Level 1 support engineer and/or a technical advisor until they are ready to go 'solo' and handle calls directly."

Certification and Licensing

Though certification is not an industry requirement, it is highly recommended. According to the Help Desk Institute, most individuals wishing to qualify to work in a support/help desk environment will need to obtain certification within a month of being on the job. A number of organizations offer several different types of certification. The Computing Technology Industry Association, for example, offers the A+ certification for entry-level computer service technicians. Help Desk Institute has training courses and offers a number of certifications for those working in support and help desk positions.

To become certified, you will need to pass a written test and in some cases may need a certain amount of work experience. Although going through the certification process is voluntary, becoming certified will most likely be to your advantage. It will show your commitment to the profession as well as your level of expertise. In addition, certification may qualify you for certain jobs and lead to new employment opportunities.

Internships and Volunteerships

Internships in technical support are not abundant. There may be some summer opportunities in computer companies, especially in geographical areas where computer companies are clustered. Technical support positions require so much in-house training that it is usually considered a bad investment to employ people only in the short-term. In areas like the Silicon Valley in northern California, however, job turnaround may be great, causing a steady demand for specialists and perhaps a willingness on the part of the employer to accept interns.

Technical school or university students might be required to complete part of their curricula by working in school-organized internships or co-op programs, which vary greatly by school. If your school doesn't organize such programs, you can work with your career services office to find summer or off-quarter employment.

> ### Best Support Web Sites
>
> The Association of Support Professionals (ASP) annually evaluates Web sites that provide online technical support. The following Web sites have been chosen at least four times by the ASP as among the "Ten Best Web Support Sites."
>
> **Cognos**
> http://support.cognos.com/en/support/index.html?lid=//services//support
>
> **Dell**
> http://www.support.dell.com
>
> **Hewlett Packard**
> http://welcome.hp.com/country/us/en/support.html
>
> **Symantec**
> http://www.symantec.com/techsupp

Any opportunity you have to practice technical support skills should be taken. One way to test technical support prowess is to offer to help friends and relatives when they run into problems on their computers. You might also offer user support and training to a religious or non-profit organization.

WHO WILL HIRE ME?

"I have gotten most every job interview from knowing someone that could help me get my foot in the door," Michael Canty says. "I've landed almost every job I have interviewed for by concentrating on core interview skills and preparing accordingly."

Technical support specialists work in any medium- to large-sized business or corporation that maintains an in-house computer information service or technical support department. Commercial databases and online services, retail stores, catalog companies, insurance companies, banks, financial institutions, hospitals, governmental agencies, universities, public and private school systems, and any other big service industry firm are some of the organizations that hire technical support specialists.

Other big employers of technical support specialists are computer companies, including those specializing in the research, development, or manufacture of hardware, software, and peripherals. As mentioned above, many computer companies tend to be established in the same geographical areas. Research Triangle in North Carolina and the Silicon Valley in northern California are two of the major ones. Potential employers can be identified simply by taking note of brand names on a walk through a computer store or perusal of a computer magazine.

Commercial online service providers like America Online are also good prospective employers of technical support specialists. Most local Internet providers also have a technical support staff. Companies that produce CD-ROMs and computer games employ a support staff as well.

You can consult the classified listings in your local newspapers as well as in computer trade magazines. Another way to find a job is to check out the many Web sites for computer-industry jobseekers. You might also browse online job postings for individual companies.

In the geographical clusters of computer companies, many job openings are made known by word of mouth. Network with employed computer professionals and try to get in the information loop. Talk to instructors and counselors in your school's career services office.

WHERE CAN I GO FROM HERE?

After working in an entry-level technical support position, you have a good chance of being promoted to *support supervisor*. This position entails more complicated technical work as well as performing some managerial duties like scheduling appointments with clients and vendors and ordering supplies. Supervisors usually do more technical writing than specialists, preparing performance reports for programmers and design analysts. They may also train new employees or participate as teachers in training workshops offered to customers.

Technical support specialists might use their positions to springboard to an area requiring more specialization and a higher level of training. Some may become *certified network engineers* (*CNEs*). CNEs determine and analyze client networking needs, select appropriate hardware and software, make any necessary changes, supervise installation and initial operations of the system, and sometimes provide training to network users. Many technical support specialists develop the basic knowledge needed to succeed in the additional education and certification programs required of these positions.

Software engineering is another field that technical support specialists might consider. *Software engineers* and *engineering specialists* use computers to solve problems, increase productivity, and allow for business efficiency. They meet with clients to determine the specific nature of the problem, give presentations of software proposals and demonstrations of finished products, and consult with other engineers in the regular course of their work. A bachelor's degree or equivalent work experience is usually required for these positions.

Having enjoyed a long and productive career, Mark Ellis plans to retire in the next 5 or 10 years. "I plan to do a great deal of writing," he says. "I have already developed a number of white papers [documentation of technology uses or solutions to problems] on technical support operations and have just finished coauthoring a book for Help Desk Institute."

WHAT ARE THE SALARY RANGES?

Technical support specialist jobs are plentiful in areas where clusters of computer companies are located, such as northern California and Seattle, Washington. Median annual earnings for technical support specialists were $40,430 in 2004, according to the U.S. Department of Labor. The highest 10 percent earned more than $69,110, while the lowest 10 percent earned less than $24,190. Those who have more education, responsibility, and expertise have the potential to earn much more.

Technical support specialists earned the following median annual salaries by industry in 2004 (according to the U.S. Department of Labor): software publishers, $44,890; computer systems design and related services, $42,750; colleges and universities, $37,940; and elementary and secondary schools, $35,500.

Most specialists work for companies that provide a complete benefits package, which may include health care coverage, a pension plan, paid sick leave and vacation days, and educational expense reimbursement.

Related Jobs

- computer network administrators and engineers
- computer programmers
- computer scientists
- computer security coordinators
- computer systems hardware analysts
- data communications analysts
- data recovery planners
- database design specialists
- database specialists
- microcomputer support specialists
- quality assurance specialists
- software engineering specialists
- software engineers
- systems analysts
- user analyst supervisors

WHAT IS THE JOB OUTLOOK?

The U.S. Department of Labor predicts that the technical support specialist position will grow faster than the average for of all occupations through 2014. As long as new technological inventions enter the market, there will be the need for technical support specialists to solve problems. Many companies cite the shortage of information technology (IT) professionals as one of the most significant obstacles to business success. As a result, those with solid computer skills have many options when entering the workplace. Though some of the more talented workers are stepping into jobs right out of high school, most industry experts say this is rare, and that some basis of college education is required for promotion and higher salaries.

The number of technical support specialists hired varies according to a number of factors. When the computer industry experiences higher sales or when a new product hits the market, companies will need additional technical support specialists, since increased sales automatically means increased calls to technical support. But even when sales at one company are down, job opportunities are still strong for technically flexible applicants. The key is to keep up-to-date on the newest technologies by surfing the Internet and talking with other computer professionals.

As large service industries continue to invest in computer systems as an automated alternative to record keeping and forms management, technical support positions there will increase in number as well. Computer companies are beginning to offer longer warranties and full-coverage service contracts to new customers as a strategy to distinguish their product from the competitors.' To fulfill these contractual obligations, computer companies will hire more technical support staff or subcontract the work out to computer service companies described above.

Webmasters

SUMMARY

Definition
Webmasters design, implement, and maintain Internet Web sites.

Alternative Job Titles
None

Salary Range
$44,775 to $63,738 to $76,668+

Educational Requirements
Some postsecondary training

Certification or Licensing
Voluntary

Employment Outlook
Much faster than the average

High School Subjects
Art
Computer science
English (writing/literature)
Mathematics

Personal Interests
Building things
Computers
Photography
Writing

"Five years ago," says Bivens Swift, a webmaster for nearly a decade, "I went back to school and learned desktop application development. This was an important step in my career as I have been able to take on more complicated projects, and I have been able to provide proprietary solutions that make things easier for my clients."

That training came in handy when he was working at an Internet start-up where he was dealing with several SQL servers holding more than 100 gigabytes of data. Many of these databases required daily updating and, in many cases, the updates could not be handled by stored procedures. To solve the problem, he wrote a Visual Basic application, which ran on another server and communicated with all SQL servers to perform the daily updates. The application also e-mailed reports and alerts as needed to inform him about server performance or accessibility issues.

This application has since been amended several times. It now performs hundreds of operations per day and is a major component of the successful and efficient operation of the business.

WHAT DOES A WEBMASTER DO?

Webmasters design, implement, and maintain Internet Web sites for corporations, educational institutions, not-for-profit organizations, government agencies, or other institutions. Webmasters should have working knowledge of network configurations, interface, graphic design, software development, business, writing, marketing, and project management. The function of a webmaster encompasses so many different responsibilities, so the position is often held by a team of individuals in a large organization.

Because the idea of designing and maintaining a Web site is relatively new, there is no complete, definitive job description for webmasters. Many of their job responsibilities depend on the goals and needs of the particular organization for which they work. There are, however, some basic duties that are common to almost all webmasters.

Webmasters, specifically site managers, first secure space on the Web for the site they are developing. They do this by contracting with an Internet service provider. The provider serves as a sort of storage facility for the organization's online information, usually charging a set monthly fee for a specified amount of megabyte space. The webmaster may also be responsible for establishing a URL (Uniform Resource Locator) for the Web site he or she is developing. The URL serves as the site's online "address" and must be registered with InterNIC, the Web URL registration service.

The webmaster is responsible for developing the actual Web site for his or her organization. In some cases, this may involve actually writing the text content of the pages. More commonly, however, the webmaster is given the text to be used and is merely responsible for programming it in such a way that it can be displayed on a Web page. In larger companies webmasters specialize in content, adaptation, and presentation of data.

In order for text to be displayed on a Web page, it must be formatted using HyperText Markup Language (HTML). HTML is a system of coding text so that the computer that is "reading" it knows how to display it. Text could be coded to be a certain size or color or to be italicized or boldface. Paragraphs, line breaks, alignment, and margins are other examples of text attributes that must be coded in HTML.

Although it is less and less common, some webmasters code text manually by actually typing the various commands into the body of the text. This method is time-consuming, however, and mistakes are easily made. More often, webmasters use a software program that automatically codes text. Some word processing programs, such as WordPerfect, even offer HTML options.

Along with coding the text, the webmaster must lay out the elements of the Web site in such a way that it is visually pleasing, well organized, and easy to navigate. He or she may use various colors, background patterns, images, tables, or charts. These graphic elements can come from image files already on the Web, software clip art files, or images scanned into the computer with an electronic scanner. In some cases, when an organization is using the Web site to promote its product or service, the webmaster may work with a marketing specialist or department to develop a page.

Some Web sites have several directories or "layers." That is, an organization may have several Web pages, organized in a sort of "tree," with its home page connected, via hypertext links, to other pages, which may in turn be linked to other pages. The webmaster is responsible for organizing the pages in such a way that a visitor can easily browse through them and find what he or she is looking for. Such webmasters are called *programmers* and *developers;* they are also responsible for creating Web tools and special Web functionality.

Webmasters who work for organizations that have several different Web sites may be responsible for making sure that the "style" or appearance of all the pages is the same. This is often referred to as "house style." In large organizations, such as universities, where many different departments may be developing and maintaining their own pages, it is especially important that the webmaster monitor these pages to ensure consistency and conformity to the organization's requirements. In almost every case, the webmaster has the final authority for the content and appearance of his or her organization's Web site. He or she must carefully edit, proofread, and check the appearance of every page.

Besides designing and setting up Web sites, most webmasters are charged with maintaining and updating existing sites. Most sites contain information that changes regularly; some change daily or even hourly. Depending on his or her employer and the type of Web site, the webmaster may spend a good deal of time updating and remodeling pages. He or she is also responsible for ensuring that the hyperlinks contained within the Web site lead to the sites they should. Since it is common for links to change or become obsolete, the webmaster usually performs a link check every few weeks.

Other job duties vary, depending on the employer and the position. Most web-

---

A Brief History of the Internet

The Internet developed from ARPANET, an experimental computer network established in the 1960s by the U.S. Department of Defense. By the late 1980s, the Internet was being used by many government and educational institutions.

The World Wide Web was the brainchild of physicist Tim Berners-Lee, who developed a way to organize information in a more logical fashion by using hypertext to link portions of documents to one another. Although Berners-Lee formed his idea of the Web in 1989, it was another four years before the first Web browser (Mosaic) made it possible for people to navigate the Web simply. Businesses quickly realized the commercial potential of the Web and soon developed their own Web sites.

No one person or organization is in charge of the Internet and what's on it. Each Web site, however, needs an individual or team of workers to gather, organize, and maintain online data. These specialists, called *webmasters,* manage sites for businesses of all sizes, nonprofit organizations, schools, government agencies, and private individuals.

masters are responsible for receiving and answering e-mail messages from visitors to the organization's Web site. Some webmasters keep logs and create reports on when and how often their pages are visited and by whom. Depending on the company, Web sites count anywhere from 300 to 1.4 billion visits, or "hits," per month. Some create and maintain order forms or online "shopping carts" that allow Web site visitors to purchase products or services. Some may train other employees on how to create or update Web pages. Finally, webmasters may be responsible for developing and adhering to a budget for their departments.

WHAT IS IT LIKE TO BE A WEBMASTER?

Swift Bivens has been a webmaster for nine years. He also serves as the director of the World Organization of Webmasters Native American Technical Education Initiative, which seeks to educate Native Americans about opportunities in Information Technology. "In 1994," he explains, "I experienced the Internet for the very first time. I was very intrigued by this new medium. Over time, I became aware of the term 'webmaster.' I saw it located on the bottom or many Web pages. I always wondered what it meant and eventually learned it stood for the creator of the Web page. I had been a freelance graphic designer with a strong background in computer graphic design, including typography and art history. I saw that the webmaster was a perfect union between the creative mind and the technical mind, and knew that I wanted to be a webmaster. I bought my first design software and began learning my new craft."

Swift builds every part of every Web site that comes to his desk. "This includes," he explains, "all graphic design, HTML, CSS, flash animation, dynamic scripting such as ASP or DHTML, database design using Microsoft SQL server utilizing TSQL, and also any e-commerce integration. I also build the occasional small Visual Basic application to automate certain processes. I am always programming, testing, or deploying Internet solutions for clients. I also provide Internet marketing solutions as well as consulting services."

Swift starts a typical work day by checking e-mails, which are normally filled with communications with other staff members, clients, or other business affairs. He then attends a morning staff meeting where he discusses the day's assignments and coordinates with other staff members and management. "I then begin one of several different tasks, depending on the day," he says. "I usually perform some kind of tech support for clients or other staff members. I also maintain our network of servers, so occasionally I will need to perform software or hardware installations or regular maintenance. I often take sales calls to new potential clients, where I help define their project's needs and discuss our service offerings. I spend most of my day programming. I always have one or more projects in various states of construction going at any time. I prioritize all my projects so that I meet all deadlines."

Swift must create a lot of documentation for his work. "I have to document every minute of my day so that clients get billed correctly for my work and the company can track my productivity," he says. "A significant amount of my time goes to administrative responsibilities and client relations; therefore, it is important to maintain a steady flow of billable hours. I also document all maintenance activities I perform so that another staff member can perform my duties if necessary." Swift also documents all communication with clients and includes notations about the client's current project status and places them in the client's file.

Because technology changes so rapidly, this job is constantly evolving. Webmasters must spend time reading and learning about new developments in online communication. "I buy lots of software and books," Swift says. "Most of my initial education was from self-teaching since formalized education in this field was not available." Webmasters may be continually working with new computer software or hardware. Their actual job responsibilities may even change, as the capabilities of both the organization and the World Wide Web itself expand. It is important that these employees be flexible and willing to learn and grow with the technology that drives their work.

Because they don't deal with the general public, most webmasters are allowed to wear fairly casual attire and to work in a relaxed atmosphere. In most cases, the job calls for standard working hours, although there may be times when overtime is required.

To Be a Successful Webmaster, You Should . . .

- be creative and have a strong sense for design
- have good writing skills
- be willing to continually learn throughout your career
- have an aptitude for marketing
- be attentive to detail
- be able to communicate and work well with others

DO I HAVE WHAT IT TAKES TO BE A WEBMASTER?

Webmasters should be creative. It is important for a Web page to be well designed in order to attract attention. Good writing skills and an aptitude for marketing are also excellent qualities for anyone considering a career in Web site design.

Although much of the webmaster's day may be spent alone, it is nonetheless important that he or she be able to communicate and work well with others. Depending on the organization for which he or she works, the webmaster may have periodic meetings with graphic designers, marketing specialists, writers, or other professionals who have input into the Web site's development. In many larger organizations, there is a team of webmasters rather than just one. Although each team member works alone on his or her own specific duties, the members may meet frequently to discuss and coordinate their activities.

HOW DO I BECOME A WEBMASTER?

Education

High School

High school students who are interested in becoming webmasters should take as many computer science classes as they can. Mathematics classes are also helpful. Finally, because writing skills are important in this career, English classes are good choices.

Swift recommends that high school students learn as many facets of webmaster technologies as possible. "The more you know about networking and programming," he says, "the better. Try to learn both Windows and Unix technologies such as ASP, PHP, SQL, and MySQL. Get very familiar with CSS, DHTML, and browser compatibility issues. Make sure you write good, clean, and commented code with a strong emphasis on server performance."

Postsecondary Training

A number of community colleges, colleges, and universities offer classes and certificate programs for webmasters, but there is no standard educational path or requirement for becoming a webmaster. While many have bachelor's degrees in computer science, information systems, or computer programming, liberal arts degrees, such as English, are not uncommon. There are also webmasters who have degrees in engineering, mathematics, and marketing.

In addition to taking college-level classes to prepare for the field, you will probably need to pursue continuing education throughout your life since Web-based technology is constantly changing. "I think it is a good idea to attend school to learn new skills whenever it is possible and feasible," Swift says. "Programming languages can usually be acquired without formal education, but networking skills often require complex and expensive equipment. Many new technologies can be self-taught, but sometimes the hands-on approach you get with formal training is the best."

Certification and Licensing

There is strong debate within the industry regarding certification. Some, mostly corporate chief executive officers, favor certification. They view certification as a way to gauge an employee's skill and Web expertise. Others argue, however, that it is nearly impossible to test knowledge of technology that is constantly changing and improving. Despite the difference of opinion, webmaster certification programs are available at many colleges, universities, and technical schools throughout the United States. Programs vary in length, anywhere from three weeks to nine months or more. Topics covered include client/server technology, Web development, programs, and software and hardware. The International Webmasters Association and World Organization of Webmasters also offer voluntary certification programs.

Should Webmasters be certified? Though it's currently not a prerequisite for employment, certification can only enhance a candidate's chance at landing a webmaster position.

What most webmasters have in common is a strong knowledge of computer technology. Most people who enter this field are already well versed in computer operating systems, programming languages, computer graphics, and Internet standards. When considering candidates for the position of webmaster, employers usually require at least two years of experience with World Wide Web technologies. In some cases, employers require that candidates already have experience in designing and maintaining Web sites. It is, in fact, most common for someone to move into the position of webmaster from another computer-related job in the same organization.

Internships and Volunteerships

Students who attend formal postsecondary training programs typically participate in internships that are set up as a result of a formal relationship between the academic institution and companies that employ webmasters. Interns usually receive little or no pay, but they do receive the intangible benefits of work experience and the opportunity to network with and learn from experienced webmasters.

WHO WILL HIRE ME?

The majority of webmasters working today are full-time employees who are employed by Web design companies, businesses, schools or universities, not-for-profit organizations, government agencies—in short, any organization that requires a presence on the World Wide Web. Webmasters may also work as freelancers or operate their own Web design businesses.

Most people become webmasters by moving into the position from another computer-related position within the same company. Since most large organizations already use computers for various functions, they may employ a person or several people to serve as computer "specialists." If these organizations decide to develop their own Web sites, they frequently assign the task to one of these employees who is already experienced with the computer system. Often, the person who ultimately becomes an organization's webmaster at first just takes on the job in addition to his or her other, already-established duties.

Another way that individuals find jobs in this field is through online postings of job openings. Many companies post webmaster position openings online because the candidates they hope to attract are very likely to use the Internet for a job search. Therefore, the prospective webmaster should use the World Wide Web to check job-related newsgroups. He or she might also use a Web search engine to locate openings.

Swift also highly recommends technical placement companies as a job search tool for webmasters. "Whenever I am looking for work," he says, "I post my resume on several key Web sites, like Dice.com, HotJobs.com, Monster.com, and CareerBuilder.com. Once my resume hits the board, I get a ton of e-mail from technical recruiters who are looking to add me to their database of clients. Many jobs submitted to these agencies cannot be found anywhere else. They are usually higher paying jobs as well." Swift says that most jobs offered by technical recruiters are contract positions that range from 1 to 18 months in duration. "Many companies hire contract programmers and then move them to full-time employees once they have established their worth to the company," he says.

WHERE CAN I GO FROM HERE?

Experienced webmasters employed by a large organization may be able to advance to the position of *chief Web officer*. These workers supervise a team of webmasters and are responsible for every aspect of a company's presence on the Web. Others might advance by starting their own business, designing Web sites on a contract basis for several clients rather than working exclusively for one organization.

Opportunities for webmasters of the future are endless due to the continuing development of online technology. As understanding and use of the World Wide Web increase, there may be new or expanded job duties for individuals with expertise in this field. People working today as webmasters may be required in a few years to perform jobs that don't even exist yet.

Swift is currently working on various online business models. "I hope to come up with a hot new business model, which

Related Jobs

- computer programmers
- computer systems programmer/analysts
- computer trainers
- desktop publishing specialists
- graphic designers
- graphics programmers
- hardware engineers
- Internet developers
- Internet security specialists
- software designers
- software engineers
- systems setup specialists
- technical support specialists
- technical writers and editors

has strong potential for viral marketing [free marketing that creates a "buzz" about a new product or service via print, online, and other delivery methods] to make it extremely profitable," he says. "Depending on how profitable the business model is, I will either work to improve it or sell it. I would like to then teach others about this incredible industry."

WHAT ARE THE SALARY RANGES?

According to Salary.com, the average salary for webmasters in 2005 was $63,738. Salaries ranged from $53,588 to $76,668. Many webmasters, however, move into the position from another position within their company, or have taken on the task in addition to other duties. These employees are often paid approximately the same salary they were already making in their old position.

According to the National Association of Colleges and Employers, the starting salary for graduates with a bachelor's degree in computer science was $50,820 in 2005; in computer systems analysis, $46,189; and in information sciences and systems, $44,775.

Depending on the organization for which they work, webmasters may receive a benefits package in addition to salary. A typical benefits package includes paid vacations and holidays, medical insurance, and perhaps a pension plan.

WHAT IS THE JOB OUTLOOK?

According to the U.S. Department of Labor, the field of computer and data processing services is projected to be the fastest growing industry for the next decade. As a result, the employment rate of webmasters and other computer specialists is expected to grow much faster than the average rate for all occupations through 2014.

There can be no doubt that computer, and specifically online, technology will continue its rapid growth for the next several years. The number of computer-related jobs, including that of webmaster, should also increase. As more and more businesses, not-for-profit organizations, educational institutions, and government agencies choose to "go online," the total number of Web sites will grow, as will the need for experts to design them. Companies are now viewing Web sites not as temporary experiments, but rather as important and necessary business and marketing tools. Growth will be largest for *Internet content developers* (webmasters responsible for the information displayed on a Web site) and chief Web officers.

One thing to keep in mind, however, is that when technology advances extremely rapidly, it tends to make old methods of doing things obsolete. If current trends continue, the responsibilities of the webmaster will be carried out by a group or department instead of by a single employee, in order to keep up with the demands of the position. It is possible that in the next few years, changes in technology will make the Web sites we are now familiar with a thing of the past. Another possibility is that, like desktop publishing, user-friendly software programs will make Web site design so easy and efficient that it no longer requires an "expert" to do it well. Webmasters who are concerned with job security should be willing to continue learning and using the very latest developments in technology so that they are prepared to move into the future of online communication, whatever it may be.

SECTION 3

Do It Yourself

The opportunities for exploring your future career right now are only limited by your imagination. You can take apart and rebuild a computer, help a neighbor troubleshoot hardware or software problems, design and build a Web site, tour a software company, participate in computer or science competitions, design your own computer game, job shadow computer professionals, visit computer- and technology-oriented museums, get a job at a computer store (such as CompUSA, Radio Shack, and Best Buy), start or join a computer club at school, take college-level computer classes, join professional associations . . . you get the idea. As you can see, there is no room for excuses when it comes to exploring options in the computer industry. So read on for details about these and other exciting opportunities.

❑ READ BOOKS AND PERIODICALS

Looking for information on computer engineering careers, motherboards, viruses, online gaming, wireless networks, Bill Gates, trends in Web design, and other subjects? Then crack open a book or magazine to get the lowdown on these and other topics. Your high school or community library contains countless books and periodicals about computers. Ask your librarian to direct you to the best resources. For a great list of books and periodicals about computers, check out Section 4: "What Can I Do Right Now?" Get Involved: Read a Book.

❑ SURF THE WEB

By surfing the Internet, you're actually killing two birds with one stone. First, every time you surf the Internet, you learn more about how to use your computer and the Web. And if you want to become a computer professional, you really need to master these basic skills. Second, the Internet is one of the greatest repositories of information about computers ever created—and it is constantly changing! So what can you find on the Internet? Computer associations, discussion groups and blogs, competitions, educational programs, glossaries, company information, worker profiles and interviews, museums, and the list goes on and on. So log on and begin educating yourself about computers! To help get you started, we've prepared a list of what we think are the best computer sites on the Web. Check out Section 4: "What Can I Do Right Now?" Get Involved: Surf the Web for more info.

❑ TAKE COMPUTER SCIENCE CLASSES

This suggestion is almost a no-brainer, but be sure to take every computer class in high school that you can. If you don't, you're passing up a wealth of knowledge and training that will help you learn more about computers and prepare for college. Typical classes might include introduction to computer science, desktop publishing, word processing, spreadsheets/databases, network administration, Web page design, software applications (such as Word, Excel, and PowerPoint), and programming languages (C++, Java, etc,). Some high schools, such as Bogan Computer Technical High School in Chicago, Illinois, may even offer advanced courses such as Cisco Network Design and Oracle Computer Science. In addition to classroom instruction, your teacher can direct you to colleges that have strong computer science programs, competitions, career options, and almost anything else that you can think of that's related to computers.

❏ DEVELOP A MANIA FOR MATH

Math ability is one of the keys to success in the computer industry, so if this isn't your favorite subject and you think you may want to be a computer professional, then it's time to get extra help after class. No matter how good you are at fixing things or understanding complex problems, if your math skills are poor, you can't be a computer professional. Why? The scientific principles that govern many areas of computer science rely on the accurate execution of, you guessed it, mathematical equations and formulas. You can't do one without the other. Don't worry, though. With a little hard work and determination, you can certainly conquer math. The more you do it, the easier it gets. Better yet, try and find ways to use your math skills, polished or not. Using practical, real examples to which you can apply the math is one of the best ways to make any subject come alive.

If you're already a whiz at math, then you're well on your way. Keep it up. But don't grow complacent and let your spark fizzle; keep pushing yourself, keep giving your math-savvy mind new challenges.

❏ JOIN COMPUTER, MATH, AND SCIENCE CLUBS

Many junior high and high schools have computer clubs that meet after school. These are great places to advance your computer skills beyond the classroom. And how about fueling a little healthy competition? Some clubs even participate in competitions with other local high schools. Talk to the computer science teachers at your school about getting involved. If your school doesn't already have a computer club, start one yourself. Enlist the help of one of your computer science teachers; most likely, they'll be happy to assist, or at least steer you in the right direction. Like other school clubs or teams, a computer club needs the leadership of a teacher, especially if you're thinking of using school equipment and facilities.

You might also consider joining a chapter of the Computer Clubhouse, an after-school club sponsored by computer giant Intel, "where young people from underserved communities work with adult mentors to explore their own ideas, develop skills, and build confidence in themselves through the use of technology." There are approximately 100 such clubs located throughout the United States—maybe there's one near you. For more information on this great program, visit http://www.computerclubhouse.org.

If you're interested in computer or electrical engineering, you might also want to check out the Junior Engineering Technical Society, which offers a variety of programs and competitions for high school students. Visit http://www.jets.org for more information.

❏ VISIT A MUSEUM

Many cities have science and technology museums where young people and adults can participate in interactive exhibits that teach principles of computer science and computer engineering. Ask one of your teachers to organize a field trip to the museum—maybe volunteer to coordinate a field trip with a particular lesson. Of course, you can always check out museums on your own or with some friends. In these museums you'll find fun and exciting exhibits that show the inner mechanics of computers and other related technology; explain how the Internet works; take a look at the past and future of computer games; profile famous computer innovators such as Charles Babbage, Ada Augusta King, Herman Hollerith, Steve Jobs, Bill Gates, and Tim Berners-Lee; and countless other topics. Check out the following museums to get started.

Computer History Museum
1401 North Shoreline Boulevard
Mountain View, CA 94043
650-810-1010
info@computerhistory.org
http://www.computerhistory.org

The Computer History Museum was founded in 1996. It has a collection of more than 4,000 artifacts, 10,000 images, and 4,000 linear feet of cataloged documentation and gigabytes of software. Items in its collection include a Hollerith census machine, a WWII Enigma, a see-through PalmPilot, a Cray-3 supercomputer, and a computer-generated Mona Lisa. A recent exhibit, "Visible Storage," traced the development of technology from pre-computing to supercomputing. In addition to regular tours, the museum offers lectures, seminars, workshops, and a speaker series. Check out its Web site for further information and online exhibits.

Museum of Science and Industry
57th Street and Lake Shore Drive
Chicago, IL 60637
773-684-1414
msi@msichicago.org
http://www.msichicago.org

The Museum of Science and Industry, founded in 1933, is one of the oldest science museums in the Western Hemisphere. One recent exhibit, "Game On: The History, Culture and Future of Video Games," featured a look at the fascinating world of video games, which included an interactive tour where visitors could play more than 100 vintage arcade and video games. Another, "Networld," took an in-depth look at the world of the Internet. In addition to brick-and-mortar and online exhibits, the museum offers lectures, seminars, and workshops. Visit its Web site for additional information.

Museum of Science–Boston
Science Park
Boston, MA 02114
617-723-2500

information@mos.org
http://www.mos.org

Founded in 1830, the Museum of Science–Boston offers more than 400 interactive exhibits annually. Recent exhibits in its Current Science & Technology Center focused on the International Space Station, space shuttles, and electricity. Visitors to the museum can also check out the Cahners ComputerPlace, a hands-on computer discovery exhibit that showcases a variety of software titles and encourages learning and creativity through demonstrations and hands-on activities. Check out the museum's Web site for online exhibits and more information.

Museums often provide opportunities for the curious young scientist beyond the museum's in-house or online exhibits. Some sponsor science clubs where you can have a much more active role in designing and running experiments. Some of the larger museums like the Museum of Science and Industry (http://www.msichicago.org/info/HR/volunteer_opps.html) have teen volunteer programs in which qualified teens work in facilitating museum-organized activities for younger children. The Computer History Museum (http://www.computerhistory.org/volunteers) and the Museum of Science–Boston (http://www.mos.org/doc/1216) also offer volunteer opportunities to high school students.

Volunteering is a great way to get involved with the museum, to really learn a subject, and to meet people in the industry. Which brings up an interesting point: You might even be able to spend your entire career working at a museum. Computer professionals help create interactive exhibits, work as curators, maintain databases and networks, and otherwise assist with technology-related concerns.

❏ FAMILIARIZE YOURSELF WITH COMPUTERS

Computer technology changes fast, and it's important to be familiar with the latest hardware and software. Bone up on your knowledge of computers and peripherals—especially if you're interested in the more technical aspects of the industry, such as computer engineering and design. Ask your computer science teacher or a parent to teach you computer basics or check out books and the Web for further information. Visit How Stuff Works: Computer Stuff (http://computer.howstuffworks.com) to get started.

❏ JOIN AN ASSOCIATION

Many computer associations offer membership to high school and college students. Membership benefits include the chance to participate in association-sponsored competitions, seminars, and conferences; subscriptions to magazines (some geared specifically toward students); mentoring and networking opportunities; and access to financial aid.

The Association for Computing Machinery (http://www.acm.org/membership/student) and the IEEE Computer Society (http://www.computer.org/students) offer excellent programs for students interested in computer science. The Association for Computing

Machinery (ACM) offers membership to both high school and college students. High school members receive student publications, access to the ACM's online career center, and free training courses. College students can join chapters at schools across the United States. They have access to hundreds of online courses and books, can participate in competitions and conferences, and are eligible for scholarships, among other benefits. The IEEE Computer Society offers membership to college students, who receive access to publications, career resources, scholarships, and other benefits. Visit Section 4: "Look to the Pros" for more information on associations that offer student membership.

❑ PARTICIPATE IN SUMMER PROGRAMS

Itching to go to college to start studying computer science? If so, you're in luck. Hundreds of colleges and universities offer early training programs for students interested in computer science—some of these programs even offer college credit! Participation in these residential and commuter programs allows you to learn more about specific computer fields, talk with professors and industry professionals, and meet other young people who are interested in the field. Summer programs typically consist of workshops, seminars, experiments, and other activities that introduce you to computer science. Some classes may focus on theory, while others may have you taking apart a computer or building a Web site from scratch. Summer programs are covered in depth in Section 4: "What Can I Do Right Now?" Get Involved: A Directory of Camps, Programs, Competitions, and Other Opportunities. Visit the section for further information.

❑ LAND AN INTERNSHIP

It's never too early to start looking for an internship—even if you're still in high school. Fair warning: There are many more internships available for college students, but that shouldn't prevent you from trying to find a local company, museum, or manufacturer that would be willing to exchange experience for a little extra help. Start with the obvious places. Ask your computer, science, and math teachers if they know of any companies in the area that offer internships or might be interested in having another pair of eyes, ears, and hands to help with projects. Contact computer professionals whom you, your parents, or teachers know. Where do they work? Can their company or workplace use your help? Don't quit until you find that elusive internship!

For more information on internships, visit http://www.acm.org/membership/career/internship.html.

❑ CONDUCT AN INFORMATION INTERVIEW OR JOB SHADOW A WORKER

Talking with computer professionals and shadowing them for a day will help you learn more about the pros and cons of work in this field. Information interviews consist of a phone or in-person conversation with a professional about his or her job. You can ask workers these and other questions:

- Can you describe your typical workday?
- What is most rewarding about your position? Most challenging?
- Who are your major clients? Major competitors?
- What training or education should I pursue to prepare for this field?
- From your perspective, what are some of the most important issues affecting the future of this field today?

Remember to do the following when conducting an information interview:

- Dress (if you are conducting the interview in person) and act appropriately.
- Arrive or call on time.
- Have written questions prepared.
- Listen closely and don't interrupt the person while he or she is talking.
- Have a notepad and pen ready to record the person's responses.
- Don't overstay your welcome (if the person has volunteered 20 minutes of his or her time, then stick to that time frame).
- Be sure to thank the person both verbally and in writing (send a thank you via mail soon after the interview) for his or her time.

For more advice on information interviewing, visit http://jobsearch.about.com/cs/infointerviews or http://www.quintcareers.com/informational_interviewing.html.

Job shadowing simply means observing someone at his or her job. In the case of computer professionals, you might shadow them as they work in offices, laboratories, factories, technical support centers, computer game companies, and other locales. Remember to do the following when shadowing a worker:

- Dress and act appropriately.
- Arrive on time.
- Take plenty of notes.
- Be positive (if the job seems boring, don't say so!).
- Follow the ground rules established by the interviewee.
- Thank the person both verbally and in writing for the opportunity.

Ask your computer, math, or science teacher to help you arrange an information interview or job shadowing opportunity. Perhaps one of your parents has a friend who is a computer professional whom you can job shadow. You can also take the initiative and call or e-mail the public relations department of a nearby computer company to see if they can refer you to one of their workers (some companies already have such programs in place). Some computer associations may also offer these opportunities to student members.

For more information on job shadowing, visit http://www.jobshadow.org.

❑ GET A JOB

Take your internship experiences to the next level and look for paid jobs that not only use your growing computer experience, but also provide you with the opportunity to add to your existing knowledge.

Challenge yourself. Begin by contacting the same firms you used to search for internships. Now that you have some practical experience under your belt, they may be more inclined to offer you an internship or, better yet, a paying position.

Don't think small, but be realistic. As hard as it is to get internships as a high school student, it's even more difficult to get jobs. If you're finding that employers are saving those choice positions for college students, aim just a little bit lower. Let employers know how interested you are in learning from the ground up and you just might find yourself learning how to test computer games—and taking home a nice paycheck.

Technician-level jobs or positions as apprentices to technicians are other good options. Keep in mind that you will be competing with men and women who have trained in technical schools for some of these jobs, but with solid grades and an obvious desire to learn, your chances are strong.

❑ ADDITIONAL SUGGESTIONS

Still looking for ways to learn more about computers? Try these activities relating to the following careers.

Computer and Video Game Designers

- Write your own stories, puzzles, and games to help you develop your storytelling and problem-solving skills.
- Play computer and video games in a variety of genres. Write down what you like and dislike about each game and why. Think about how you would redesign the game if you had the opportunity.
- Try to develop copies of easy games, such as *Pong* and *Pac-Man*; try to change a game that has an editor (games such as *Klik & Play*, *Empire*, and *Doom* allow players to modify them to create new circumstances); design and create your own game.

Computer Service Technicians

- Clean your computer using brushes and a vacuum.
- Install a new hard drive, CD drive, or other component to your computer.
- Install a new software program on your computer.

Computer Engineers

- Troubleshoot problems with your computer and peripherals.
- Install a new hard drive, sound card, or other component to your computer.
- Install a new software program on your computer.

Computer Network Administrators

- Try hooking up a mini-network at home or school, configuring computers, printers, modems, and other peripherals into a coherent system.

Computer Programmers

- Learn computer-programming language, such as COBOL, FORTRAN, Java, and C++.
- Write a basic computer program.

Computer System Programmer/Analysts

- Analyze the hardware and software on your computer to determine if it needs to be updated. Write a report about your findings and then create an action plan that details the upgrades you will undertake.
- Follow this action plan to upgrade your computer.

Quality Assurance Testers

- Gain wide exposure to computer systems and programs of all kinds.
- Become comfortable using Windows and Mac programs, and learn how to operate every part of your computer.
- Look for bugs in your software at home and practice writing them up.

Software Designers

- Study various types of software. Write down what you like and dislike about each, and find ways to improve them.
- Design and program your own applications, such as simple games and utility programs.

Technical Support Specialists

- Take a computer technology course at a local technical/vocational school. This will give you hands-on exposure to typical technical support training.
- If you are experiencing problems with your own hardware or software, call the manufacturer's technical support department. Pay close attention to how the support specialist handles the call, and ask as many questions as the specialist has time to answer.
- Help friends and neighbors troubleshoot and solve their computer problems.

Webmasters

- Spend time surfing the World Wide Web. By studying a variety of Web sites to see how they look and operate, you can begin to get a feel for what goes into a home page.
- Critique existing sites. Write down what you like and dislike about each site and what you would do to improve them.
- Design your own personal Web page. Many Internet servers offer their users the option of designing and maintaining a personal Web page for a very low fee. A personal page can contain virtually anything that you want to include, from snapshots of friends and audio files of favorite music, to hypertext links and other favorite sites. Check out http://www.wigglebits.com for tips on getting started.

SECTION 4

What Can I Do Right Now?

Get Involved: A Directory of Camps, Programs, Competitions, and Other Opportunities

Now that you've read about some of the different careers available in computer science, you may be anxious to experience this line of work for yourself, to find out what it's really like. Or, perhaps you already feel certain that this is the career path for you and want to get started on it right away. Whichever is the case, this section is for you! There are plenty of things you can do right now to learn about computer careers while gaining valuable experience. Just as important, you'll get to meet new friends and see new places, too.

In the following pages you will find programs designed to pique your interest in computer science and start preparing you for a career. You already know that this field is complex and highly technical, and that to work in it you need a solid education. Since the first step toward a computer career will be gaining that education, we've found more than 60 programs that will start you on your way. Some are special introductory sessions, others are actual college courses—one of them may be right for you. Take time to read over the listings and see how each compares to your situation: how committed you are to computer science, how much of your money and free time you're willing to devote to it, and how the program will help you after high school. These listings are divided into categories, with the type of program printed right after its name or the name of the sponsoring organization.

❏ THE CATEGORIES

Camps

When you see an activity that is classified as a camp, don't automatically start packing your tent and mosquito repellent. Where academic study is involved, the term "camp" often simply means a residential program including both educational and recreational activities. It's sometimes hard to differentiate between such camps and other study programs, but if the sponsoring organization calls it a camp, so do we!

College Courses/Summer Study

These terms are linked because most college courses offered to students your age must take place in the summer, when you are out of school. At the same time, many summer study programs are sponsored by colleges and universities that want to attract future students and give them a head start in higher education. Summer study of almost any type is a good idea because it keeps your mind and your study skills sharp over the long vacation. Summer study at a college offers any number of additional benefits, including giving you the tools to make a well-informed decision about your future academic career. Study options, including some impressive college and university programs, account for most of the listings in this section—primarily because higher education is so crucial to every computer career.

Competitions

Competitions are fairly self-explanatory, but you should know that there are only a few in this book, for two reasons: one, a number of computer competitions are part of general science contests too numerous to mention, and two, many computer competitions are at the local and regional levels and so again are impractical to list here. What this means, however, is that if you are interested in entering a competition, you shouldn't have much trouble finding one yourself. Your guidance counselor or computer, math, or science teachers can help you start searching in your area.

Conferences

Conferences for high school students are usually difficult to track down because most are for professionals in the field who gather to share new information and ideas with each other. Don't be discouraged, though. A number of professional organizations with student branches invite those student members to their conferences and plan special events for them. Some student branches even run their own conferences; check the directory of student organizations at the end of this section for possible leads. This is an option worth pursuing because conferences focus on some of the most current information available and also give you the chance to meet professionals who can answer your questions and even offer advice.

Employment and Internship Opportunities

As you may already know from experience, employment opportunities for teenagers can be very limited. This is particularly true in computer science, which requires workers with bachelor's and even graduate degrees. Even internships are most often reserved for college students who have completed at least one or two years of study in the field. Still, if you're very determined to find an internship or paid position in computer science, there may be ways to find one. See the "Do It Yourself" section in this book for some suggestions.

Field Experience

This is something of a catchall category for activities that don't exactly fit the other descriptions. But anything called a *field experience* in this book is always a good opportunity to get out and explore the work of computer professionals.

Membership

When an organization is in this category, it simply means that you are welcome to pay your dues and become a card-carrying member. Formally joining any organization brings the benefits of meeting others who share your interests, finding opportunities to get involved, and keeping up with current events. Depending on how active you are, the contacts you make and the experiences you gain may help when the time comes to apply to colleges or look for a job.

In some organizations, you pay a special student rate and receive benefits similar to regular members. Many organizations, however, are now starting student branches with their own benefits and publications. As in any field, make sure you understand exactly what the benefits of membership are before you join.

Finally, don't let membership dues discourage you from making contact with these organizations. Some charge dues as low as $5 because they know that students are perpetually short of funds. When the annual dues are higher, think of the money as an investment in your future and then consider if it is too much to pay.

Incidentally...

We have included in these pages a few listings for localized programs and activities that are actually connected to larger movements or organizations. For example, some programs listed here are run by university branches of the Society of Women Engineers (SWE)—a national organization. Others are part of the Minority Introduction to Engineering (MITE) program. If you're interested in SWE or MITE, check with the colleges and universities that interest you to see if they have a branch of their own.

❏ PROGRAM DESCRIPTIONS

Once you've started to look at the individual listings themselves, you'll find that they contain a lot of information. Naturally, there is a general description of each program, but wherever possible we have also included the following details.

Application Information

Each listing notes how far in advance you'll need to apply for the program or position, but the simple rule is to apply as far in advance as possible. This ensures that you won't miss out on a great opportunity simply because other people got there ahead of you. It also means that you will get a timely decision on your application, so if you are not accepted, you'll still have some time to apply elsewhere. As for the things that make up your application—essays, recommendations, etc.—we've tried to tell you what's involved, but be sure to contact the program about specific requirements before you submit anything.

Background Information

This includes such information as the date the program was established, the name of the organization that is sponsoring it financially, and the faculty and staff who will be there for you. This can help you—and your family—gauge the quality and reliability of the program.

Classes and Activities

Classes and activities change from year to year, depending on popularity, availability of instructors, and many other factors. Nevertheless, colleges and universities quite consistently offer the same or similar classes, even in their summer sessions. Courses like Introduction to Computer Programming and Computer Science

101, for example, are simply indispensable. So you can look through the listings and see which programs offer foundational courses like these and which offer courses on more variable topics. As for activities, we note when you have access to recreational facilities on campus, and it's usually a given that special social and cultural activities will be arranged for most programs.

Contact Information

Wherever possible, we have given the title of the person whom you should contact instead of the name because people change jobs so frequently. If no title is given and you are telephoning an organization, simply tell the person who answers the phone the name of the program that interests you and he or she will forward your call. If you are writing, include the line "Attention: Summer Study Program" (or whatever is appropriate after "Attention") somewhere on the envelope. This will help to ensure that your letter goes to the person in charge of that program.

Credit

Where academic programs are concerned, we sometimes note that high school or college credit is available to those who have completed them. This means that the program can count toward your high school diploma or a future college degree just like a regular course. Obviously, this can be very useful, but it's important to note that rules about accepting such credit vary from school to school. Before you commit to a program offering high school credit, check with your guidance counselor to see if it is acceptable to your school. As for programs offering college credit, check with your chosen college (if you have one) to see if they will accept it.

Eligibility and Qualifications

The main eligibility requirement to be concerned about is age or grade in school. A term frequently used in relation to grade level is "rising," as in "rising senior": someone who will be a senior when the next school year begins. This is especially important where summer programs are concerned. A number of university-based programs make admissions decisions partly in consideration of GPA, class rank, and standardized test scores. This is mentioned in the listings, but you must contact the program for specific numbers. If you are worried that your GPA or your ACT scores, for example, aren't good enough, don't let them stop you from applying to programs that consider such things in the admissions process. Often, a fine essay or even an example of your dedication and eagerness can compensate for statistical weaknesses.

Facilities

We tell you where you'll be living, studying, eating, and having fun during these programs, but there isn't enough room to go into all the details. Some of those details can be important: what is and isn't accessible for people with disabilities, whether the site of a summer program has air-conditioning, and how modern the laboratory and computer equipment are.

You can expect most program brochures and application materials to address these concerns, but if you still have questions about the facilities, just call the program's administration and ask.

Financial Details

While a few of the programs listed here are fully underwritten by collegiate and corporate sponsors, most of them rely on you for at least some of their funding. The 2005 prices and fees are given here, but you should bear in mind that costs rise slightly almost every year. You and your parents must take costs into consideration when choosing a program. We always try to note where financial aid is available, but really, most programs will do their best to ensure that a shortage of funds does not prevent you from taking part.

Minorities

In the not-so-distant past, computer science and computer engineering were fields populated almost solely by Caucasian males—that is most certainly not the case today. Still, colleges and universities are working to promote even more diversity in the field, so there are any number of programs encouraging applicants of every gender, race, and ethnic background. When a computer department bills its summer session as a "minority program," however, you must determine just who is a minority. If you have an Asian heritage, you are a minority in the U.S. population, but not necessarily in computer science or engineering: Asian-Americans are so well represented in the field that the MITE program, among others, does not include them. In short, if you are interested in minority programs, make sure you know how they define the term.

Residential Versus Commuter Options

Simply put, some programs prefer that participating students live with other participants and staff members; others do not; and still others leave the decision entirely to the students themselves. As a rule, residential programs are suitable for young people who live out of town or even out of state, as well as for local residents. They generally provide a better overview of college life than programs in which you're only on campus for a few hours a day, and they're a way to test how well you cope with living away from home. Commuter programs may be viable only if you live near the program site or if you can stay with relatives who do. Bear in mind that for residential programs especially, the travel between your home and the location of the activity is almost always your responsibility and can significantly increase the cost of participation.

Finally...

Ultimately, there are three important things to bear in mind concerning all of the programs listed in this volume. The first is that things change. Staff members come and go, funding is added or withdrawn, and supply and demand determine which programs continue and which terminate. Dates, times, and costs vary widely because of a number of factors.

The information we give you, although as current and detailed as possible, is just not enough on which to base your final decision. If you are interested in a program, you simply must write, call, fax, or e-mail the organization concerned to get the latest and most complete information available. This has the added benefit of putting you in touch with someone who can deal with your individual questions and problems.

Another important point to keep in mind when considering these programs is that the people who run them provided the information printed here. The editors of this book haven't attended the programs and don't endorse them: We simply give you the information with which to begin your own research. And after all, we can't pass judgment because you're the only one who can decide which programs are right for you.

The final thing to bear in mind is that the programs listed here are just the tip of the iceberg. No book can possibly cover all of the opportunities that are available to you—partly because they are so numerous and are constantly coming and going, but partly because some are waiting to be discovered. For instance, you may be very interested in taking a college course but don't see the college that interests you in the listings. Call their Admissions Office! Even if they don't have a special program for high school students, they might be able to make some kind of arrangements for you to visit or sit in on a class. Use the ideas behind these listings and take the initiative to turn them into opportunities!

❑ THE PROGRAMS

Academic Study Associates (ASA)
College Courses/Summer Study

Academic Study Associates has been offering residential and commuter pre-college summer programs for young people for more than 20 years. It offers college credit classes and enrichment opportunities in a variety of academic fields, including computers, mathematics, and science, at the University of Massachusetts–Amherst, the University of California–Berkeley, Emory University, and Oxford University. In addition to classroom/studio work, students participate in field trips, mini-clinics, and extracurricular activities. Programs are usually three to four weeks in length. Fees and deadlines vary for these programs—visit the ASA Web site for further details. Options are also available for middle school students.

ASA Programs
Academic Study Associates
375 West Broadway
New York, NY 10012-4324
800-752-2250
summer@asaprograms.com
http://www.asaprograms.com/home/asa_home.asp

American Collegiate Adventures (ACA) at the University of Wisconsin in Madison
College Courses/Summer Study

American Collegiate Adventures offers high school students the chance to experience and prepare for college during summer vacation. Adventures are based at the University of Wisconsin in Madison; they vary in length from three to six weeks. Participants attend college-level courses taught by university faculty during the week (for college credit or enrichment) and visit regional colleges and recreation sites over the weekend. All students live in comfortable en suite accommodations, just down the hall from an ACA resident staff member. Courses vary but recently included Power of Computer Programming, Web Design, and Desktop Publishing and Web Design—perfect for those planning to pursue a degree in computer science or related fields. Programs in Italy and Spain are also available. Contact American Collegiate Adventures for current course listings, prices, and application procedures.

American Collegiate Adventures
1811 West North Avenue, Suite 201
Chicago, IL 60622-0202
800-509-7867
info@acasummer.com
http://www.zfc-consulting.com/webprojects/americanadventures

American Indian Science & Engineering Society
Conference, Membership

The American Indian Science & Engineering Society (AISES) is a nonprofit organization founded in 1977 to encourage young American Indians to pursue careers in science, technology, and engineering. AISES welcomes students from kindergarten to 12th grade (whom they refer to as "pre-college students") as members; dues are only $10 per year. Pre-college student members can participate in many special programs, including the National American Indian Science and Engineering Fair, and attend the annual AISES Annual Conference, which features High School Day and a career fair. AISES also has a number of programs designed for entire classes and their teachers, so talk to your science or math teacher about getting involved with the society. You can also contact them yourself or visit their Web site for more information.

American Indian Science & Engineering Society
PO Box 9828
Albuquerque, NM 87119-9828
505-765-1052
http://www.aises.org

Association for Computing Machinery
Membership

The Association for Computing Machinery offers several membership options to high school and college students. High school members at the Student Lite level receive student publications, access to the association's online career center, and free training courses.

Association for Computing Machinery
1515 Broadway
New York, NY 10036-8901
800-342-6626

sigs@acm.org
http://www.acm.org

Boston University High School Honors Program
College Course/Summer Study

Rising high school seniors can participate in the High School Honors Program, which offers six-week, for-credit undergraduate study at the university. Students take two for-credit classes (up to eight credits) alongside regular Boston College students, live in dorms on campus, and participate in extracurricular activities and tours of local attractions. Recent courses included Introduction to Computers, Introduction to Computer Science, Windows Programming Paradigms, Computer Networks, Engineering Computation with C++, Computer-Aided Design and Manufacture, Software Design, and Introduction to Computer Science with Java. The program typically begins in early July. Students who demonstrate financial need may be eligible for financial aid. Tuition for the program is approximately $3,550, with registration/program fees ($350) and room and board options ($1,598 to $1,718) extra. Visit the university's Summer Programs Web site for more information.

Boston University High School Honors Program
755 Commonwealth Avenue
Boston, MA 02215-1401
617-353-5124
summer@bu.edu
http://www.bu.edu/summer/highschool

The Center for Excellence in Education at Massachusetts Institute of Technology
Field Experience

The goal of the Center for Excellence in Education (CEE) is to nurture future leaders in science, technology, and business. And it won't cost you a dime: All of CEE's programs are absolutely free. Since 1984, the CEE has sponsored the Research Science Institute, a six-week residential summer program held at the Massachusetts Institute of Technology. Seventy-five high school students with scientific and technological promise are chosen from a field of more than 700 applicants to participate in the program, conducting projects with scientists and researchers. You can read more about specific research projects at the Center's Web site.

The Center for Excellence in Education
8201 Greensboro Drive, Suite 215
McLean, VA 22102-3813
703-448-9062
cee@cee.org
http://www.cee.org

Challenge Program at St. Vincent College
College Course/Summer Study

The Challenge Program, offered by St. Vincent College, is just what its name implies. Challenge gives gifted, creative, and talented students in grades 9 through 12 the opportunity to explore new and stimulating subjects that most high schools just can't cover. If you qualify for this program and are highly motivated, you can spend one week in July on the campus of St. Vincent College taking courses like Dreamweaver (Web site creation) and Digital Publishing. Should you choose, you may live on campus, meeting and socializing with other students who share your ambitions and interests. Resident students pay a total of about $600 for the week, while commuters pay closer to $500. For more information about Challenge and details of this year's course offerings, contact the program coordinator. There is a similar Challenge program for students in the sixth through ninth grades, usually held one week before the high school session.

Challenge Program at St. Vincent College
Attn: Program Coordinator
300 Fraser Purchase Road
Latrobe, PA 15650-2690
724-532-6600
http://www.stvincent.edu/challenge_home

College and Careers Program at the Rochester Institute of Technology
College Course/Summer Study

The Rochester Institute of Technology (RIT) offers its College and Careers Program for rising seniors who want to experience college life and explore career options in engineering. The program, in existence since 1990, allows you to spend a Friday and Saturday on campus, living in the dorms and attending four sessions on the career areas of your choice. Each year, some sessions focus on the liberal arts and sciences, but between 10 and 20 sessions focus on engineering and technology. In each session, participants work with RIT students and faculty to gain some hands-on experience in the topic area. This residential program is held twice each summer, usually once in July and again in August. The registration deadline is one week before the start of the program, but space is limited and students are accepted on a first-come, first-served basis. For further information about the program and specific sessions on offer, contact the RIT admissions office.

College and Careers Program
Rochester Institute of Technology
Office of Admissions
60 Lomb Memorial Drive
Rochester, NY 14623-5604
585-475-6631
admissions@rit.edu
https://ambassador.rit.edu/careers2006/

Computer History Museum
Field Experience

The Computer History Museum offers volunteer opportunities to people of all ages. Volunteers perform basic clerical work and assist at lectures, receptions, tours, and special functions. Contact the museum for more information.

Computer History Museum
1401 North Shoreline Boulevard
Mountain View, CA 94043-1311
650-810-1010
info@computerhistory.org
http://www.computerhistory.org/volunteers

Cornell University Summer College for High School Students
College Course/Summer Study

As part of its Summer College for High School Students, Cornell University offers an Exploration in Engineering for students who have completed their sophomore, junior, or senior years. The Summer College seminar runs for six weeks from late June until early August. It is largely a residential program designed to acquaint you with all aspects of college life. The Exploration in Engineering seminar is one of several such seminars offered by Cornell to allow students to survey various disciplines within the field and speak with working professionals. The seminar meets several times per week and includes laboratory projects and field trips. In addition, Summer College participants take two college-level courses of their own choosing, one of which should be in computer science or mathematics to complement the engineering focus. You must bear in mind that these are regular undergraduate courses condensed into a very short time span, so they are especially challenging and demanding. Cornell University awards letter grades and full undergraduate credit for the two courses you complete. Residents live and eat on campus, and enjoy access to the university's recreational facilities and special activities. Academic fees total around $4,785, while housing, food, and recreation fees amount to an additional $2,465. Books, travel, and an application fee are extra. A very limited amount of financial aid is available. Applications are due in early May, although Cornell advises that you submit them well in advance of the deadline; those applying for financial aid must submit their applications by April 1. Further information and details of the application procedure are available from the Summer College office.

Cornell University Summer College for High School Students
Summer College
B20 Day Hall
Ithaca, NY 14853-2801
607-255-6203
http://www.sce.cornell.edu/sc

Dickinson College Pre-College Summer Programs
College Course/Summer Study

Rising high school juniors and seniors who are interested in exploring computer science and other fields may want to participate in Pre-College Summer Programs at Dickinson College. The month-long program, available in both residential and commuter options, exposes young people to college-level classes in their field of interest. Recent computer-related courses included Introduction to Computer Science/Lab and Introduction to Physics. The residential program costs approximately $5,000, which includes accommodations in Dickinson College dormitories, a full meal plan, special events, and field trips. Additional fees for spending money and books are required. Costs for the commuter options were yet to be determined as of press time; contact the director of Summer Programs for further information. Some financial aid is available.

Summer Programs
Attn: Director of Summer Programs
Dickinson College
PO Box 1773
Carlisle, PA 17013-2896
717-254-8782
summer@dickinson.edu
http://www.dickinson.edu/summer/precollege.html

DigiPen Summer Workshops at DigiPen Institute of Technology
College Courses/Summer Study

High school and college students who are interested in game programming and 3-D computer animation can attend two-week residential workshops at DigiPen Institute of Technology. Recent workshops included Junior Game Developer, Video Game Programming, 3-D Animation, and Robotics. In addition to attending workshops, participants get the opportunity to tour Nintendo of America, participate in game tournaments, and attend movie nights in DigiPen's auditorium. Each workshop costs approximately $850; lodging and meals are extra. Contact the institute for more information.

DigiPen Summer Workshops
DigiPen Institute of Technology
5001 - 150th Avenue, NE
Redmond, WA 98052-5170
425-558-0299
workshops@digipen.edu
http://www.digipen.edu

Early Experience Program at the University of Denver
College Course/Summer Study

The University of Denver invites academically gifted high school students interested in computer science and other subjects to apply for its Early Experience Program, which involves participating in university-level classes during the school year and especially during the summer. This is a commuter-only program. Interested students must submit a completed application (with essay), official high school transcript, standardized test results (PACT/ACT/PSAT/SAT), a letter of recommendation from a counselor or teacher, and have a minimum GPA of 3.0. Contact the Early Experience Program coordinator for more information, including application forms, available classes, and current fees.

Early Experience Program
Attn: Pam Campbell, Coordinator
University of Denver
Office of Academic Youth Programs
1981 South University Boulevard
Denver, CO 80208-4209
303-871-2663
pcampbe1@du.edu
http://www.du.edu/education/ces/ee.html

Exploration Summer Programs (ESP) at Yale University
College Course/Summer Study

Exploration Summer Programs has been offering academic summer enrichment programs to students for nearly 30 years. Rising high school sophomores, juniors, and seniors can participate in ESP's Senior Program at Yale University. Two three-week residential and day sessions are available and are typically held in June and July. Participants can choose from more than 80 courses in computer science and other areas of study. Recent computer-related courses included Introduction to Java Programming, Introduction to C++ Programming, and Electrical Engineering. Students entering the 11th or 12th grades can take college seminars, which provide course work that is similar to that of first-year college study. All courses and seminars are ungraded and not-for-credit. In addition to academics, students participate in extracurricular activities such as tours, sports, concerts, weekend recreational trips, college trips, and discussions of current events and other issues. Tuition for the Residential Senior Program is approximately $4,100 for one session and $7,400 for two sessions. Day-session tuition ranges from approximately $2,100 for one session to $3,795 for two sessions. A limited number of need-based partial and full scholarships are available. Programs are also available for students in grades four through nine. Contact ESP for more information.

Exploration Summer Programs
470 Washington Street, PO Box 368
Norwood, MA 02062-0368
781-762-7400
http://www.explo.org

Explorations in Engineering, Women in Engineering, Summer Youth Explorations, and American Indian Workshop at Michigan Technological University

College Course/Summer Study

Michigan Technological University (MTU) offers four opportunities for high school students to explore computers and engineering in a college setting. The residential Explorations in Engineering Program is for minority or economically disadvantaged students; freshmen, sophomores, and juniors are eligible. While living on campus for one week, participants engage in informational discussions and technical projects with MTU faculty and other professional engineers and computer scientists. The program is usually held in June or July, and applications are due in April. The only cost for the program is a $50 registration fee. The Women in Engineering Program is almost identical to the Minorities Program except, of course, that only female students are eligible. The Summer Youth Explorations program is for students in grades 6 through 11. Participants attend one of four week-long sessions usually held during the months of July or August, choosing either to commute or to live on campus. Students undertake an "exploration" in one of many career fields—including computer science and engineering—through field trips and discussions with MTU faculty and other professionals. Recent classes included Computer Network Architecture and Security, Video Game Programming, Web Design, Flash Animation, and Computer

Programming. The American Indian Workshop introduces Native Americans ages 12 to 15 to college study through the study of computers and mathematics. Contact the Youth Programs Office for more information.

Explorations in Engineering, Women in Engineering, Summer Youth Explorations, and American Indian Workshop
Michigan Technological University
Youth Programs Office, Alumni House
1400 Townsend Drive
Houghton, MI 49931-1295
906-487-2219
http://youthprograms.mtu.edu

Exploring Engineering at the University of Maryland for Women/Stepping Stones
College Course/Summer Study
The University of Maryland at College Park (UMCP) hosts Exploring Engineering at the University of Maryland for Women for one week in July. Rising juniors and seniors who are considering careers in engineering learn more about the various disciplines within the field by participating in fun activities, experiments, interesting workshops, and talking with professional engineers. Participants live on the UMCP campus. It costs about $200 and does not include the cost of transportation to and from UMCP or spending money. Scholarships are available. To be considered for the program, the university must receive a completed application form, a letter of recommendation, and a high school transcript by early April. For more information, contact the program directly. The university also offers Stepping Stones, a one-week summer day camp for students of both genders who are entering the 7th, 8th, and 9th grades. The commuter camp exposes students to the worlds of science and engineering.

Exploring Engineering at the University of Maryland for Women/Stepping Stones
Women in Engineering Program
Attn: Dr. Paige E. Smith, Director
University of Maryland
1134G Glenn L. Martin Hall
College Park, MD 20742
301-405-3931
http://www.eng.umd.edu/wie

Eye On Engineering and Computer Science at Catholic University of America
College Course/Summer Study
The Catholic University of America (CUA) offers rising seniors the chance to participate in Eye On Engineering and Computer Science. Students in the program explore the opportunities available to them in this field. During the week-long program held each July, participants take part in two research projects from a selection of subjects like robotics and artificial intelligence, and computer graphics. As a participant, you also take an active role in discussions with CUA engineering faculty and students about such topics as

engineering curricula, careers, and professional ethics. There is also time for you to take advantage of CUA's many recreational facilities and to explore campus life while living in the dormitories. Applicants to Eye On Engineering and Computer Science must submit a completed form, transcript, and one letter of recommendation by the end of April. Participants are selected primarily on the basis of their achievements in science and mathematics. The cost is about $500, which does not include transportation to and from the school. For an application and further information, contact the program.

Eye On Engineering & Computer Science
The Catholic University of America
School of Engineering
Washington, DC 20064
202-319-5160
eyeonengineering@cua.edu
http://engineering.cua.edu/activities/Engr2002

FIRST
Competitions

The nonprofit organization FIRST—For Inspiration and Recognition of Science and Technology—wants to generate an interest in science and engineering in high school students. And judging by their annual robot-building contest, interest is not a problem. Each year the rules of the competition are different, and details are kept top-secret until a kick-off workshop. Then, for six weeks, students team up with engineers from corporations and universities to brainstorm, design, construct, and test their robots. Contact FIRST to get more information.

FIRST
200 Bedford Street
Manchester, NH 03101-1132
603-666-3906
http://www.usfirst.org

Frontiers at Worcester Polytechnic Institute
College Courses/Summer Study

Frontiers is an on-campus research and learning experience for high school students who are interested in science, mathematics, and engineering. Areas of study include computer science, electrical and computer engineering, aerospace engineering, mathematics, mechanical engineering, physics, robotics, and biology and biotechnology. Participants attend classes and do lab work Monday through Friday. Participants also have the opportunity to try out one of five communication modules: creative writing, elements of writing, music, speech, and theatre. In addition to the academic program, you will attend evening workshops, live performances, field trips, movies, and tournaments. Applications are typically available in January and due in March. Tuition is about $2,000; this covers tuition, room, board, linens, transportation, and entrance fees to group activities. A $500 nonrefundable deposit is required. For more information, contact the program director.

Frontiers Program
Attn: Program Director
Worcester Polytechnic Institute
100 Institute Road
Worcester, MA 01609-2280
508-831-5286
frontiers@wpi.edu
http://www.admissions.wpi.edu/Frontiers

Future Scientists and Engineers of America
Membership

Future Scientists and Engineers of America (FSEA) is a nonprofit organization on the order of Future Farmers of America, working to encourage early participation in a chosen career field. The FSEA encourages young people in 4th through 12th grades to start student chapters in their schools. Each chapter needs a sponsor from the local community, a teacher to act as an advisor, a parent coordinator, two mentors from the local scientific or engineering community, and up to 25 student members. Naturally, with these people involved, the students in each FSEA chapter learn about the professional world and gain hands-on experience in science and engineering. If you'd like more information about the FSEA or about starting a chapter, write to them or visit their Web site.

Future Scientists and Engineers of America
8441 Monroe Avenue
Stanton, CA 90680-2615
714-229-2224
fsea@fsea.org
http://www.fsea.org

G.R.A.D.E. Camp at the University of Houston
Camps

The Cullen College of Engineering at the University of Houston offers the G.R.A.D.E (Girls Reaching and Demonstrating Excellence) Camp for female high school freshmen, sophomores, juniors, and seniors in the Houston area. The week-long commuter program, offered several times in the summer, gives girls the chance to explore engineering by participating in fun, hands-on activities. The program costs about $200; some financial aid is available. Applications are due in early April. For more information, contact the G.R.A.D.E. camp director.

G.R.A.D.E. Camp
Attn: Jenny Ruchhoeft, G.R.A.D.E. Camp Director
University of Houston
Cullen College of Engineering
E316 Engineering Building 2
Houston, TX 77204-4009
713-743-5939
grade@egr.uh.edu
http://www.egr.uh.edu/grade/?e=camp

Hila Science Camp
Camp

Hila Science Camp offers both residential and day camps in the Ottawa Valley, close to Beachburg, Ontario. Established in 1984, Hila features a variety of programs with an emphasis on science and technology. You choose a major program as your focus; options include engineering and technology, rocketry, and computer science. You can build an advanced model rocket, construct and fly a balsa model aircraft, and construct electronic circuits using circuit boards, solder, and a soldering iron. The computer science program shows you how to create digital computer images, set up your own Web page, and write computer programs. In addition to your major program, you can collect specimens, go on archeological digs, hunt for fossils, and gaze at the stars through Hila's eight-foot reflecting telescope. Residential camp lasts one week, from Sunday afternoon through the following Friday. Campers sleep in large dome-style tents, and Hila facilities include a dining hall, basketball court, rocketry and aircraft shop, computer room, and a flying field. Day camp runs Monday through Friday, 9:00 A.M. to 5:00 P.M. Hila offers seven camp sessions, beginning in late June, and all programs are offered in all sessions. A week of day camp at Hila costs about $335; contact Hila for current prices for residential camp. Kits and equipment for various programs cost extra. Supplies for the engineering and technology program, for example, cost an extra $115. Each program enrolls a maximum of 34 students on a first-come, first-served basis. If you live in the Ottawa Valley, some scholarships are available. Hila is happy to provide you with more details on all matters.

Hila Science Camp
382 Hila Road
RR #2
Pembroke, Ontario K8A 6W3
Canada
613-582-3632
hila@hilaroad.com
http://www.hilaroad.com

Idaho JEMS Summer Workshop at the University of Idaho
College Course/Summer Study

The University of Idaho College of Engineering sponsors Idaho JEMS (Junior Engineering, Math & Science program) each summer for rising seniors. During Idaho JEMS, first introduced in 1967, students live on the university campus for two weeks and take classes with College of Engineering professors. Such classes may include computer programming, engineering design, human factors, and engineering problem-solving. Successful completion of the classes leads to college engineering credits from the University of Idaho. In addition to course work, participants explore engineering through lab exercises, field trips, and guest speakers. You can experience college life to the fullest while living and dining on campus by using the university's recreational facilities and touring its colleges. There are also special barbecues and dances to promote an active social life during the Idaho JEMS program. Applicants must have at least a 3.0 GPA and three years of mathematics; you must submit a high school transcript, brief resume, and essay along with your application form. The cost of the program is about $550 including room and board, and some financial aid is available. Female and minority students are especially encouraged to apply, but the program is open to all qualified applicants. For more information and an application, contact the program director.

Idaho JEMS Summer Workshop
University of Idaho
College of Engineering

PO Box 441011, JEB B40
Moscow, ID 83844-1011
208-885-4934
isgc@uidaho.edu
http://www.uidaho.edu/engr/jems

IEEE Computer Society
Membership

The IEEE Computer Society offers membership to college students via student chapters. Student members have access to publications, career resources, and scholarships, among other benefits.

> **IEEE Computer Society**
> 1730 Massachusetts Avenue, NW
> Washington, DC 20036-1992
> 202-371-0101
> http://www.computer.org

Intel International Science and Engineering Fair
Competitions/Conference

The Intel International Science and Engineering Fair is the world's largest pre-college science fair. More than 1,300 students from approximately 40 nations compete for scholarships, tuition grants, internships, scientific field trips and a grand prize of a $50,000 college scholarship at the fair, which is held annually each May. Contact the Science Service for further details.

> **Intel International Science and Engineering Fair**
> Science Service
> 1719 N Street, NW
> Washington, DC 20036-2801
> 202-785-2255
> http://www.sciserv.org/isef

Intel Science Talent Search
Competitions

Since 1942, Science Service has held a nationwide competition for talented high school seniors who plan to pursue careers in science, engineering, math, or medicine. Those who win find themselves in illustrious company: Former winners have gone on to win Nobel Prizes, National Medals of Science, MacArthur Foundation fellowships, and memberships in the National Academy of Engineering. High school students in the United States and its territories, as well as American students abroad, are eligible to compete for more than $1 million dollars in scholarships and prizes awarded to participants, including the top one for $100,000. If you'd like to enter next year's competition, contact the Science Service for more information.

> **Intel Science Talent Search**
> Science Service
> 1719 N Street, NW
> Washington, DC 20036-2801
> 202-785-2255
> http://www.sciserv.org/sts

Intern Exchange International (IEI), Ltd.
Employment and Internship Opportunities

High school students ages 16 to 18 (including graduating seniors) who are interested in gaining real-life experience in Web site design can participate in IEI's Career-Plus Programme, a month-long summer internship in London, England. Participants work with mentors and tutors in a group setting from 10 A.M. to 4:30 P.M. each day, learning the ins and outs of Web site design. Participants learn to work with a variety of technologies, including Adobe Photoshop, Flash, and Macromedia Dreamweaver. The cost of the program is approximately $6,200 plus airfare; this fee includes tuition, housing (students live in residence halls at the University of London), breakfast and dinner daily, housekeeping service, linens and towels, special dinner events, weekend trips and excursions, group activities including scheduled theatre, and a Tube Pass. Contact Intern Exchange International for more information.

Intern Exchange International Ltd.
2606 Bridgewood Circle
Boca Raton, FL 33434-4118
561-477-2434
info@internexchange.com
http://www.internexchange.com

International Game Developers Association
Membership

The International Game Developers Association offers membership to college students and the general public (classified as a Free User Account at the IGDA Web site) who are interested in the field. Free User members can participate in online discussion forums and receive a subscription to the IGDA newsletter.

International Game Developers Association
870 Market Street, Suite 1181
San Francisco, CA 94102-3002
415-947-6235
info@igda.org
http://www.igda.org

Junior Engineering Technical Society (JETS)
Competitions, Field Experience

The Junior Engineering Technical Society (JETS) offers several different opportunities for young people in grades 9 through 12 to test and strengthen their aptitude for engineering before making college and career decisions. One of their most interesting and direct means of testing aptitude is administrating the National Engineering Aptitude Search+ (NEAS+) exam. The NEAS+ is a self-assessment of your thinking, reasoning, and understanding processes, which you can take at any point during your high school career. This not only reveals whether your skills are generally suited to an engineering career, but also what your weaknesses are so that you can work to improve them before starting college. To take this exam, you need only request the NEAS+ kit (which includes career guidance materials) from JETS; the cost is about $15.

If some of your friends share your interest in engineering, you may want to participate in JETS' Tests of Engineering Aptitude, Mathematics, and Science (TEAMS). The TEAMS program is a one-day assessment of your ability to work with others on engineering problems; results determine if your group is ranked at the local, state, or national levels. High school groups can also participate in JETS' National Engineering Design Challenge (NEDC), a year-long program and competition also leading to rankings at the local, state, and national levels. In the NEDC, you concentrate on problem-solving and team-building exercises as you consider real challenges from the world of engineering. For both the TEAMS and NEDC programs, your group needs a teacher to serve as your coach, so speak to your math and science teachers and ask them to contact JETS for detailed information.

JETS, in conjunction with the U.S. Army Research Office, also offers The Uninitiates' Introduction to Engineering Program (UNITE), which helps minority high school students prepare for college through summer classes. The classes introduce students to an educational experience that parallels that of a freshmen student in a university engineering program. Learning methods include academic classes, hands-on activities, and team-based learning. Participating schools include Colorado State University, Florida International University, New Mexico MESA, the University of Delaware, and the University of Detroit–Mercy.

Junior Engineering Technical Society
1420 King Street, Suite 405
Alexandria, VA 22314-2794
703-548-5387
info@jets.org
http://www.jets.org

Junior Scholars Program at Miami University-Oxford College
Courses/Summer Study
Academically talented high school seniors can earn six to eight semester hours of college credit and learn about university life by participating in the Junior Scholars Program at Miami University–Oxford. Students may choose from more than 40 courses, including Introduction to Computer Concepts and Programming, Pre-Calculus, and Calculus. In addition to academics, Scholars participate in social events, recreational activities, and cocurricular seminars. Program participants live in an air-conditioned residence hall. Fees range from approximately $1,750 to $2,865, depending on the number of credit hours taken and applicant's place of residence (Ohio residents receive a program discount). There is an additional fee of approximately $150 for books. The application deadline is typically in mid-May. Visit the program's Web site for additional eligibility requirements and additional details.

Junior Scholars Program at Miami University-Oxford
202 Bachelor Hall
Oxford, Ohio 45056-3414
513-529-5825
juniorscholars@muohio.edu
http://www.units.muohio.edu/jrscholars

Junior Science and Humanities Symposium (JSHS)
Conference
The Junior Science and Humanities Symposium encourages high school students (grades 9 through 12) who are gifted in the sciences, engineering, and mathematics to develop their analytical and creative skills. There are nearly 50 symposia held at locations all around the United States—including Georgetown University, the University of Toledo,

and Seattle Pacific University—so that each year some 10,000 students are able to participate. Funded by the U.S. Army Research Office since its inception in 1958 (and by the U.S. Army, Navy, and Air Force since 1995), the JSHS has little to do with the military and everything to do with research. At each individual symposium, researchers and educators from various universities and laboratories meet with the high school students (and some of their teachers) to study new scientific findings, pursue their own interests in the lab, and discuss and debate relevant issues. Participants learn how scientific and engineering research can be used to benefit humanity, and they are strongly encouraged to pursue such research in college and as a career. To provide further encouragement, one attendee at each symposium will win a scholarship of about $3,000 and the chance to present his or her own research at the national Junior Science and Humanities Symposium. Finalists from each regional JSHS win all-expenses-paid trips to the national symposium, where the top research students can win additional scholarships worth up to $16,000 and trips to the prestigious London International Youth Sciences Forum. For information about the symposium in your region and on eligibility requirements, contact the national Junior Science and Humanities Symposium.

Junior Science and Humanities Symposium (JSHS)
Academy of Applied Science
24 Warren Street
Concord, NH 03301-4048
603-228-4520
phampton@aas-world.org
http://www.jshs.org

The Making of a Scientist/The Making of an Engineer at the University of Denver
College Course/Summer Study

The University of Denver invites high school sophomores, juniors, and seniors to apply for its Making of a Scientist course or Making of an Engineer course, both of which run for three weeks in June. As a part of the university's larger Early Experience Program, the Making of a Scientist course encourages students already interested in computers and science to "explore the relationship between mathematics and computer science, and their applications to chemistry." The Making of an Engineer course is a program for students already interested in science and technology and considering putting those interests to work in an engineering career.

Participants in both courses attend lectures and laboratory sessions that provide an introduction to the tools and concepts common to most areas of computer science and engineering; there are also group outings to laboratories and industrial plants. Each student also concentrates on one particular topic, such as computer engineering, robotics, electronics, biomechanics, superconductivity, and astronomy, and meets one on one with a university professor to complete a project on that topic. The tuition cost for either course is only around $115, which includes field trips and supplies. Students can choose to reside on the University of Denver campus and pay an additional fee of about $1,100 for room, board, and social activities. Scholarships are available to needy students to cover residential and/or travel costs. Interested students must submit a completed application (with essay), official high school transcript, standardized test results (PACT/ACT/PSAT/SAT), a letter of recommendation from a counselor or teacher, and a minimum GPA of 3.0/3.5 or a "B" average. All materials should be submitted by the deadline, usually in April, to the Early Experience Program coordinator, who can also provide application forms and further information about both courses.

The Making of a Scientist/The Making of an Engineer
Attn: Pam Campbell
University of Denver
Office of Academic Youth Programs
1981 South University Boulevard
Denver, CO 80208-4209
303-871-2663
pcampbe1@du.edu
http://www.du.edu/education/ces/moe.html

Mentoring and Enrichment Seminar in Engineering Training at the University of Houston
College Course/Summer Study
The Cullen College of Engineering at the University of Houston offers the Mentoring and Enrichment Seminar in Engineering Training (MESET) for rising seniors during three weeks in June. Students planning a career in engineering who have demonstrated scientific and mathematical aptitude are eligible for this residential program. All participants attend short, formal courses in such subjects as computers, physics, problem-solving, and engineering design. There are also a number of field trips to industrial facilities on the Gulf Coast and tours of Cullen College's own facilities. On evenings and weekends, students can enjoy social events including games and picnics and also attend lectures by guest speakers. There are no tuition or room and board fees for the MESET, but participants must cover their own travel costs, weekend meals, and incidental expenses. A few transportation scholarships are available for cases of extreme hardship. To apply, students must submit an application as well as a high school transcript and letter of recommendation from their guidance counselor by a deadline that is usually in early April. For an application or more information about the program, contact the director of MESET.

Mentoring and Enrichment Seminar in Engineering Training
Attn: Director
University of Houston
E301 Engineering Building 2
Houston, TX 77204-4010
713-743-4222
http://www.egr.uh.edu/news/?e=camps

Minority Introduction to Engineering (MITE) at Tuskegee University
College Course/Summer Study
The College of Engineering, Architecture and Physical Sciences at Tuskegee University invites minority students who

are rising juniors or seniors to apply to the Minority Introduction to Engineering (MITE). MITE is a two-week summer program (check with the university for specific dates) that allows students to fully experience campus life, from living in the dormitories to studying with current staff and students. As a participant, you spend time exploring engineering and other math and science careers and attending laboratory demonstrations by engineering faculty. There is no cost for this program except for transportation to and from Tuskegee University and a $50 application fee and enrollment fee upon acceptance to the program. For further details and application information, contact the assistant to the dean for Student Development and Special Programs.

Minority Introduction to Engineering (MITE)
Attn: Assistant to the Dean for Student Development and Special Programs
Tuskegee University
Tuskegee, AL 36088-1629
334-727-8946 or 334-727-8355
http://tuskegee.edu/global/Story.asp?s=1172515

MITE at Purdue University
College Courses/Summer Study

Purdue University's MITE (Multiethnic Introduction to Engineering) runs for two weeks in mid-July. Rising seniors with a strong academic background take part in computer sessions, laboratory experiences, engineering design projects, and lectures by faculty members and engineering professionals. Participants live on campus and have access to a wide range of recreational events and facilities. MITE is fully funded, so students pay just for travel to and from Purdue, incidentals, and an administration fee. There is no formal admissions deadline, but students should apply as soon as the forms become available in May because eligible applicants are accepted on a first come, first served basis. For more information about the program and details about application procedures, contact the Minority Engineering Program.

Purdue University Multiethnic Introduction to Engineering Program
Engineering Administration Building, Room 222
400 Centennial Mall Drive
West Lafayette, IN 47907-2016
765-494-3974
mep@ecn.purdue.edu
https://engineering.purdue.edu/MEP/pre_college/mite

Museum of Science and Industry
Field Experience

The museum offers a teen volunteer program in which qualified teens work in facilitating museum-organized activities for younger children. Contact the museum's volunteer coordinator for more information.

Museum of Science and Industry
Volunteer Office
Attn: Volunteer Coordinator
57th Street and Lake Shore Drive
Chicago, IL 60637

773-684-1414
http://www.msichicago.org/info/HR/volunteer_opps.html

National Association of Precollege Directors
College Course/Summer Study, Field Experience
The National Association of Precollege Directors (NAPD) is a nonprofit group trying to increase the number of ethnically underrepresented students (Latino/Hispanic American, African-American, Native American) who pursue college degrees in engineering, mathematics, and technology. Its programs—collaborations between high schools, universities, and corporations—include in-school math instruction to ensure that students are on a college-entrance track; science and technology projects conducted with professors or engineers; students "shadowing" professionals throughout a day at work; and intensive summer programs on college campuses. To get a sense of the incredible variety of participants and projects, contact the NAPD for more information.

National Association of Precollege Directors
The Johns Hopkins University
Applied Physics Laboratory
Johns Hopkins Road
Laurel, MD 20723-6099

National Collegiate Conference
Conference
The Association of Information Technology Professionals sponsors an annual conference for its 2,500 college student chapter members. At the conference, attendees can listen to speakers discuss career options, view exhibits, participate in competitions (computer troubleshooting, network design, etc.), and network with fellow students, educators, and professionals. While this conference is usually open to only college-level students, you should consider contacting the association to see if you might be able to receive special permission to attend.

Association of Information Technology Professionals
401 North Michigan Avenue, Suite 2400
Chicago, IL 60611-4267
800-224-9371
http://www.aitp.org/ncc/ncc2005/ncc2005index.htm

National Society of Black Engineers
Membership
The National Society of Black Engineers (NSBE) welcomes young people as members and as participants in its Pre-College Initiative (PCI) program. The PCI program links professional NSBE members with students to encourage their interests in math and science. PCI student in grades 7 through 12 are eligible to become NSBE Jr. members. Membership dues are only $5 per year, for which you can join or start a local chapter and participate in such things as "camping conferences" and college admissions and financial aid workshops. The National Society of Black Engineers urges you to call or e-mail them

if you want to make the NSBE part of your career preparation.

National Society of Black Engineers
1454 Duke Street
Alexandria, VA 22314-3403
703-549-2207
info@nsbe.org
http://www.nsbe.org

Operation Catapult at Rose-Hulman Institute of Technology
College Course/Summer Study

Operation Catapult is a summer program operated by the Rose-Hulman Institute of Technology. Founded in 1874 under a different name, Rose-Hulman is today one of the country's best undergraduate colleges in science and engineering. It is a relatively small facility with a teaching (not research) faculty and is extremely selective in admitting students. Rose-Hulman's Operation Catapult is equally selective, usually extending invitations only to high school juniors who have finished in the highest percentiles on such standardized tests as the PSAT. Participants must also have completed three years of high school math and one of chemistry or physics.

There are two sessions each summer—generally the last three weeks of June and of July—with some 95 students participating in each session. Working in groups of two to four, participants try to solve a "real-world" problem in engineering or another scientific field. They are assisted by Rose-Hulman's faculty and upperclassmen and make use of the institute's excellent facilities. Throughout Operation Catapult, students also go on field trips, witness demonstrations, and hear lectures. The program is a chance to live, work, and play on a college campus as well as to meet other students from around the country. Costs total about $1,900. Operation Catapult is obviously not for everyone interested in engineering, but if you meet the academic requirements, it's a unique and challenging opportunity that merits serious consideration. Eligible students should receive an invitation from Rose-Hulman Institute of Technology; if you believe you are qualified but have not been invited, ask your guidance counselor or a teacher for direction.

Operation Catapult
Attn: Associate Director of Admissions
Rose-Hulman Institute of Technology
5500 Wabash Avenue
Terre Haute, IN 47803-3920
800-248-7448
http://www.rose-hulman.edu/catapult

Pre-College Program at Johns Hopkins University
College Courses/Summer Study

Johns Hopkins University welcomes academically talented high school students to its summer Pre-College Program. Participants in this program live on Hopkins' Homewood campus for five weeks beginning in early July. They pursue one of 27 programs leading to college credit; those interested in computers should strongly consider enrolling in the Computer Science Program. Recent courses included Computer Literacy, Introduction to Programming in C/C++,

Automata and Computation Theory, and Computer System Fundamentals. Course work is supplemented by presentations by research scientists and laboratory tours. All participants in the Pre-College Program also attend workshops on college admissions, time management, and diversity. Students who live in the greater Baltimore area have the option of commuting. Contact the Office of Summer Programs for financial aid information, costs, and deadlines. As of July 1, applicants must be at least 15, have completed their sophomore, junior, or senior year, and have a minimum GPA of 3.0. All applicants must submit an application form, essay, transcript, two recommendations, and a nonrefundable application fee (rates vary by date of submission).

Pre-College Program
Johns Hopkins University
Wyman Park Building, Suite G4
3400 North Charles Street
Baltimore, MD 21218-2685
800-548-0548
summer@jhu.edu
http://www.jhu.edu/~sumprog/pre-college

Science Olympiad

Competitions

The Science Olympiad is a national competition based in schools. It involves various science disciplines, including computers and technology, physics, biology, earth science, and chemistry. School teams feed into regional and state tournaments, and the winners at the state level go on to the national competition. Some schools have many teams, all of which compete in their state Science Olympiad. Only one team per school, however, is allowed to represent its state at the national contest, and each state gets a slot. There are four divisions of Science Olympiad: Divisions A1 and A2 for younger students, Division B for grades six through nine, and Division C for grades nine through twelve. There is no national competition for Division A.

A school team membership fee must be submitted with a completed membership form 30 days before your regional or state tournament. The fee entitles your school to a copy of the Science Olympiad Coaches and Rules Manual plus the eligibility to have up to 15 students at the first level of your state or regional contest. Fees vary from state to state. The National Science Olympiad is held in a different site every year, and your school team is fully responsible for transportation, lodging, and food.

Specific rules have been developed for each event and must be read carefully. There are numerous, different events in each division. You and your teammates can choose the events you want to enter and prepare yourselves accordingly. Winners receive medals, trophies, and some scholarships.

For a list of all Science Olympiad state directors and a membership form, go to the Science Olympiad Web site. You can also write or call the national office for information.

Science Olympiad, Inc.
National Office
2 Trans Am Plaza Drive, Suite 215
Oakbrook Terrace, IL 60181-4296

248-651-4013
http://www.soinc.org

Secondary Student Training Program (SSTP) Research Participation at the University of Iowa
College Course/Summer Study

The University of Iowa invites those who have completed grade 10 or 11 to apply to its Secondary Student Training Program (SSTP). The program allows students to explore a particular area of science, such as computer science or engineering. Participants work with university faculty in one of the many laboratories on campus, studying and conducting research projects for approximately 40 hours per week. At the end of the program, which usually runs from late June to early August, you present your project to a formal gathering of faculty, staff, and fellow SSTP participants. Throughout the program you also take part in various seminars on career choices and the scientific profession, and a variety of recreational activities designed especially for SSTP participants. Students live in the University of Iowa dormitories and use many of the facilities on campus. The admissions process is highly competitive and is based on an essay, transcript, and recommendations. Those who complete the program have the option of receiving college credit from the University of Iowa. Applications are due by mid-March, and applicants will be notified of the decisions by mid-May. Tuition fees, room, and board generally total around $2,000; spending money and transportation to and from the university are not included. Financial aid is available. For an application form, financial aid information, and to discuss possible research projects, contact the Secondary Student Training Program.

Secondary Student Training Program
University of Iowa
E203 Seashore Hall
Iowa City, IA 52242-1316
800-553-4692, ext. 5-3876
william-swain@uiowa.edu
http://www.uiowa.edu/~provost/oi/sstp

Seminar for Top Engineering Prospects at Purdue University
Camp

Purdue University's Department of Engineering Education offers the Seminar for Top Engineering Prospects (STEP), which allows high school students entering their senior year in high school the chance to explore various engineering disciplines and careers. Students will participate in tours, demonstrations, classroom experiences, projects, and discussions with engineering faculty members. Applicants must have completed three years of high school mathematics and one year of chemistry or physics. Sessions last one week and are typically held in July. The registration fee is about $495, which covers room, board, and tuition. Need-based scholarships are available.

Seminar for Top Engineering Prospects
Purdue University
Attn: Deb Felix
Engineering Administration
  Building, Room 212

400 Central Mall Drive
West Lafayette, IN 47907-2016
765-494-3976
step@ecn.purdue.edu
https://engineering.purdue.edu/ENE/SpecialPrograms/ProspectiveStudents/step

Shadow Day at the University of Michigan
Field Experience

The Society of Women Engineers at the University of Michigan hosts a Shadow Day experience. During the school year, high school girls can take part in a Shadow Day. Participants "shadow" a female computer engineering student at the University of Michigan for the whole day or even overnight. The itinerary usually includes a tour of the College of Engineering and a typical day of classes. The cost is only $12, which covers meals. If you are interested in a Shadow Day, contact the high school relations chair.

Shadow Day
Attn: High School Relations Chair
Society of Women Engineers
University of Michigan
1226 EECS Building
1301 Beal Avenue
Ann Arbor, MI 48109-1226
734-763-5027
dannelly@umich.edu
http://www.engin.umich.edu/soc/swe

SkillsUSA
Competitions

SkillsUSA offers "local, state and national competitions in which students demonstrate occupational and leadership skills." Students who participate in its SkillsUSA Championships can compete in categories such as 3-D Visualization and Animation, Computer Maintenance Technology, Electronics Applications, Electronics Technology, Internetworking, Robotics and Automation Technology, Technical Computer Applications, and Web Design. SkillsUSA works directly with high schools and colleges, so ask your guidance counselor or teacher if it is an option for you. Visit the SkillsUSA Web site for more information.

SkillsUSA
PO Box 3000
Leesburg, VA 20177-0300
703-777-8810
http://www.skillsusa.org/

Smith Summer Science and Engineering Program at Smith College
College Courses/Summer Study

Female high school students who are interested in careers in science and engineering can participate in Smith College's Science and Engineering Program. Students in this month-long residential program take either two two-week-long research courses or one four-week-long research course. One recent course was Designing Intelligent Robots, an introduction to robot design and introductory programming. Participants give two oral presentations about their work, one at the midpoint of the program and one at the conclusion of the program. In their free time, students participate in a variety of extracurricular activities, such as sports, nature walks, movie nights, museum tours, and cultural activities. For more information on the program, contact the director of educational outreach.

Smith Summer Science and Engineering Program
Attn: Director of Educational Outreach
Smith College
Clark Hall
Northampton, MA 01063-6353
413-585-3060
gscordil@smith.edu
http://www.smith.edu/summerprograms/ssep

Student Introduction to Engineering at North Carolina State University

College Course/Summer Study

The Student Introduction to Engineering (SITE) is a summer program sponsored by the College of Engineering at North Carolina State University (NCSU). Open to rising juniors and seniors from all backgrounds, SITE offers high school students a realistic look at the professional lives of engineers and the preparation needed to pursue such a career via 11 programs, including Computer Science, Aerospace Engineering, Autonomous Robotics, Civil Engineering/Construction Management, Materials Science and Engineering, Mechatronics, Biological Engineering, Chemical Engineering, Textiles (including Textile Engineering), Wolfpack Motorsports, and a Young Investigators Program in Nuclear Technology

As a participant, you spend one week living on the NCSU campus and participating in discussions and demonstrations in its lecture halls and laboratories. You also meet with engineering students and practicing engineers to learn what you can expect in the years to come. NCSU provides information on college admissions and financial aid to all the students in the SITE program. The cost of participation is about $550, which includes room, board, tuition, gymnasium access, and insurance coverage. Some financial assistance is available. The same material is covered in three different SITE sessions, which run in June and July. To apply, select the session you want and submit the application form by early April. Applicants are judged on the basis of scholastic performance, interest in math and science, teacher recommendations, and standardized test scores. Underrepresented minorities (Hispanic Americans, African Americans, and Native Americans, and women) are strongly encouraged to apply. For more information and a copy of the application form, contact the SITE coordinator.

Student Introduction to Engineering (SITE) at North Carolina State University
Attn: SITE Coordinator
College of Engineering
Campus Box 7904
Raleigh, NC 27695-7904
919-515-9669
http://www.engr.ncsu.edu/summerprograms

Summer at Delphi
Camps/College Courses/Summer Study

Whether you're trying to catch up or get ahead on a course, Summer at Delphi may offer the opportunity you need. The Delphian School is a private, nonsectarian day and residential school for students ages 5 to 17, but its summer session is open to students (boarding school ages, 8 to 18; day school ages 5 to 18) from other schools around the country. Delphi adheres to the educational philosophy of L. Ron Hubbard, who created innovative study methods and emphasized the responsibility of the individual for his or her own academic success. Many of the courses offered for high school students during Summer at Delphi are perfectly suited for those considering a computer career; recent classes included Computer Programming and Electronics. You can also work on such fundamentals as algebra and composition. Each course curriculum is personally tailored to your needs, so you are challenged but not held back or left behind by other students. All students, however, participate in computer training, service projects, and various trips and activities. You may enroll as a day or resident student.

The Delphian School also offers a weeklong Computer Camp where participants learn about computer basics, Web design, computer programming, and how to use the Internet for research.

Contact the School for program costs and dates, to discuss its educational philosophy, and to determine if it is right for you.

Summer at Delphi
The Delphian School
20950 SW Rock Creek Road
Sheridan, OR 97378-9740
800-626-6610
summer@delphian.org
http://www.summeratdelphi.org

Summer College for High School Students at Syracuse University
College Course/Summer Study

The Syracuse University Summer College for High School Students features an Engineering and Computer Science Program for those who have just completed their sophomore, junior, or senior year. The Summer College runs for six weeks and offers a residential option so participants can experience campus life while still in high school. The Engineering and Computer Science Program has several aims: to introduce you to the many specialties within the computer science and engineering professions; to help you match your aptitudes with possible careers; and to prepare you for college, both academically and socially. Participants take two courses: everyone takes the Survey of Engineering Problems course, as well as a liberal arts and sciences course of their choice to complement it. All students take part in a number of computer science- and engineering-related field trips and group design projects, the results of which are presented at the end of the course. Syracuse University awards college credit for completion of the two courses. Admission is competitive and is based on recommendations, test scores, and transcripts. The total cost of the residential program is about $5,300; the commuter option costs about $3,800. Some scholarships are available. The application deadline is in mid-May, or mid-April for those seeking financial aid. For further information, contact the Summer College.

Syracuse University Summer College for High School Students
111 Waverly Avenue, Suite 240
Syracuse, NY 13244-2320
315-443-5297
summcoll@syr.edu
http://summercollege.syr.edu/engineering.html

Summer High School Engineering Institute at Michigan State University

College Course/Summer Study

Since 1963, the College of Engineering at Michigan State University (MSU) has offered the High School Engineering Institute to rising juniors and seniors each summer. Taking place in July, the program gives students with strong interests in math and science the chance to explore engineering as a career. Participants live on campus and participate in hands-on activities, discussions, and laboratories with MSU faculty members and graduate assistants. During the course of the institute, you are exposed to eight engineering disciplines offered at the university, including electrical engineering and computer science. There are also opportunities to experience the social life on campus, enjoy the recreational facilities, and learn more about the entire college admissions process. Admittance to the program is subject to considerations of academic performance, class rank, and the recommendation of a teacher or counselor. Applications must be submitted in May (check the Web site for an exact date) along with a $100 deposit (to be refunded if you are not accepted into the institute). Costs of the program total around $450, from which the deposit is deducted. A limited amount of financial aid is available to those students otherwise unable to afford the program. Contact the High School Engineering Institute for the latest information and an application.

Summer High School Engineering Institute
Michigan State University
College of Engineering
East Lansing, MI 48824-1226
517-355-6616, ext. 1
radforda@egr.msu.edu
http://www.egr.msu.edu/egr/programs/bachelors/hsei.php

Summer Institute in Science and Engineering at Alfred University

College Course/Summer Study

The Summer Institute in Science and Engineering for High School Juniors is held on the Alfred University campus for one week at the end of July. By "juniors," the university means both rising juniors and those who have just completed their junior year (i.e., rising seniors). Participants live in campus dormitories and participate in 7 hands-on labs they have selected from a choice of about 25; past lab topics have included

Integrated Circuit Design and Construction/Care/Feeding of Electric Machinery. Students must apply for the Summer Institute by the beginning of June, submitting an application form, transcript, and two letters of recommendation from high school teachers. The total cost for tuition and room and board is approximately $495 (which includes a $75 deposit), and some financial aid is available. Participants who submit a paper on a given topic before the first day of the institute will be in competition for a four-year scholarship to Alfred University, the winner to be decided based on the quality of the writing. Contact the director of the Summer Institute for more information.

Summer Institute in Science and Engineering
Attn: Director
New York State College of Ceramics
  at Alfred University
Office of Continuing Education
2 Pine Street
Alfred, NY 14802-1296
607-871-2425
wightman@alfred.edu
http://www.alfred.edu/summer/html/
  scienceandengineering.html

Summer Program for Secondary School Program at Harvard University
College Course/Summer Study

High school students who have completed their sophomore, junior, or senior years may apply to Harvard's Summer Program for Secondary School Program. Students who live on campus take either two four-unit courses or one eight-unit course for college credit. Commuting students may take only one four-unit course for college credit. Recent computer-related courses included Algorithms and Data Structures, Fundamentals of Web site Development, Elements of Computer Science Using Java, and Intensive Introduction to Computer Science Using Java. In addition to academics, students can participate in extracurricular activities such as intramural sports, a trivia bowl, a talent show, and dances. Tuition for the program ranges from $2,125 (per four-unit course) to $4,250 (per eight-unit course). A nonrefundable registration fee ($50), health insurance ($110), and room and board ($3,725) are extra. The application deadline for this program is mid-June. Contact the program for more information.

Summer Program for Secondary School Program
Harvard University
51 Brattle Street
Cambridge, MA 02138-3701
617-495-3192
ssp@hudce.harvard.edu
http://www.summer.harvard.
  edu/2005/programs/ssp.jsp

Summer Scholars Program at Wright State University (WSU)
College Courses/Summer Study

If you are a rising junior or senior who is considering a computer career, you can participate in WSU's Summer Scholars Program, where you can take up to eight credit hours of college-level course work. Past courses included Computer Science, Economics, Biology, Chemistry, Communication, English, French, Geology, German, History, Mathematics, and more. Students are required to pay half of the total tuition; the Summer Scholars Program pays for the other half. Two one-month sessions and one two-month session are available. The application deadline is typically in April. Contact the WSU Office of Pre-College Programs for more information.

Summer Scholars Program at Wright State University
Office of Pre-College Programs
120 Millett Hall
3640 Colonel Glenn Highway
Dayton, OH 45435-0001
937-775-3135
precollege@wright.edu
http://www.wright.edu/academics/precollege

Summer Study at Pennsylvania State University
College Course/Summer Study

High school students who are interested in computer science, mathematics, and other fields can apply to participate in Penn State's Summer Study programs. The six-and-a-half-week College Credit Program begins in late June and recently offered the following mathematics-related classes: Finite Mathematics, General View of Mathematics, and Intermediate Algebra. Students typically choose one college credit course (for three or four credits) and either an enrichment class/workshop or The Kaplan SAT prep class. Students who have completed the 10th, 11th, and 12th grades are eligible to apply. The three-and-a-half-week Non-Credit Enrichment Program is held in early July and features computer-related classes such as Animaniacs: Introduction to Computer Animation and Home Sweet Homepage: Web Page Design. Students who have completed the 9th, 10th, and 11th grades are eligible for the program. Tuition for the College Credit Program is approximately $6,000, while tuition for the Non-Credit Enrichment Program is approximately $4,000. Limited financial aid is available. Contact the program for more information.

Summer Study Program
900 Walt Whitman Road
Melville, NY 11747-2293
800-666-2556
info@summerstudy.com
http://www.summerstudy.com/pennstate

Talented and Gifted Program/College Experience Program at Southern Methodist University (SMU)
College Course/Summer Study

Students in grades 8 through 10 can participate in SMU's Talented and Gifted Program. The two-and-a-half week residential program allows students to learn more about various fields, including art. Recent science-related courses included Introduction to Mathematical Sciences, Engineering and Design, and Rocketry. Although high school credit is not universally granted for participation in the program, some school districts have granted such credit to participating students. The program fee is approximately $2,450 (which includes tuition, room and board, books, and supplies). Some financial aid is available.

Gifted and highly motivated high school student who have completed the 10th or 11th grade can participate in SMU's College Experience Program. The five-week residential program allows students to experience college-level instruction and earn up to six college credits. Students take courses from SMU's regular class schedule and also participate in an intensive interdisciplinary study. Applicants must submit an academic transcript, recommendations, an essay, and PSAT, SAT, or ACT scores. Tuition for the program is approximately $1,900; an additional $1,300 for room and board is required.

Summer Programs
Southern Methodist University
PO Box 750383
Dallas, TX 75275-0383
214-768-0123
http://www.smu.edu/continuing_education/youth

Visit in Engineering Week (VIEW) Summer Program at Pennsylvania State University

College Course/Summer Study

The Pennsylvania State University invites rising freshman, sophomores, and juniors to apply to its Visit in Engineering Week (VIEW) residential summer program. Participants must be academically talented, motivated, and genuinely interested in computer engineering or other engineering disciplines. Members of an underrepresented minority group are especially encouraged to apply. There are three week-long VIEW sessions each summer for current juniors; freshmen and sophomores are invited to participate in a three-day program. Each session provides experiences in design, modeling and implementation, communications, group dynamics, and project management. Participants explore many different areas within the field of engineering and also sample college life as an engineering student. All fees, including tuition, and room and board, are underwritten by corporate sponsors, so VIEW is free to all students. You must submit an application form, transcript, and essay by the end of April to the program director, who is also available to answer your questions.

Visit in Engineering Week (VIEW) Summer Program
Multicultural Engineering Programs
Attn: Program Director
Pennsylvania State University
208 Hammond Building
University Park, PA 16802-1401
800-848-9223
http://www.engr.psu.edu/mep/VIEW.htm

Women in Engineering Program at Purdue University

Camp/Field Experience

Purdue's Women in Engineering Program (WIEP) offers two pre-college camps for female high school students who are interested in learning more about engineering. The LEAP Summer Camp is for girls entering 7th through 9th grades. Campers may view engineering laboratories on campus, design a Web page, design and program a robot, and reassemble a computer from its parts. The five-day camp is usually held in June or July.

EDGE Summer Camp (Exciting Discoveries for Girls in Engineering) is offered to girls entering their sophomore and junior years of high school. Campers will tour engineering laboratories and a production facility, build their own electronics device, and program an experiment using Lego Investigator, among other activities. The six-day camp is typically held in June.

The WIEP also sponsors a Preview Day for female high school juniors who are interested in learning more about Purdue University and its engineering programs. Attendees receive a tour of the College's engineering facilities and get to meet engineering students and educators. Information about the following engineering disciplines is available: aeronautical and astronautical, agricultural and biological, biomedical, chemical, civil, construction, electrical and computer, industrial, materials, mechanical, and nuclear. The Preview Day is typically held in April.

Contact the WIEP for more information on program costs.

Women In Engineering Program
Purdue University
Civil Engineering Building, Room G167
550 Stadium Mall Drive
West Lafayette, IN 47907-2051
765-494-3889
puwie@ecn.purdue.edu
https://engineering.purdue.edu/WIEP

Women's Technology Program at Massachusetts Institute of Technology
Summer Study

This residential summer program, sponsored by the Massachusetts Institute of Technology (MIT) Department of Electrical Engineering and Computer Science, seeks to introduce high school girls to computer science and electrical engineering. Students who have completed the 11th grade are eligible to participate in the four-week program, which includes classes in computer science, electrical engineering, and mathematics taught by women Ph.D. candidates, guest speakers and lab tours, hands-on experiments, and team-based projects. Forty participants are selected each year. Students are expected to be able to handle college-level material, but they do not have to have prior experience in computer programming, physics, or engineering. The cost of the program is approximately $2,000, which includes books, lab materials, food, and housing. Transportation to and from MIT is not covered. Financial aid is available.

Women's Technology Program
Attn: Director
Massachusetts Institute of Technology
MIT Room 38-491
77 Massachusetts Avenue
Cambridge, MA 02139-4301
617-253-5580

wtp@mit.edu
http://wtp.mit.edu

Worldwide Youth in Science and Engineering (WYSE) at the University of Illinois–Urbana-Champaign
College Course/Summer Study

The College of Engineering at the University of Illinois-Champaign-Urbana sponsors a Worldwide Youth in Science and Engineering (WYSE) program twice each summer. Rising high school juniors or seniors are eligible for the program, which is subtitled: "Exploring Your Options... Tomorrow's Careers in Science and Engineering." The week-long program features visits to each department within the College of Engineering, where faculty, graduates, and undergraduates conduct presentations, discussions, and hands-on activities concerning their particular area. Participants can make personal appointments with faculty members in engineering and nonengineering fields alike. Students live and eat on campus. Participants are selected according to the following factors: GPA, class ranking, curriculum, PSAT/SAT/ACT scores, letters of recommendation, and a personal essay. Applications are due at the beginning of May and applying earlier is encouraged. The all-inclusive fee for the program is about $600; some financial aid is available for women and minority students. The university also offers Discover Engineering, a similar one-week residential camp for rising sophomores. For more information about the programs, contact the program director.

Worldwide Youth in Science and Engineering (WYSE) at the University of Illinois–Urbana-Champaign

Attn: Program Director
210 Engineering Hall
1308 West Green Street
Urbana, IL 61801-2936
800-843-5410
wyse@uiuc.edu
http://www.engr.uiuc.edu/wyse

Young Scholars Program: Engineering at the University of Maryland
College Course/Summer Study

The Young Scholars Program is sponsored by the University of Maryland for motivated high school juniors and seniors. Participants in the three-week program spend July exploring the field of engineering and taking a college-level course. College credit is awarded to students who satisfactorily complete the course. Participants live in the residence halls at the University of Maryland and take their meals on campus or in selected College Park restaurants. To apply, you must submit an application form, an essay, two letters of recommendation, a current transcript, and an application fee of $50 by mid-May. Admissions decisions are based primarily on the recommendations, a GPA of 3.0 or better, and overall academic ability. For further details (including information on cost of tuition) and an application form, visit the Web site below or contact the Summer Sessions and Special Programs staff.

Summer Sessions and Special Programs
University of Maryland
Mitchell Building, 1st Floor
College Park, MD 20742
301-314-8240
http://www.summer.umd.edu/youngscholars

In addition to the aforementioned programs, visit the following Web sites for searchable databases or lists of even more opportunities:

American Society for Engineering Education
http://www.engineeringk12.org/educators/making_engineers_cool/search.cfm

Engineers Make it Real
http://www.engineerinyou.com

Sloan Career Cornerstone Center/Pre-College Career Planning/Programs and Projects
http://www.careercornerstone.org/pcprogproj.htm

Society of Women Engineers
http://www.swe.org/stellent/idcplg?IdcService=SS_GET_PAGE&nodeId=89&ssSourceNodeId=5

Read a Book

When it comes to finding out about computers, don't overlook a book. (You're reading one now, after all.) What follows is a short, annotated list of books and periodicals related to computers. The books range from biographies of well-known computer professionals, to books about what it's like to work in a variety of computer careers, to volumes on specific topics. Don't be afraid to check out the professional journals, either. The technical stuff may be way above your head right now, but if you take the time to become familiar with one or two, you're bound to pick up some of what is important to computer professionals, not to mention begin to feel like a part of their world, which is what you're interested in, right?

We've tried to include recent materials as well as old favorites. Always check for the latest editions, and, if you find an author you like, ask your librarian to help you find more. Keep reading good books!

❑ BOOKS

Allen, Huey, and Joanne C. Wachter. *Careers in the Computer Field.* Hauppauge, N.Y.: Barron's Educational Series, 2000. This book highlights computer jobs that do not require a college degree.

Bates, Bob. *Game Design: The Art & Business of Creating Games.* Boston, Mass.: Muska & Lipman/Premier-Trade, 2002. Offers detailed instructions on how to turn an idea for a computer or video game into a finished product. Also includes information on marketing and sales.

Berners-Lee, Tim. *Weaving the Web: The Original Design and Ultimate Destiny of the World Wide Web.* New York: HarperBusiness, 2000. Entertaining and informative memoir from the man credited with inventing the Web. Read this book to learn how now-familiar terms such as "URL" and "WWW," among others, got their start.

Burns, Julie Kling. *Opportunities in Computer Careers.* New York: McGraw-Hill, 2001. Informative guide on different careers available in the field, with job descriptions, employment outlooks, and salary ranges.

Campbell-Kelly, Martin. *From Airline Reservations to Sonic the Hedgehog: A History of the Software Industry.* Cambridge, Mass.: The MIT Press, 2004. Informative book covering the history and development of the computer software industry.

Ceruzzi, Paul E. *A History of Modern Computing.* 2nd ed. Cambridge, Mass.: The MIT Press, 2003. This book takes the reader from the early days of electronic digital computers of the 1940s through the dot-com crash.

Deutschman, Alan. *The Second Coming of Steve Jobs.* New York: Broadway, 2001. Engaging biography of Apple cofounder Steve Jobs. Drawing from nearly 100 interviews of Jobs' colleagues and closest friends, this book covers his rise and fall, and rise again, within the computer and entertainment industries.

Dustin, Elfriede. *Effective Software Testing: 50 Specific Ways to Improve Your Testing.* Upper Saddle River, N.J.: Addison-Wesley Publishing Company, 2002. Offers 50 best practices and solutions for quality assurance professionals. Key topics discussed include test planning, documentation, unit testing, and nonfunctional testing.

Editors of the VGM Career Books. *Resumes for Computer Careers.* 2nd ed. New York: McGraw-Hill, 2002. Includes more than 100 sample resumes and cover letters tailored for workers in the computer industry.

Elmasri, Ramez, and Shamkant B. Navathe. *Fundamentals of Database Systems.* 4th ed. Upper Saddle River, N.J.: Addison-Wesley Publishing, 2003. This popular textbook for entry-level database management students covers the most recent innovations in database technology.

Floyd, Thomas L. *Electronics Fundamentals: Circuits, Devices, and Applications.* 6th ed. Upper Saddle River, N.J.: Prentice Hall, 2003. An extensive examination of electrical and electronic concepts that focuses on fundamental principles and their applications.

Freedman, Alan. *Computer Glossary: The Complete Illustrated Dictionary.* 9th ed. New York: American Management Association, 2000. If you have a computer question, grab this resource. Filled with more than 6,000 terms, illustrations, cross references, and profiles of industry giants.

Gardner, Garth. *Careers in Computer Graphics & Animation.* Washington, D.C.: Garth Gardner Company, 2001. This informative book includes more than 130 job descriptions in graphics, design, and animation. Also includes salary information and education requirements.

———. *Gardner's Guide to Colleges for Multimedia & Animation.* 4th ed. Washington, D.C.: Garth Gardner Company, 2004. This directory provides information on computer graphics and animation undergraduate and graduate programs at U.S. community colleges, colleges, and universities.

Gilster, Ron. *PC Technician Black Book: The PC Technician's Secret Weapon.* Scottsdale, Ariz.: The Coriolis Group, 2001. A useful reference book for almost every computer or peripheral-device problem. Each unit addresses a particular computer complaint, the symptoms, tools needed, and the step-by-step fix. This book is especially suited for the beginning computer enthusiast.

Greenia, Mark W. *History of Computing: An Encyclopedia of the People and Machines that Made Computer History.* Revised CD-ROM ed. Antilope, Calif.: Lexikon Services, 2001. Provides a detailed look at the history of computers, spanning early adding machines to the systems we use today. Includes illustrations, an extensive glossary, and a 101-question quiz to test your knowledge of the industry.

Hambley, Allan R. *Electrical Engineering: Principles and Applications.* 3rd ed. Upper Saddle River, N.J.: Prentice Hall, 2004. User-friendly text providing a solid foundation in the basics of circuits, electronics (radio and digital), and electromechanics.

Hawkins, Lori, and Betsy Dowling. *100 Jobs in Technology.* New York: MacMillan, 1996. Among the many careers and jobs listed in this comprehensive book are: CD-ROM producer, environmental engineer, physicist, Internet access provider, and biotechnology researcher.

Ifrah, Georges. *The Universal History of Computing: From the Abacus to the Quantum Computer.* Hoboken, N.J.: Wiley, 2002. The author, a scholar and former math teacher, details the development of counting and manipulation of numbers from early counting machines to the supercomputers of today.

Iovine, John. *Robots, Androids, and Animatrons: 12 Incredible Projects You Can Build.* 2nd ed. New York: McGraw-Hill/TAB Electronics, 2001. This guide provides an introduction to such concepts as robotics, motion control, sensors, and neural intelligence, and gives the reader 12 impressive projects to try on their own.

Kurose, James F., and Keith W. Ross. *Computer Networking: A Top-Down Approach Featuring the Internet.* 3rd ed. Upper Saddle River, N.J.: Addison-Wesley Publishing, 2004. The authors, using a top-down approach, explain the structure and function of application, transport, network and link layers of the Internet Protocol Stack. Wireless and mobile networks, encryption, and network security are also covered in this edition. This book is geared for beginners, but contains enough details on the latest technology to interest the network professional.

Levy, Steven. *Hackers: Heroes of the Computer Revolution.* New York: Penguin Putnam, 2001. The author profiles such "computer nerds" as Bill Gates, Steve Wozniak, and MIT's Model Railroad Club, to present an entertaining history of hackers and their so called "hacker ethic." In the context of this book, hackers are defined as early computer visionaries who devised unique and creative ways to advance technology for the common good, as well as for commercial profit.

Linzmayer, Owen. *Apple Confidential 2.0: The Definitive History of the World's Most Colorful Company.* 2nd ed. San Francisco: No Starch Press, 2004. The author, having covered the Apple company for almost 20 years, presents a thorough history of the computer giant. Includes "insider details" about the company's founders—Steve Jobs, Steve Wozniak, among others. A must-read for all Apple fans.

Marks, Aaron. *The Complete Guide to Game Audio: For Composers, Musicians, Sound Designers, and Game Developers.* Gilroy, Calif.: CMP Books, 2001. Provides an overview of music and sound effects techniques used to create computer and video games. A companion CD-ROM features audio and cinematic examples, sample business contracts, and more.

McComb, Gordon. *Robot Builder's Sourcebook: Over 2,500 Sources for Robotic Parts.* New York: McGraw-Hill/TAB Electronics, 2002. This book provides the robot/engineering enthusiast not only with places to find robotic parts, but also contains information on robot building and the related technology involved.

Miller, Rex, and Mark R. Miller. *Electronics the Easy Way.* 4th ed. Hauppauge, N.Y.: Barron's Educational Series, 2002. A useful and easy-to-read guide for anyone interested in electronics.

Minasi, Mark. *The Complete PC Upgrade & Maintenance Guide.* 15th ed. Alameda, Calif.: Sybex, Inc., 2004. Learn how to keep disasters from happening—or at least fix them when they do occur—with this industry favorite. Topics such as protecting your system from viruses and upgrading memory are tackled in easy-to-follow language and steps. This edition also comes with a companion CD with instructions on important PC upgrades and maintenance tasks.

Pasternak, Ceel, and Linda Thornburg. *Cool Careers for Girls in Computers.* Manassas Park, Va.: Impact Publications, 1999. This book profiles 10 women of different ages and ethnic backgrounds, each successful in different areas of the computer industry. Profiles include job descriptions and educational requirements, as well as other details needed to succeed in a once male-dominated industry. Geared for girls in grades five to eight.

Rafiquzzaman, Mohamed. *Preparing for an Outstanding Career in Computers.* Diamond Bar, Calif.: Rafi Systems, 2001. Presented in a question-and-answer format, this book covers different aspects of computers—from terminology to types of systems.

Rollings, Andrew, and Ernest Adams. *Andrew Rollings and Ernest Adams on Game Design.* Berkeley, Calif.: New Riders Publishing, 2003. A useful publication for novice and experienced game designers. Covers game concepts and worlds, character design, storytelling, and genres.

Spainhour, Stephen, and Robert Eckstein. *Webmaster in a Nutshell.* 3rd ed. Sebastopol, Calif.: O'Reilly, 2002. Covers issues that are of critical importance to today's webmasters.

Stair, Lila B., and Leslie Stair. *Careers in Computers.* 3rd ed. New York: McGraw-Hill, 2002. Informative guide on different career options in the computer industry, with job descriptions, salary ranges, and employment outlooks.

Wang, Wally. *Beginning Programming for Dummies.* 2nd ed. New York: For Dummies, 2001. A good reference for computer programming novices. Easy to follow and informative, with CD-ROM companion.

Whittaker, James A. *How to Break Software: A Practical Guide to Testing.* Upper Saddle River, N.J.: Addison-Wesley Publishing Company, 2002. Provides suggestions and tools to help professionals think "outside the box" when testing software.

Wurster, Christian. *Computers: An Illustrated History.* Los Angeles: Taschen, 2002. Illustrated history of computers, interfaces, and computer design. Includes a complete alphabetical listing of influential computer firms.

❑ PERIODICALS

ASEE PRISM. Published monthly by the American Society for Engineering Education, 1818 N Street, NW, Suite 600, Washington, DC 20036-2479, 202-331-3500, prism@asee.org. Offers information on trends in engineering education and employment. Read sample articles at http://www.prismmagazine.org.

ACM CareerNews. Published biweekly by the Association for Computing Machinery (ACM), 1515 Broadway, New York, NY 10036, 800-342-6626, careernews-request@acm.org, http://www.acm.org/careernews. Features career news and resources for students and professionals. Available free to both ACM members and nonmembers.

ACM Queue. Published 10 times annually by the Association for Computing Machinery (ACM), 1515 Broadway, New York, NY 10036, 800-342-6626, acmhelp@acm.org. Provides information on the latest computing trends. Read sample articles by visiting http://www.acmqueue.org. Free subscriptions are available.

ACM Student Quick Takes. E-mail newsletter that is published quarterly by the Association for Computing Machinery (ACM), 1515 Broadway, New York, NY 10036, 800-342-6626, acmhelp@acm.org. Features information on ACM activities, programs, and other topics of interest. This publication is only available to ACM student members. Visit http://www.acm.org/membership/student/sqt.html to read back issues.

Computer. Published monthly by the IEEE Computer Society, 10662 Los Vaqueros Circle, PO Box 3014, Los Alamitos, CA 90720-1314, 800-272-6657. Covers a variety of topics in computer science, computer engineering, technology, and applications. Visit http://www.computer.org/computer to read sample articles.

Computer Graphics World. Published monthly by the PennWell Corporation, 1421 South Sheridan Road, Tulsa, OK 74112, 800-280-6446, editorial@cgw.com. Offers cover stories, product reviews, and profiles of professionals. Read sample articles at http://www.cgw.com.

Computers in Entertainment. Published quarterly by the Association for Computing Machinery (ACM), 1515

Broadway, New York, NY 10036, 800-342-6626, acmhelp@acm.org. Covers topics such as animation, animatronics, digital asset management, digital cinema, digital rights management, games, interactive television, Internet, movies, music, performing arts, robotics, toys, and virtual reality. You can preview issues by visiting http://www.acm.org/pubs/cie.html.

Crossroads: The International ACM Student Magazine. Published quarterly by the Association for Computing Machinery (ACM), 1515 Broadway, New York, NY 10036, 800-342-6626, crossroads@acm.org. Student-written publication that covers computer-related topics. Features educational and career articles, opinion columns, and reviews of books, software, and conferences. Read it online at http://www.acm.org/crossroads.

EE Times Online. Published by CMP Media LLC, 600 Community Drive, Manhasset, NY 11030, 516-562-5000. An excellent guide to the semiconductors, systems, software, design, and technology industries that offers day-to-day news, career advice, product analysis, features, and columns. Updated daily at http://www.eet.com.

eLearn Magazine. Published by the Association for Computing Machinery (ACM), 1515 Broadway, New York, NY 10036, 800-342-6626. Online publication for providers and consumers of online learning. Features articles, regular columns, and tutorials. Sample articles are available at http://www.elearnmag.org.

Electronic Products: The Engineer's Magazine of Product Technology. Published monthly by Hearst Business Communications, Inc., 50 Charles Lindbergh Boulevard, Suite 100, Uniondale, NY 11553, http://electronicproducts.com. Details both the latest developments in electronics and unusual or new applications of products or technologies.

Engineers. Published quarterly by the American Association of Engineering Societies, 1620 I Street, NW, Suite 210, Washington, DC 20006, 202-296-2237, http://www.aaes.org. Reports on engineering surveys conducted by the organization.

Game Developer. Published 11 times annually by CMP Media LLC, 600 Community Drive, Manhasset, NY 11030, http://www.gdmag.com. One of the most popular publications for computer and video game developers. Features technical solutions, product reviews, interviews with industry professionals, and more.

Information Security. Published monthly by TechTarget, 117 Kendrick Street, Suite 800, Needham, MA 02494, 888-804-5501. Features a variety of information for computer security professionals, including security strategies and tactics, product reviews, and more. A free subscription can be obtained by visiting http://informationsecurity.techtarget.com.

IEEE Internet Computing. Published bimonthly by the IEEE Computer Society, 10662 Los Vaqueros Circle, PO Box 3014, Los Alamitos, CA

90720-1314, 800-272-6657, help@computer.org. Professional publication for Internet practitioners. Features useful articles, book reviews, and columns. Visit http://www.computer.org/internet to read sample articles.

IEEE Software. Published monthly by the IEEE Computer Society, 10662 Los Vaqueros Circle, PO Box 3014, Los Alamitos, CA 90720-1314, 800-272-6657, help@computer.org. Professional publication for software practitioners. Features useful articles, columns, and book reviews. Visit http://www.computer.org/software to read sample articles.

IT Professional. Published bimonthly by the IEEE Computer Society, 10662 Los Vaqueros Circle, PO Box 3014, Los Alamitos, CA 90720-1314, 800-272-6657, help@computer.org. Professional publication for Information Technology professionals. Sample articles are available at http://www.computer.org/itpro.

Journal of Engineering Education. Published quarterly by the American Society for Engineering Education, 1818 N Street, NW, Suite 600, Washington, DC 20036-2479, http://www.asee.org/about/publications/jee. A scholarly journal that provides information on the status of engineering education, including current trends and innovations.

Journal of Technology Education. Published twice annually by the *Journal of Technology Education,* Department of Industry and Technology, Millersville University, PO Box 1002, Millersville, PA 17551-0302, http://scholar.lib.vt.edu/ejournals/JTE. Provides a forum for scholarly discussion of technology education research, philosophy, theory, and practice. Includes book reviews, articles, and interviews.

Looking.Forward. Published quarterly by the IEEE Computer Society, 1730 Massachusetts Avenue, NW, Washington, DC 20036-1992. Student-written e-zine that focuses on developments in the computer industry. Issues are available at http://www.computer.org/students/looking.

MacWorld. Published monthly by Mac Publishing, PO Box 37781, Boone, IA, 50037-0781 800-288-6848, customer_service@macworld.com. This award-winning magazine offers a variety of resources to Mac users including practical how-tos, feature stories, troubleshooting tips and tricks, industry news and trends, and more. Sample articles can be read at http://www.macworld.com.

Microsoft Certified Professional Magazine. Published monthly by 101communications, 9121 Oakdale Avenue, Chatsworth, CA 91311, 818-734-1520, info@101com., http://www.101com.com. Provides information about the Windows Server System and related technology to computer professionals—many of whom hold Microsoft certification.

Network Computing. Published 26 times annually by CMP Media LLC, 600 Community Drive, Manhasset, NY 11030, , networkcomputing@bellevue.com. Features articles, book reviews, buying guides for computer network professionals, and more. Visit http://www.networkcomputing.com to read sample articles.

PC Today. Published monthly by Sandhills Publishing Company, 131 West Grand Drive, Lincoln, NE 68521, 800-733-3809, customer.service@pctoday.com. Award-winning magazine for PC users that includes in-depth coverage of Windows, tutorials and tips from experts, news about new operating systems, and software reviews. Visit http://www.pctoday.com to read sample articles.

The Pre-Engineering Times. Published monthly by the Junior Engineering Technical Society (JETS), 1420 King Street, Suite 405, Alexandria, VA 22314, 703-548-5387. Offers information for students and educators on engineering disciplines, profiles of interesting engineers and engineering programs, scholarship opportunities, Web links, engineering salaries, and much more. Available for free at http://www.jets.org/publications/petimes.cfm.

SWE, Magazine of the Society of Women Engineers. Published five times annually by the Society of Women Engineers (SWE), 230 East Ohio, Suite 400, Chicago, IL 60611-3265, 312-596-5223, hq@swe.org, http://www.swe.org. Offers stories on the achievements of women engineers, career development resources, and career guidance for students.

SupportWorld. Published bimonthly by the Help Desk Institute, 6385 Corporate Drive, Suite 301, Colorado Springs, CO 80919, 800-248-5667, http://www.thinkhdi.com/publications/supportWorldMagazine. A professional resource for help-desk professionals that includes interviews with industry leaders, articles about tools and techniques, and listings of industry events.

Today's Engineer Webzine. Published online monthly by the Institute of Electrical and Electronics Engineers, 1828 L Street, NW, Suite 1202, Washington, DC 20036-5104. Discusses topics—such as professionalism, management skills, engineering performance, engineering skills and competencies, product development practices, project management issues, innovation and entrepreneurship, and business practices—that are of interest to today's engineers. Available online at http://www.todaysengineer.org.

Ubiquity. Published online weekly by the Association for Computing Machinery (ACM), 1515 Broadway, New York, NY 10036, 800-342-6626, ubiquity@acm.org. Serves as an electronic forum for computer industry professionals. Includes interviews, book excerpts, and book reviews. Read sample issues by visiting http://www.acm.org/ubiquity/. Free subscriptions are available.

Upgrade. Published monthly by the Software & Information Industry Association, 1090 Vermont Avenue, NW, Sixth Floor, Washington, DC 20005-4095. Professional publication that provides information on the software and information industry. Read sample articles at http://www.siia.net/upgrade.

Winds of Change. Published five times (including a *College Guide*) a year by American Indian Science and Engineering Society Publishing, Inc., 4450 Arapahoe Avenue, Suite 100, Boulder, CO 80303. Information on career and educational advancement for American Indians and Native Alaskans/Hawaiians. Read selected articles at http://www.wocmag.org/.

WOW Newsletter. Published monthly by the World Organization of Webmasters, 9580 Oak Avenue Parkway, Suite 7-177, Folsom, CA 95630. Features useful articles on salaries, new technology, and industry events. Read sample articles at http://www.joinwow.org/newsletter.

Surf the Web

You must use the Internet to do research and to explore. The Web offers a wealth of information on computers and often does it in a way where you can actually have fun while learning. This chapter gets you started with an annotated list of Web sites related to computers. Try a few. Follow the links. Maybe even venture as far as asking questions in a chat room. The more you read about and interact with computer professionals, the better prepared you'll be when you're old enough to participate as a professional.

One caveat: You probably already know that URLs change all the time. If a Web address listed below is out of date, try searching on the site's name or other key words. Chances are if it's still out there, you'll find it. If it's not, maybe you'll find something better!

❑ THE LIST

All Engineering Schools
http://www.allengineeringschools.com

Visit this site for a one-stop online shop of different engineering programs (including computer science and electrical/electronics engineering), from bachelor's degrees to doctoral programs. Search by degree program, state, or among their short list of featured programs. Each school listing includes contact information, a link to its Web site, and details about each engineering program offered. Visit the Q&A section for basic information about choosing a program, short descriptions of different specialties within engineering, and tips on applying to a school.

Blobz Guide to Electric Circuits
http://www.andythelwell.com/blobz

This educational and entertaining game will teach you the basics about electrical engineering, such as open versus closed circuits, different power supplies, and how to interpret circuit diagrams. Read the short "lesson" about the subject, try the lesson activity, and then take the short quiz to see if you were really paying attention. What makes this site work is it's interactive, and information is doled out in small, easy-to-understand bites. Get all five quizzes right to receive a bonus prize.

ASEE Engineering K12 Center
http://www.engineeringk12.org

Sponsored by the American Society for Engineering Education (ASEE), this Web site supplies exactly the information "precollege engineers" are looking for. Go to the Students section and browse the Engineering Alphabet, featuring information on different jobs (including computer/software engineering) within the engineering field. Also interesting is Engineer Spotlight, which includes biographies of young engineers and details about a typical day on the job.

In the Education section, read about the high school courses you'll need to get accepted into a good engineering institution, and the SAT or ACT scores you should shoot for.

In case you're wondering whether you'll be able to handle those engineering courses in college, you can take a science/math aptitude test online at this site. If you make it over that hurdle, there's specific information to help you pick the right engineering school and secrets on getting admitted. Then link right to the Web pages of hundreds of colleges and universities in the United States that offer strong engineering programs.

Of course, you'll need to pay for college, and this site has thought of that, too. Visit the section Finding and Affording the Right School for links to the Web sites of the U.S. Department of Education and various federal loan, grant, and work-study programs.

Breaking In: Preparing For Your Career in Games
http://www.igda.org/breakingin

Are you exploring the possibility of a career in computer and video games? If so, this Web site is the place to go! This site breaks the industry into different paths—audio, design, production, programming, visual arts, and administration—and provides job descriptions, salary information, and profiles of people working in that field.

Don't forget to check out the Resources section. It provides helpful career advice, books to read, and links to schools with computer/game programs nationwide. A very useful site.

Building a School Web Site
http://www.wigglebits.com

Wanda Wigglebits took out the intimidating, and sometimes boring, techno-talk and left simplified, step-by step instructions on how to build a Web site. After a short history about the Web, then a crash course on HTML language, search engines, and animation, you suddenly have a Web site.

Computer History Museum
http://www.computerhistory.org

Created by the Computer History Museum in Mountain View, California, this site features a variety of virtual exhibits, including a timeline that explores the development of computers from 1945 to 1990, a detailed look at the history of the Internet, and features on microprocessors and visible storage. The site contains thousands of images of computers and related technology and is highly recommended for those who are interested in the past and future of computers.

ComputerGirl
http://www.computergirl.us

ComputerGirl seeks to encourage female high school students to pursue rewarding careers in the computer industry. It offers a wealth of resources at its Web site, including advice from role models in the field; information on organizations, mentoring, and scholarships; and answers to frequently asked questions about the career, such as: Why are women needed in computer fields? Do all IT engineers have to work in isolation and in small cubicles for long hours?; and, What kind of precollege experience should I have? Its Learning Center offers tutorials on computer knowledge that may seem daunting to young women (and men) who might be interested in the field. Topics include e-mail, downloading music, Web page design, operating systems, computer languages, and computer terms. Young women who are interested in computer science should definitely visit this site.

Engineer Girl
http://www.engineergirl.org

This site, developed by the National Academy of Engineering, aims to promote engineering to all people at any age, but particularly to women and girls. Did you know that a woman named Emily Roebling supervised construction of the Brooklyn Bridge? Or, that a famous Hollywood actress helped pave the way for current wireless technology? Check out the site to read other curious stories about projects created by women engineers and fun facts about the field. In the Features in the Women Engineers section, you can read day-in-the-life accounts of women engineers (including computer engineers), as well as recommendations for preparing for college and a career in the sciences. In the Becoming an Engineer section, test your knowledge of engineering through an online quiz or in the puzzles and games section, where you can build a satellite or conduct experiments from the comfort of your own computer.

How Stuff Works: Computer Stuff
http://computer.howstuffworks.com

If you spend a lot of time wondering how computers and other technology actually work, this site should also be on your short list of Web sites to explore. Complex computer and technological concepts are carefully broken down and examined, including photos and links to current and past news items about the field. The ins and outs of a variety of technology and processes are discussed in detail, including file compression, CD burners, RAM, computer viruses, Web servers, DSL, e-mail, blogs, Internet search engines, and much more.

Imagine
http://www.jhu.edu/~gifted/imagine

Imagine is a bimonthly journal for the go-getter high school student with his or her eye on the future. Its tag line, "Opportunities and resources for academically talented youth," says it all.

If you're always searching for good academic programs, competitions, and internships, this publication can keep you well informed on what's available and when you need to apply. There's an entertaining College Review series in which student contributors evaluate individual colleges and universities, and also a Career Options series featuring interviews with professionals.

Along with the current issue, selected portions of back issues can be read online. Previous issues have included articles about the USA Computing Olympiad and the ThinkQuest Competition, as well as general tips on entering academic competitions and choosing summer academic programs. For $30 a year, you can subscribe and get the printed journal delivered to your home—or for free, you can just read back issues online.

IEEE Computer Society: Careers In Computing
http://www.computer.org/education/careers.htm

The IEEE Computer Society's vision is "to be the leading provider of technical information and services" to computer professionals—and based on its Web site, the organization is on the right track. A digital library is offered, as well as online technical courses and certification study forums. The Education section is especially helpful to students interested in a computer career and gives advice that ranges from precollege courses and summer programs and competitions to employment possibilities in different professional environments.

IEEE Virtual Museum
http://www.ieee-virtual-museum.org

This site is sponsored by the Institute of Electrical and Electronic Engineers (IEEE), a leading authority on everything technical from computer engineering to biomedical technology. Don't worry—the museum is still a fun place to visit. Geared towards students in middle to high school, their teachers, and the general public, the museum's exhibits are presented to enhance the understanding of electrical engineering and information science through its history. The exhibit "Women and the Communications Industry," for example, traces the path of women working as early railroad telegraphers and key-punch operators in the mid-1900s to those working as computer engineers today.

Junior Engineering Technical Society (JETS)
http://www.jets.org

This site, another great resource brought to you by the American Society for Engineering Education, offers an unbelievable amount of useful and interesting information for junior high and high school students interested in electrical engineering and other engineering specialties. The mission of JETS is to increase college enrollment in the technology and engineering fields by providing opportunities for students to explore these careers while they're still in high school.

On the left-hand menu bar on the JETS home page, click on the icon JETS Programs. Next, click on TEAMS (Tests of Engineering Aptitude, Mathematics, and Science) to learn about this program in which teams of students work with an engineering mentor, then participate in an open-book, open-discussion engineering problem competition. The National

Engineering Design Challenge (NEDC in JETS Programs) is another program that challenges teams of students working with an advisor to design, fabricate, and demonstrate a working solution to a social need. Finally, take the self-administered National Engineering Aptitude Search (NEAS+ in JETS Programs) to determine if your education is on the right track.

For each of these programs, you can view sample problems and their solutions. In addition, many brochures are posted online, including "Engineering is For You!" which provides descriptions of different disciplines and ways to "try on" engineering, and several different Engineering Specialty Brochures, which explain in more detail jobs in different areas of the engineering field. In addition to these online publications, JETS also offers a broad range of brochures, books, and videos for sale.

National Inventors Hall of Fame
http://www.invent.org/hall_of_fame/1_0_0_hall_of_fame.asp

Sponsored by the National Inventors Hall of Fame located in Akron, Ohio, this Web site presents inventors and their life- and time-saving achievements. Navigating this site is a little cumbersome, but there's a lot of information here. Computer enthusiasts may want to learn more about Douglas Engelbart—inventor of the computer mouse, among many others. Visitors can get hands-on experience as an inventor by checking out programs such as Camp Invention (geared for school age students) or Collegiate Inventors (college students).

Past Notable Women of Computing
http://www.cs.yale.edu/homes/tap/past-women-cs.html

This no-frills site spotlights a dozen women who have made important contributions to the field. Also provides links to other relevant computer sites.

Peterson's Guide to Summer Programs for Teenagers
http://www.petersons.com/summerop

Your commitment to a brilliant academic future might waver when you visit some sections of this site. Along with great information about computer-focused summer programs, you'll be tantalized by summer camps that revolve around activities that are less mentally rigorous, such as white water rafting or touring France by bicycle. Shake it off. You're here to further your education, and this site offers good tips on assessing any summer program or camp you're considering.

Search Peterson's database of programs to find a camp that suits your interests. Under several computer-oriented headings (including computer programming, computer science-advanced placement, computers, and engineering), you'll find a list of links to dozens of topics. Click on a topic and then a specific program or camp for a quick overview description. In some instances you'll get a more in-depth description, along with photographs, applications, and online brochures. Limiting your search to your home state is also easy to do: you can sift through Peterson's database by geographic region or alphabetically.

Pioneers of Computing
http://vmoc.museophile.com/pioneers

This site provides links to people who have made valuable contributions to the computer industry. Biographies range from 17th-century mathematicians to industry superhero Bill Gates. Some illustrations are provided.

A Sightseer's Guide to Engineering
http://www.engineeringsights.org

The National Society of Professional Engineers and National Engineers Week developed this fun and interactive site to explore the work of engineers nationwide. Click on the map to see projects from a particular state, such as the Museum of Science and Industry in Illinois, or the Space Center Houston - Johnson Space Center in Texas. The photos alone are worth checking out in addition to the informative listings of fun facts about the featured location, contact information, and hours of operation (when applicable).

Sloan Career Cornerstone Center: Electrical Engineering and Computer Science
http://www.careercornerstone.org/eleceng/eleceng.htm

The Sloan Career Cornerstone Center is a nonprofit resource center for those interested in a career in technology, science, mathematics, or engineering. Want to explore the career of computer engineer? Use the Discipline Quick Jump and learn more about educational requirements, job security, and salary expectations. Also, don't miss the Pre-College section of this Web site. It offers a wealth of information geared toward high school students. Working professionals recall which high school classes helped them succeed in college and in the workplace. This section also provides links to a variety of high school-level contests, programs and projects, as well as available scholarships and grants.

U.S. News & World Report: America's Best Colleges 2006
http://www.usnews.com/usnews/edu/college/majors/majors_index_brief.php

Use this free online service to search schools by national ranking, location, name, or major. (The link above will allow you to search by major.) The Computer and Information Sciences and Support Services subsection alone lists hundreds of schools that offer computer-related programs, and each school link includes contact information and details about services and facilities, campus life, mission, and extracurriculars offered. Note: In order to read the full account information about each school, you must either buy the print publication or pay for the Premium Online Edition.

Yahoo! Computer Science
http://dir.yahoo.com/science/computer_science

It might seem odd to include the popular search engine Yahoo! among a list of computer-related Web sites, but Yahoo! has done a tremendous amount of legwork for you. If you're interested in artificial intelligence, for example, then scan through the nearly 200 sites currently included here. Supercomputing and parallel computing posts an impressive 103 sites. Even real-time computing offers six sites you probably wouldn't have known to look for otherwise. In addition to sites about engineering professions, you'll also find computer-related education sites, events, journals, and magazines.

Ask for Money

By the time most students start thinking about applying for scholarships, they have already extolled their personal and academic virtues to such lengths in essays and interviews for college applications that even their own grandmothers wouldn't recognize them. The thought of filling out yet another application form fills students with dread. And why bother? Won't the same five or six kids who have been fighting over grade point averages since the fifth grade walk away with all the really good scholarships?

The truth is, most of the scholarships available to high school and college students are being offered because an organization wants to promote interest in a particular field, encourage more students to become qualified to enter it, and help those students afford an education. Certainly, having a good grade point average is a valuable asset, and many organizations that grant scholarships request that only applicants with a minimum grade point average apply. More often than not, however, grade point averages aren't even mentioned; the focus is on the area of interest and what a student has done to distinguish himself or herself in that area. In fact, sometimes the only requirement is that the scholarship applicant must be studying in a particular area.

❑ GUIDELINES

When applying for scholarships there are a few simple guidelines that can help ease the process considerably.

Plan Ahead

The absolute worst thing you can do is wait until the last minute. For one thing, obtaining recommendations or other supporting data in time to meet an application deadline is incredibly difficult. For another, no one does his or her best thinking or writing under pressure. So get off to a good start by reviewing scholarship applications as early as possible—months, even a year, in advance. If the current scholarship information isn't available, ask for a copy of last year's version. Once you have the scholarship information or application in hand, give it a thorough read. Try to determine how your experience or situation best fits into the scholarship, or if it even fits at all. Don't waste your time applying for a scholarship in literature if you couldn't finish *Great Expectations.*

If possible, research the award or scholarship, including past recipients and, where applicable, the person in whose name the scholarship is offered. Often, scholarships are established to memorialize an individual who majored in religious studies or who loved history, for example, but in other cases, the scholarship is to memorialize the work of an individual. In those cases, try to get a feel for the spirit of the person's work. If you have any similar interests or experiences, don't hesitate to mention these.

Talk to others who received the scholarship, or to students currently studying in the same area or field of interest in which the scholarship is offered, and try to gain insight into possible applications or work related to that field. When you're working on the essay addressing why you want this scholarship, you'll have real answers—"I would benefit from receiving this scholarship because studying computer science will help me develop technology that allows users to surf the Web faster."

Take your time writing the essays. Make sure you are answering the question or questions on the application and not merely restating facts about yourself. Don't be afraid to get creative; try to imagine what you would think of if you had to sift through hundreds of applications. What would you want to know about the candidate? What would convince you that someone was deserving of the scholarship? Work through several drafts and have someone whose advice you respect—a parent, teacher, or guidance counselor—review the essay for grammar and content.

Finally, if you know in advance which scholarships you want to apply for, there might still be time to stack the deck in your favor by getting an internship, volunteering, or working part time. The bottom line is that the more you know about a scholarship and the sooner you learn it, the greater your advantage.

Follow Directions

Think of it this way: Many of the organizations that offer scholarships devote 99.9 percent of their time to something other than the scholarship for which you are applying. Don't make a nuisance of yourself by pestering them for information. Simply follow the directions as they are presented to you. If the scholarship application specifies that you write for further information, then write for it—don't call.

Pay close attention to whether you're applying for an award, a scholarship, a prize, or financial aid. Often these words are used interchangeably, but just as often they have different meanings. An award is usually given for something you have done: built a park or helped distribute meals to the elderly; or something you have created: a design, an essay, a short film, a screenplay, or an invention. On the other hand, a scholarship is frequently a renewable sum of money that is given to a person to help defray the costs of college. Scholarships are given to candidates who meet the necessary criteria based on essays, eligibility, grades, or sometimes all three.

Supply all the necessary documents, information, and fees, and meet the deadlines. You won't win any scholarships by forgetting to include a recommendation from a teacher or failing to postmark the application by the deadline. Get it right the first time, and get it done on time.

Apply Early

Once you have the application in hand, don't dawdle. If you've requested it far enough in advance, there shouldn't be any reason for you not to turn it in well in advance of the deadline. If it comes down to two candidates, your timeliness just might be the deciding factor. Don't wait, and don't hesitate.

Be Yourself

Don't make promises you can't keep. There are plenty of hefty scholarships available, but if they all require you to study something that you don't enjoy, you'll be miserable in college. And the side effects from switching majors after you've accepted a scholarship could be even worse. Be yourself.

Don't Limit Yourself

There are many sources for scholarships, beginning with your guidance counselor and ending with the Internet. All of the search engines have education categories. Start there and search by keywords, such as "financial aid," "scholarship," and "award." And go beyond the scholarships listed on these pages.

If you know of an organization related to or involved with the field of your choice, write a letter asking if they offer scholarships. If they don't offer scholarships, don't stop there. Write them another letter, or better yet, schedule a meeting with the president or someone in the public relations office and ask if they would be willing to sponsor a scholarship for you. Of course, you'll need to prepare yourself well for such a meeting because you're selling a priceless commodity—yourself. Be confident. Tell them all about yourself, what you want to study and why, and let them know what you would be willing to do in exchange—volunteer at their favorite charity, write up reports on your progress in school, or work part-time on school breaks, full-time during the summer. Explain why you're a wise investment.

❑ THE LIST

Air Force ROTC
Scholarship Actions Branch
551 East Maxwell Boulevard
Maxwell AFB, AL 36112-5917
866-423-7682
http://www.afrotc.com

The Air Force ROTC provides a wide range of four-year scholarships (ranging from partial to full tuition) to high school students planning to study computer science, engineering, physics, or other majors in college. Scholarships are also available to college and enlisted students. Visit the Air Force ROTC Web site to apply.

American Indian Science and Engineering Society (AISES)
PO Box 9828
Albuquerque, NM 87119-9828
505-765-1052
http://www.aises.org/highered/scholarships

The AISES offers a variety of scholarships to Native American students at the undergraduate and graduate level. Applicants must be student members. Contact the society for more information and to download applications.

American Institute of Aeronautics and Astronautics (AIAA) Foundation
1801 Alexander Bell Drive, Suite 500
Reston, VA 20191-4344
800-639-2422
http://www.aiaa.org/content.cfm?pageid=211

College sophomores, juniors, and seniors and graduate students interested in pursuing careers in aeronautics, astronautics, engineering, and related fields are eligible to apply for a variety of scholarships that range from $2,000 to $10,000. Contact the AIAA Foundation for more information.

American Legion Auxiliary
777 North Meridian Street, Third Floor
Indianapolis, IN 46204
317-955-3845
alahq@legion-aux.org
http://www.legion-aux.org/scholarships/index.aspx

Various state auxiliaries of the American Legion offer scholarships to help students prepare for various careers. Most require that candidates be associated with the organization in some way, whether as a child, spouse, etc., of a military veteran. Interested students should contact the auxiliary for further information.

American Radio Relay League Foundation
225 Main Street
Newington, CT 06111
860-594-0200
http://www.arrl.org/arrlf

Members of the league who are majoring in computer science, engineering, science, or related fields are eligible for a variety of scholarships. Awards range from $500 to $10,000.

Army ROTC
800-USA-ROTC
http://www.goarmy.com/rotc/scholarships.jsp

Students planning to pursue or currently pursuing a bachelor's degree in computer science and other fields may apply for scholarships that pay tuition and some living expenses. Recipients must agree to accept a commission and serve in the army on active duty or in a reserve component (U.S. Army Reserve or Army National Guard).

Association for Computing Machinery (ACM)
1515 Broadway
New York, NY 10036-5701
800-342-6626
sigs@acm.org
http://www.acm.org

The association, in cooperation with Upsilon Pi Epsilon and the Honor Society for Computing Sciences, offers $1,000 scholarships to undergraduate and graduate students studying computer science and related disciplines. Contact ACM for more information.

AWIS Educational Foundation
1200 New York Avenue, NW,
   Suite 650
Washington, DC 20005
202-326-8940
awis@awis.org
http://www.awis.org/careers/
   edfoundation.html#undergraduate

Female high school seniors who plan to study computer science or engineering in college can apply for several scholarships from the foundation. Applicants must be U.S. citizens, have at least a 3.75 GPA (on a 4.0 scale), and have a minimum SAT score of 1200 or a minimum ACT score of 25. Visit the foundation's Web site to apply online.

Association on American Indian Affairs
Scholarship Coordinator
966 Hungerford Drive, Suite 12-B
Rockville, MD 20850
240-314-7155
general.aaia@verizon.net
http://www.indian-affairs.org

Undergraduate and graduate Native American students who are pursuing a wide variety of college majors (including computer science) can apply for several different scholarships ranging from $500 to $1,500. All applicants must provide proof of Native American heritage. Visit the association's Web site for more information.

Collegeboard.com
http://apps.collegeboard.com/
   cbsearch_ss/welcome.jsp

This testing service (PSAT, SAT, etc.) also offers a scholarship search engine. It features scholarships (not all computer-related) worth more than $3 billion. You can search by specific major and a variety of other criteria.

✓**CollegeNET**
http://www.collegenet.com/

CollegeNET features 600,000 scholarships (not all computer-related) worth more than $1.6 billion. You can search by keyword (such as "computer science") or by creating a personality profile of your interests.

Daughters of the American Revolution (DAR)
Scholarship Committee
1776 D Street, NW
Washington, DC 20006-5303
202-628-1776
http://www.dar.org

General scholarships are available to students who have been accepted or who are currently enrolled in a college or university in the United States. Selection criteria include academic excellence, commitment to field of study, and financial need; applicants need not be affiliated with DAR. Scholarships are also available for Native American students. Contact DAR for more information.

Electronic Document Systems Foundation
608 Silver Spur Road, Suite 280
Rolling Hills Estates, CA 90274-3616
310-265-5510
http://www.edsf.org/
   scholarshipAwards.cfm

Undergraduate and graduate students who are pursuing study in document preparation, graphic communication and arts, e-commerce, imaging science, printing, Web authoring, electronic publishing, computer science, or telecommunications are eligible to apply for scholarships that range from $1,000 to $3,500. Application requirements vary by scholarship. Contact the foundation for more information and to apply online.

FastWeb
http://fastweb.monster.com

FastWeb is one of the largest scholarship search engines around. It features 600,000 scholarships (not all computer-related) worth more than $1 billion. To use this resource, you will need to register (free).

✓Foundation for the Carolinas
217 South Tryon Street
Charlotte, NC 28201
704-973-4500
http://www.fftc.org

The foundation administers more than 70 scholarship funds that offer awards to undergraduate and graduate students pursuing study in computer technology and other disciplines. Visit its Web site for a searchable list of awards.

Golden Key International Honor Society
621 North Avenue, NE, Suite 100
Atlanta, GA 30308
800-377-2401
http://www.goldenkey.org

Golden Key is an academic honor society that offers its members "opportunities for individual growth through leadership, career development, networking, and service." It awards more than $400,000 in scholarships annually through 17 different award programs. Membership in the society is selective; only the top 15 percent of college juniors and seniors—who may be pursuing education in any college major—are considered for membership by the organization. There is a one-time membership fee of $60 to $65. Contact the society for more information.

✓GuaranteedScholarships.com
http://www.guaranteed-scholarships.com

This Web site offers lists (by college) of scholarships, grants, and financial aid (not all computer-related) that "require no interview, essay, portfolio, audition, competition, or other secondary requirement."

Hawaii Community Foundation
1164 Bishop Street, Suite 800
Honolulu, HI 96813
808-537-633
scholarships@hcf-hawaii.org
http://www.hawaiicommunity
  foundation.org/scholar/
  scholar.php

The foundation offers a variety of scholarships for high school seniors and college students planning to study or currently studying computer science and other majors in college. Applicants must be residents of Hawaii, demonstrate financial need, and plan to attend a two- or four-year college. Visit the foundation's Web site for more information and to apply online.

Hispanic College Fund (HCF)
1717 Pennsylvania Avenue, NW, Suite 460
Washington, DC 20006
800-644-4223
hcf-info@hispanicfund.org
http://www.hispanicfund.org

The Hispanic College Fund, in collaboration with several major corporations, offers a variety of scholarships for high school seniors and college students planning to attend or currently studying computer science and other majors. Applicants must be Hispanic, live in the United States or Puerto Rico, and have a GPA of at least 3.0 on a 4.0 scale. Contact the HCF for more information.

Illinois Career Resource Network
http://www.ilworkinfo.com/icrn.htm

Created by the Illinois Department of Employment Security, this useful site offers a great scholarship search engine, as well as detailed information on careers (including computer careers). You can search for computer-related scholarships based on computer majors and keywords. This site is available to everyone, not just Illinois residents; you can get a password by simply visiting the site. The Illinois Career Information System is just one example of sites created by state departments of employment security (or departments of labor) to assist students with financial- and career-related issues. After checking out this site, visit your state's department of labor Web site to see what they offer.

Institute of Electrical and Electronics Engineers (IEEE)
1828 L Street, NW, Suite 1202
Washington, DC 20036-5104
202-785-0017
ieeeusa@ieee.org
http://www.ieee.org/portal/site/mainsite/menuitem.818c0c39e85ef176fb2275875bac26c8/index.jsp?&pName=corp_level1&path=membership/students&file=sc_scholarships.xml&xsl=generic.xsl

The institute offers a variety of scholarships and fellowships to its student members who are pursuing education in electrical and electronic engineering and computer science. Applicants must be undergraduate or graduate students. Contact IEEE for more information.

IEEE Computer Society
1730 Massachusetts Avenue, NW
Washington, DC 20036-1992
202-371-0101
http://www.computer.org

Four $3,000 Richard E. Merwin Scholarships are available to college juniors and seniors who are studying electrical engineering, computer engineering, computer science, or a well-defined computer-related field. Applicants must be members of an IEEE Computer Society student chapter and have a GPA of at least 2.5. Contact the society for more information.

International Technology Education Association

1914 Association Drive, Suite 201
Reston, VA 20191-1539
703-860-2100
itea@iteaconnect.org
http://www.iteawww.org/l.html

The association offers the $1,000 Undergraduate Scholarship in Technology Education and the $1,000 Litherland/FTE Scholarship to undergraduates who are studying technology education. Applicants must be members of the association to be eligible for the scholarships. Contact the association for additional information.

Korean-American Scientists and Engineers Association (KSEA)

1952 Gallows Road, Suite 300
Vienna, VA 22182
703-748-1221
sejong@ksea.org
https://www.ksea.org/KSEA/indexe.asp?p=3

The association offers several scholarships to undergraduate and graduate students of Korean heritage who are studying science, engineering, or related fields. Applicants must be members of the KSEA. Contact the association for additional information and a downloadable application

Marine Corps Scholarship Foundation

PO Box 3008
Princeton, NJ 08543-3008
800-292-7777
mcsfnj@mcsf.org
http://www.mcsf.org/site/c.doIGLOOuGnF/b.1300199/k.BF7E/Home.htm

The foundation helps children of marines and former marines with scholarships of up to $5,000 for study in computer science and other health fields. To be eligible, you must be a high school graduate or registered as an undergraduate student at an accredited college or vocational/technical institute. Additionally, your total family gross income may not exceed $61,000. Contact the foundation for further details.

Microsoft Corporation

Microsoft Scholarship Program
One Microsoft Way
Redmond, WA 98052-6399
scholars@microsoft.com
http://www.microsoft.com/college/ss_overview.mspx

Microsoft awards approximately $500,000 in scholarships annually to current undergraduate students who are studying computer science and related technical disciplines. The following scholarships are available: General Scholarships, Women's Scholarships, Underrepresented Minority Scholarships, and Scholarships for Students with Disabilities. Visit Microsoft's Web site for more information.

National Action Council for Minorities in Engineering (NACME)

440 Hamilton Avenue, Suite 302
White Plains, NY 10601-1813
914-539-4010
scholarships@nacme.org
http://www.guidemenacme.org/guideme/parents/scholar.jsp

The NACME offers information on the scholarship process for high school students interested in computer engineering and other engineering specialties. It encourages students to e-mail the NACME Scholarship Source with scholarship-related questions. A searchable scholarship database is available at its Web site.

National Federation of the Blind
Scholarship Committee
805 Fifth Avenue
Grinnell, IA 50112-1653
641-236-3366
http://www.nfb.org/sch_intro.htm

Scholarships ranging from $3,000 to $12,000 are available to blind high school seniors and undergraduates who are interested in or who are currently studying computer science or engineering. Contact the federation for further details. Visit the federation's Web site for an application.

National Security Agency (NSA)
Stokes Educational Scholarship
  Program
9800 Savage Road, Suite 6779
Ft. George G. Meade, MD 20755-6779
410-854-4725
http://www.nsa.gov/careers/students_4.cfm

High school seniors who plan to study computer science, computer or electrical engineering, or mathematics in college may apply for the Stokes Educational Scholarship Program. Students who are accepted into the program work in their area of interest at the NSA during summer vacations; the NSA pays for college tuition, books and selected expenses, and for travel during summer work periods. Upon college graduation, participants in the program must work for the NSA for at least one-and-one-half times their length of study. Scholarship programs are also available for current undergraduate and graduate students. Contact the NSA for more information.

National Society of Black Engineers (NSBE)
1454 Duke Street
Alexandria, VA 22314
703-549-2207
scholarships@nsbe.org
http://www.nsbe.org/programs/index.php#scholarships

High school and college student members of the NSBE are eligible to apply for a variety of scholarships that range in value from $500 to $5,000. Visit the society's Web site for a complete list.

National Society of Professional Engineers
1420 King Street
Alexandria, VA 22314-2794
703-684-2800
http://www.nspe.org/scholarships/sc-home.asp

The society offers a variety of scholarships (ranging from $1,000 to $10,000) to high school seniors and undergraduate and graduate students who are interested in pursuing careers in engineering. High school students will be most interested in learning more about the Maureen L. and Howard N. Blitman P.E. Scholarship to Promote Diversity in Engineering ($5,000, ethnic minorities), the Auxiliaries Scholarship ($2,000 a year for four years, females), and the Virginia D. Henry Memorial Scholarship ($1,000, females). Visit the society's application page, http://www.nspe.org/scholarships/sc1-appl.asp, to fill out an online application.

National Urban League (NUL)
120 Wall Street, 8th floor
New York, NY 10005
212-558-5300
info@nul.org
http://www.nul.org/scholarships.html

This civil rights organization offers a scholarship in association with the University of Rochester and a list of minority-focused scholarships from other organizations. Minority high school seniors and undergraduate and graduate students are eligible for these awards. Visit the NUL's Web site for more information.

Navy: Education: Earn Money For College
http://www.navy.com/education/earnmoneyforcollege

The navy offers a variety of funding programs for college study. Contact your local recruiter or visit its Web site for details.

Sallie Mae
http://www.collegeanswer.com

This Web site offers a scholarship database of more than 2.4 million awards (not all computer-related) worth more than $14 billion. You must register (free) to use the database.

Scholarship America
4960 Viking Drive, Suite 110
Edina, MN 55435-5314
800-279-2083
http://www.scholarshipamerica.org

This organization works through its local Dollars for Scholars chapters in 41 states and the District of Columbia. To date, it has awarded more than $1 billion in scholarships to more than one million students. Visit Scholarship America's Web site for more information.

Scholarships.com
http://www.scholarships.com

Scholarships.com offers a free college scholarship search engine (although you must register to use it) and financial aid information.

Sigma Xi Scientific Research Society
PO Box 13975
3106 East NC Highway 54
Research Triangle Park, NC 27709
800-243-6534
giar@sigmaxi.org
http://www.sigmaxi.org/programs/giar/index.shtml

The society provides grants of up to $1,000 to support student research efforts in the sciences and engineering via its Grants-in-Aid of Research Program. College undergraduates and graduate students are eligible. Visit the society's Web site for an application.

Society for Technical Communication
Attn: Scholarships
901 North Stuart Street, Suite 904
Arlington, VA 22203-1802
703-522-4114
stc@stc.org
http://www.stc.org/edu/scholarshipInfo01.asp

Scholarships of $1,000 are awarded to undergraduate (who have been in college for at least one year) and graduate students studying technical communication. Visit the society's Web site for further details and to apply online.

Society of Hispanic Professional Engineers/Hispanic Scholarship Fund
5400 East Olympic Boulevard, Suite 210
Los Angeles, CA 90022
323-725-3970
http://oneshpe.shpe.org/wps/portal/national

The society partners with the Hispanic Scholarship Fund to offer scholarships to Hispanic high school seniors and undergraduate and graduate students pursuing degrees in computer science, engineering, mathematics, and science. Visit the society's Web site to learn more.

Society of Women Engineers (SWE)
230 East Ohio Street, Suite 400
Chicago, IL 60611-3265
312-596-5223
http://www.swe.org/stellent/idcplg?IdcService=SS_GET_PAGE&nodeId=9&ssSourceNodeId=5

Female high school seniors and college students who plan to study or who are currently studying computer science or engineering are eligible for a variety of scholarships ranging from $1,000 to $10,000. Visit the SWE Web site for details and an application.

Triangle Education Foundation (TEF)
Chairman, Scholarship & Loan Committee
120 South Center Street
Plainfield, IN 46168-1214
http://www.triangle.org/tef/programs/scholarships

The foundation offers a variety of scholarships (ranging from $1,000 to $8,000) to undergraduate and graduate student-members who are currently studying computer science, engineering, and other "hard sciences." The foundation also offers loans. Contact the TEF for more information and to download applications.

United Negro College Fund (UNCF)
http://www.uncf.org/scholarships

Visitors to the UNCF Web site can search for thousands of scholarships and grants, many of which are administered by the UNCF. High school seniors and undergraduate and graduate students are eligible. The search engine allows you to search by major, state, scholarship title, grade level, and achievement score.

Upsilon Pi Epsilon
c/o Orlando S. Madrigal
California State University-Chico

158 Wetlands Edge Road
American Canyon, CA 94503
530- 518-8488
upe@acm.org
http://www.acm.org/upe/scholarship.htm

This international honor society for the computing and information disciplines offers several scholarships to undergraduate and graduate students studying computer science and related disciplines. Contact the society for additional information and a downloadable application.

Virginia Society of Professional Engineers
5206 Markel Road, Suite 300
Richmond, VA 23230
804-673-4545
vspe@aol.com
http://www.vspe.org

Students who are attending one of the eight engineering schools in Virginia are eligible to apply for a $1,000 scholarship. The schools are George Mason University, Old Dominion University, Hampton University, University of Virginia, Virginia Commonwealth University, Virginia Military Institute, Virginia Polytechnic Institute & State University, and Virginia State University. Contact the Society for more information.

Yes I Can! Foundation for Exceptional Children
1110 North Glebe Road, Suite 300
Arlington, Virginia 22201-5704
800-224-6830
yesican@cec.sped.org
http://yesican.sped.org

The foundation offers scholarships to high school and college students who have disabilities. Contact the foundation for more information.

Look to the Pros

The following professional organizations offer a variety of materials, from career brochures to lists of accredited schools to salary surveys. Many of them also publish journals and newsletters that you should become familiar with. A number also have annual conferences that you might be able to attend. (While you may not be able to attend a conference as a participant, it may be possible to cover one for your school or even your local paper, especially if your school has a related club.)

When contacting professional organizations, keep in mind that they all exist primarily to serve their members, be it through continuing education, professional licensure, political lobbying, or just "keeping up with the profession." While many are strongly interested in promoting their profession and passing information about it to the general public, these professional organizations are also very busy with other activities. Whether you call or write, be courteous, brief, and to the point. Know what you need and ask for it. If the organization has a Web site, check it out first. What you're looking for may be available there for downloading, or you may find a list of prices or instructions, such as sending a self-addressed, stamped envelope with your request. Finally, be aware that organizations, like people, move. To save time when writing, first confirm the address, preferably with a quick phone call to the organization itself ("Hello, I'm calling to confirm your address. . .") or a visit to its Web site.

❑ THE SOURCES

Accreditation Board for Engineering and Technology (ABET)
111 Market Place, Suite 1050
Baltimore, MD 21202-4012
410-347-7700
http://www.abet.org

Contact the ABET for a list of accredited computer and engineering schools and programs.

American Indian Science and Engineering Society
PO Box 9828
Albuquerque, NM 87119-9828
505-765-1052
http://www.aises.org

Through a variety of educational programs, the society offers financial, academic, and cultural support to American Indians and Alaska Natives interested in technology, science, and engineering from middle school through graduate school. It offers *Winds of Change,* which is published five times annually to provide information on career and educational advancement for American Indians and Native Alaskans/Hawaiians. The Annual College Guide for American Indians is published as a special *Winds of Change* issue annually. The organization also offers job listings and a resume database at its Web site.

American Society for Engineering Education (ASEE)
1818 N Street, NW, Suite 600
Washington, DC 20036-2479
202-331-3500
http://www.asee.org and http://www.engineeringk12.org/students

ASEE's precollege Web site is a guide for high school students and others interested in engineering and engineering technology careers where you can learn about the different engineering and engineering technology fields (including computer and software engineering), interesting people who got their start as engineers, what engineers actually do, and how to get (and pay for) an engineering education. One of its most useful publications is *Engineering: Go For It*, which is available for a small charge.

American Society of Certified Engineering Technicians
PO Box 1536
Brandon, MS 39043
601-824-8991
general-manager@ascet.org
http://www.ascet.org

Contact the society for information on training and certification.

Association for Computing Machinery
1515 Broadway
New York, NY 10036
800-342-6626
sigs@acm.org
http://www.acm.org

Contact the association for information on internships, student (high school and college) membership, and the student magazine, *Crossroads*.

Association of Computer Support Specialists (ACSS)
333 Mamaroneck Avenue, #129
White Plains, NY 10605
917-438-0865
http://www.acss.org

Contact the ACSS for information on computer support careers.

Association of Information Technology Professionals
401 North Michigan Avenue, Suite 2400
Chicago, IL 60611-4267
800-224-9371
aitp_hq@aitp.org
http://www.aitp.org

Visit the association's Web site for information on student (college) membership and industry news.

Association of Support Professionals
122 Barnard Avenue
Watertown, MA 02472-3414
617-924-3944
http://www.asponline.com

Visit the association's Web site for information on salaries, award-winning customer-support sites, and industry news.

Computer Science Teachers Association
PO Box 11414
New York, NY 10286-1414
800-342-6626
cstahelp@csta.acm.org
http://csta.acm.org

The CSTA is an association for K-12 computer science teachers.

Computer Security Institute
600 Harrison Street
San Francisco, CA 94107
415-947-6320
csi@cmp.com
http://www.gocsi.com

This is a professional organization for information security professionals. It provides education and training for its members.

Computing Technology Industry Association
1815 South Meyers Road, Suite 300
Oakbrook Terrace, IL 60181-5228
630-678-8300
http://www.comptia.org

Contact the association for information on certification.

Data Management Association International
PO Box 5786
Bellevue, WA 98006-5786
425-562-2636
http://www.dama.org

Contact the association for information on database management careers.

Electronic Industries Alliance
2500 Wilson Boulevard
Arlington, VA 22201-3834
703-907-7500
http://www.eia.org

Contact the alliance for information on the electronics industry.

Electronics Technicians Association International
5 Depot Street
Greencastle, IN 46135
800-288-3824
eta@eta-i.org
http://www.eta-sda.com

This organization offers information on certification and student (college) membership.

Entertainment Software Association
575 7th Street, NW, Suite 300
Washington, DC 20004
esa@theesa.com
http://www.theesa.com

Visit the association's Web site to read *Essential Facts About The Computer And Video Game Industry.*

Help Desk Institute
102 South Tejon, Suite 1200
Colorado Springs, CO 80903
800-248-5667
support@thinkhdi.com
http://www.thinkhdi.com

Visit the institute's Web site for information on training and certification, job listings, and career advice.

Independent Computer Consultants Association
11131 South Towne Square, Suite F
St. Louis, MO 63123
800-774-4222
info@icca.org
http://www.icca.org

Contact the association for information on computer consulting careers.

Institute for Certification of Computing Professionals (ICCP)
2350 East Devon Avenue, Suite 115
Des Plaines, IL 60018-4610
800-843-8227
office@iccp.org
http://www.iccp.org

Contact the ICCP for information on computer certifications.

Institute of Electrical and Electronics Engineers (IEEE)
1828 L Street, NW, Suite 1202
Washington, DC 20036-5104
202-785-0017
ieeeusa@ieee.org
http://www.ieee.org

Contact the IEEE for information on careers in electrical and electronic engineering. Its Web site has a Precollege page full of information for high school students.

IEEE Computer Society
1730 Massachusetts Avenue, NW
Washington, DC 20036-1992
202-371-0101
http://www.computer.org

Contact the society for information on careers in computer engineering, scholarships, student (college) membership, and the student newsletter, *looking.forward.*

International Game Developers Association
870 Market Street, Suite 1181
San Francisco, CA 94102-3002
415-738-2104
info@igda.org
http://www.igda.org

Contact the association for comprehensive career information, including *Breaking In: Preparing For Your Career in Games.* The Association also offers membership to college students and members of the general public who are interested in the field.

International Society of Certified Electronics Technicians
3608 Pershing Avenue
Fort Worth, TX 76107-4527
817-921-9101
info@iscet.org
http://www.iscet.org

Contact the society for information on certification and student (college) membership.

International Technology Education Association
1914 Association Drive, Suite 201
Reston, VA 20191-1539
703-860-2100

itea@iteaconnect.org
http://www.iteaconnect.org/index.html

Contact the association for career, education, and scholarship information.

International Webmasters Association
119 East Union Street, Suite F
Pasadena, CA 91103
626-449-3709
http://www.iwanet.org

Visit the association's Web site for information on certification, trial and regular membership for Webmasters, and professional development.

Junior Engineering Technical Society (JETS)
1420 King Street, Suite 405
Alexandria, VA 22314
703-548-5387
info@jets.org
http://www.jets.org

Contact the JETS for information on starting a local student chapter in your high school and for details on high school programs that provide opportunities to learn about engineering technology. JET's Guidance Brochures and Brochures for Most Engineering Specialties (both suitable for middle and high school students) may be viewed at the Web site. Titles include *Engineering and You*, *Engineering Is For You*, *Engineering Technologists and Technicians*, and *Electrical Engineering*.

National Action Council for Minorities in Engineering (NACME)
440 Hamilton Avenue, Suite 302
White Plains, NY 10601-1813
914-539-4010
http://www.nacme.org

Contact NACME for information on scholarships and career options.

National Institute for Certification in Engineering Technologies
1420 King Street
Alexandria, VA 22314-2794
888-476-4238
http://www.nicet.org

This organization offers information on certification for engineering technicians and technologists.

National Society of Black Engineers (NSBE)
1454 Duke Street
Alexandria, VA 22314
703-549-2207
info@nsbe.org
http://www.nsbe.org

Contact the NSBE for information on careers in engineering, educational programs, scholarships, activities for high school students, and student membership.

National Society of Professional Engineers (NSPE)
1420 King Street
Alexandria, VA 22314-2794
703-684-2800
http://www.nspe.org/students

Contact the NSPE for information on careers in engineering and on student memberships. Visit the Student Information page of its Web site for a variety of information of interest to high school students considering engineering.

Network Professional Association
17 South High Street, Suite 200
Columbus, OH 43215
888-NPA-NPA0
http://www.npa.org

Visit the association's Web site for career advice, job listings, and information on student (college) chapters.

Quality Assurance Institute Worldwide
2101 Park Center Drive, Suite 200
Orlando, FL 32835-7614
407-363-1111
http://www.qaiworldwide.org/

Contact the institute for information on certification.

Society for Technical Communication
901 North Stuart Street, Suite 904
Arlington, VA 22203-1802
703-522-4114 stc@stc.org
http://www.stc.org

The society is a professional organization of technical writers and editors, content developers, documentation specialists, technical illustrators, instructional designers, academics, information architects, usability and human factors professionals, visual designers, Web designers and developers, and translators. Visit its Web site for information on careers, competitions for high school students, and scholarships.

Society of Hispanic Professional Engineers (SHPE)
5400 East Olympic Boulevard, Suite 210
Los Angeles, CA 90022
323-725-3970
http://www.shpe.org

Contact the SHPE for information on its competitions and educational programs for engineering students and for information on careers in engineering.

Society of Women Engineers (SWE)
230 East Ohio Street, Suite 400
Chicago, IL 60611-3265
312-596-5223
hq@swe.org
http://www.swe.org

Contact the SWE for information on scholarships, student (college) membership, and mentor programs. The Society also offers research and statistics about the status of women in engineering.

Software and Information Industry Association
1090 Vermont Avenue, NW, Sixth Floor
Washington, DC 20005-4095
202-289-7442
http://www.siia.net

This is a trade association that represents software code and information content companies.

Upsilon Pi Epsilon
c/o Orlando S. Madrigal
California State University-Chico
158 Wetlands Edge Road
American Canyon, CA 94503
530-518-8488
upe@acm.org
http://www.acm.org/upe

This international honor society for the computing and information disciplines offers chapters for college students and scholarships.

World Organization of Webmasters (WOW)
9580 Oak Avenue Parkway, Suite 7-177
Folsom, CA 95630
916-989-2933
info@joinwow.org
http://www.joinwow.org

Visit WOW's Web site for information on training, certification, and student (college) membership.

Index

Entries and page numbers in **bold** indicate major treatment of a topic.

A

ABN AMRO 33
Accreditation Board for Engineering and Technology (ABET) 51, 91
administration, careers in 11
Adventure (video game) 21
Albert Nerken School of Engineering 32
America Online 8, 102
Apple Corporation 6, 9
applications programmers
    computer programmers 48
    software designers 88
applications software engineers. *See* computer engineers
Army, U.S. *See* U.S. Army
ARPANET 108
Artwick, Bruce 21
Assembly 22
asset managers, computer and video game designers 20
Associate Computing Professional designation 32
Association for Computing Machinery (ACM) 44, 119–120
Association of Information Technology Professionals 44
Association of Support Professionals (ASP) 102
associations, joining 119–120
Asvos, Nick 28, 30–31, 33–34
Atari 21
Audio Visual Services Corporation 30

B

Babbage, Charles 4, 5, 12
BASIC 10
bench servicers. *See* computer service technicians
Berners-Lee, Tim 108
Big Huge Games 20, 22
Binary Automatic Computer (BINAC) 5–6
Bivens, Swift 109–110, 112–113
Bushnell, Nolan 21
business and commercial applications programmers. *See* computer programmers
Byron, Lord 4

C

CAD/CAM technology 29
Calculating-Tabling-Recording Company 5
California Polytechnic State University 32
Camacho, Stella 36, 39, 41–44
camps, programs, and competitions, directory of 126–161
    categories, described 126–128
    program descriptions 128–131
        specific programs, including addresses 131–161
Canty, Michael 95, 97–100, 102
CareerBuilder.com 112
careers 18–114
    administration 11
    design 10
    generally 10–13
    programming 10
    sales 12–13
    service 11–12
Carmen Sandiego (video game) 21
C/C++ 10, 22, 24, 48
CD ROM technology 22, 48
certified network engineers (CNEs) 103
chief computer programmers 53, 54
chief Web officer 113
Cisco 33, 43
Clark, Arthur C. 12
clubs, joining 117–118
COBOL 10, 47, 48, 49
competitions, directory of. *See* camps, programs, and competitions, directory of
CompTIA 43
CompTIA A+ 62
computer administrators 11
computer and video game designers 13, **18–27**
    activities related to 122
    asset managers 20
    career advancement 26
    education 24
    high school requirements 24
    hiring 25–26
    history of computer and video games 21–22
    how to become 24–25
    industry stats 25
    internships and volunteerships 25
    job outlook 27
    postsecondary training 24
    production team 20
    related jobs 27
    salary ranges 26–27
    skills 23
    success, qualities necessary for 23
    what it is like to be a computer and video game designer 20–21

computer and video game programmers. *See* computer programmers
Computer Clubhouse 117
computer engineers 10, **28–35**
   activities related to 122
   applications software engineers, generally 29
   career advancement 33–34
   certification and licensing 32–33
   computer managers, generally 34
   education 31–32
   hardware engineers, generally 29
   hardware managers, generally 34
   high school requirements 31
   hiring 33
   how to become 31–33
   internships and volunteerships 33
   job, described 29–30
   job outlook 35
   mental disabilities, hiring of people with 29
   network engineers, generally 29–30
   postsecondary training 31–32
   project team leaders 33
   related jobs 34
   salary ranges 34–35
   skills 31
   software engineers
      career advancement 101, 103
      generally 29
      quality assurance testers 82
   success, qualities necessary for 31
   systems software engineers, generally 29
   top computer engineering programs in U.S. 32
   what it is like to be a computer engineer 30–31
computer managers, generally 34
computer network administrators 36–46
   activities related to 122
   career advancement 44–45
   certification and licensing 43
   data recover operators, generally 38–39
   education 41–43
   enterprise computer network engineers 44
   high school requirements 41–42
   hiring 43–44
   history of computer networks 40
   how to become 41–43
   information systems manager 45
   internships and volunteerships 43
   job, described 36–39
   job outlook 45–46
   lingo of 37
   multimedia administrators 44
   multiple administrators 44
   network control operators, generally 39
   network security specialists, generally 38
   postsecondary training 42–43
   related jobs 45
   salary ranges 45
   skills 41
   success, qualities necessary for 42
   what it is like to be a computer network administrator 39–41

computer network engineers 101
computer network security administrators. *See* computer network administrators
computer network specialists. *See* computer network administrators
computer programmers 10, **47–56,** 87. *See also* computer systems programmer/analysts
   activities related to 122
   applications programmers, generally 48
   business and commercial applications programmers, generally 48
   career advancement 53, 54
   certification and licensing 52
   chief computer programmers 53, 54
   computer and videogame programmers 49
   debugging, defined 48
   education 51–52
   engineering and scientific applications programmers, generally 48
   high school requirements 51
   hiring 53–54
   how to become 51–53
   internships and volunteerships 52–53
   job, described 47–49
   job outlook 55–56
   lingo of 49
   postsecondary training 51–52
   programs, defined 47
   related jobs 55
   skills 50
   success, qualities necessary for 50
   systems programmers 9, 10, 48
   webmasters 108
   what it is like to be a computer programmer 49–50
   work settings 52
computer scientists 10
computer servicers. *See* computer service technicians
computer service technicians 11–12, **57–65**
   activities related to 122
   bench servicers, generally 58
   career advancement 63–64
   certification and licensing 62
   computer sales representatives 63, 64
   education 61–62
   field service representatives, generally 58
   high school requirements 61
   hiring 62–63
   how to become 61–62
   internships and volunteerships 62
   job, described 57–58
   job outlook 64–65
   lingo of 58
   maintenance managers 63
   maintenance supervisors 63
   postsecondary training 61–62
   related jobs 64
   salary ranges 64
   skills 60–61
   success, qualities necessary for 60
   what it is like to be a computer service technician 58–59
Computer Space (video game) 21

computer support specialists 11
computer systems programmer/analysts 66–75
   activities related to 123
   career advancement 73–74
      specific jobs 72
   certification and licensing 72
   database design analysts 72
   education 70–71
   high school requirements 70–71
   hiring 73
   how to become 70–72
   internships and volunteerships 72–73
   job, described 67–69
   job outlook 75
   lead programmer/analysts 72
   lingo of 68
   managers of information systems 72
   postsecondary training 71–72
   programmer analysts, career advancement 53
   pros and cons of being 71
   related jobs 74
   salary ranges 74
   senior systems programmers/analysts 72
   skills 70
   success, qualities necessary for 70
   systems analysts 10
      career advancement 53, 54
   what it is like to be a computer systems programmer/analyst 69–70
computer technology, familiarizing self with 119
Computing Technology Industry Association 62, 101
Contact A+ Plus Computing 58–59
Cooper Union for the Advancement of Science and Art Albert Nerken School of Engineering 32
Crawford, Chris 21

D

database design analysts 72
data communications analysts. *See* computer network administrators
data recovery operators. *See* computer network administrators
debugging, defined 48
Defense Department. *See* U.S. Department of Defense
Deloitte 14
design careers 10
developers 108
Dice.com 112
DigiPen Institute of Technology 24
Digital Equipment Corporation 11
directors of network services. *See* computer engineers
disk operating system (DOS) 7–8
Disney 26
Donkey Kong (video game) 21
Doom (video game) 22, 122
DOS. *See* disk operating system (DOS)
Dungeons and Dragons (video game) 21

E

Electronic Arts and Activision 21, 25–26
Electronic Numerical Integrator and Calculator (ENIAC) 5

Ellis, Mark 96, 98–100, 103
Empire (video game) 122
employment opportunities, generally 13–14
end-user consultants. *See* technical support specialists
engineering and scientific applications programmers. *See* computer programmers
engineering specialists 103
enterprise computer network engineers 44
Ernst & Young 14
exploring future career 116–123
   clubs, joining 117–118
   computer classes 116–117
   computer technology, familiarizing self with 119
   information interviews 120–121
   internships 120
   job, paid 121–122
   job shadowing worker 120–121
   mathematical ability, developing 117
   museums, visiting 118–119
   reading books and periodicals 116
   summer programs, participation in 120
   surfing the Web 116

F

field service representatives. *See* computer service technicians
Flight Simulator (video game) 21
FORTRAN 10, 48
fun facts 12

G

Gama Network 26
Gamasutra.com 26
game designers. *See* computer and video game designers
Game Developers Conference 25, 26
Game Developer (magazine) 26
Game Jobs 25
Garriott, Richard 21
Gates, Bill 117
general information on computers 4–8
Good, I. J. 12

H

Haeder, Dan 60, 64–65
hardware engineers. *See* computer engineers
hardware managers, generally 34
hardware, structure of the industry and 8
Harvard University 12
Harvey Mudd College 32
Help Desk Institute 101
help-desk representatives. *See* technical support specialists
help desk technicians 11
Hewlett Packard Co. 44
history of computers 4–8
Hollerith, Herman 4, 5
Hopper, Grace Murray 12
HotJobs.com 112
HyperCard 22
HyperText Markup Language (HTML) 107, 109

I

Ibaraki, Stephen 41, 42, 45
IBM. *See* International Business Machines (IBM)
IEEE Computer Society 12, 44, 119
industry outlook, generally 14–15
information brokers 13
information center specialists. *See* technical support specialists
information interviews 120–121
Institute for Certification of Computing Professionals (ICCP)
    computer engineers 32
    computer programmers 52
    computer systems programmer/analysts 72
Institute of Electrical and Electronics Engineers Computer Society
    Certified Software Development Professional 32, 91
Interactive Digital Software Association 26
Interactive System Productivity Facility (ISPF) 47
International Business Machines (IBM) 5–6, 11
    introduction of personal computer 12
International Society of Certified Electronics Technicians 62
International Webmasters Association 111
Internet
    growth of 6, 14
    history of 108
Internet consultants 13
Internet content developers 114
Internet executives 13
Internet quality assurance specialists 13
Internet security specialists 13
Internet store managers 13
internships 120
intranet, growth of 14

J

Jacquard, Joseph-Marie 4
Java 24
job, paid, while exploring future career 121–122
Job Control Language 47
job shadowing worker 120–121
Jobs, Steve 6, 21
Junior Engineering Technical Society 118

K

Kaufman, Doug 18–20, 22–26
Kay, Alan 21
King, Ada Augusta (Countess of Lovelace) 4, 12
Klik & Play (video game) 122
Kronos, Inc. 96, 100

L

Laboratory for Recreational Computing (LARC) 24
Labor Department. *See* U.S. Department of Labor
LAN support 30
lead programmer/analysts 72
Leibnitz, Gottfried Wilhelm von 4
lingo to learn 5, 7
LPI (Linux Professional Institute) 43

M

Macintosh computer 6
Mac system 7
Macworld (magazine) 44, 80, 83
Madden NFL (video game) 24
Makdah, Imad 66, 69, 71–73
managers of information systems 72
Mark II computer 12
mathematical ability, developing 117
mental disabilities, hiring of people with 29
microcomputer support specialists. *See* technical support specialists
Microsoft Corporation 7, 9, 43, 44, 54
Minsky, Marvin 12
Mitchell Technical Institute 60
Monster.com 112
M.U.L.E. (video game) 21
multimedia administrators 44
multiple administrators, computer networks 44
museums 118–119

N

National Association of Colleges and Employers
    computer engineers 34
    computer programmers 54
    computer systems programmer/analysts 74
    webmasters 114
National Museum of American History 12
National Occupational Employment and Wage Estimates 34–35, 93
Nerken School of Engineering 32
Netscape 9
Network Computing (magazine) 42
Network Computing Online (e-newsletter) 42
Network Computing Report (e-newsletter) 42
Network Computing's IT Pro Downloads (e-newsletter) 42
Network Computing's Mobile Observer (e-newsletter) 42
network control operators. *See* computer network administrators
network engineers. *See* computer engineers
Network Professional Association 41, 44
network programmers. *See* computer network administrators
network security specialists. *See* computer network administrators
North Texas, University of
    Laboratory for Recreational Computing (LARC) 24
Novell 43, 44
NPD Group 26

O

Occupational Outlook Handbook
    computer engineers 33, 35
    software designers 93
Oliver, George 86–89, 92, 94
Olson, Ken 11
online journalists 13
online researchers 13

P

Pac-Man (video game) 21, 122
Pascal, Blaise 4

Index   201

PC/LAN connectivity 30
PC Magazine (magazine) 80, 83
PC World (magazine) 44, 80, 83
Pennsylvania, University of 5
Pong (video game) 21, 122
Popular Mechanics (magazine) 11
printers 8
production team, computer and video game designers 20
professional organizations 190–196
programmer analysts. *See* computer systems programmer/analysts
programming careers 10
programs, directory of. *See* camps, programs, and competitions, directory of
project team leaders
    computer engineers 33
    software designers 92
punched cards 4–5, 49

Q

quality assurance analysts 77–78
quality assurance engineers 82
Quality Assurance Institute Worldwide 82
quality assurance supervisors 82
quality assurance testers 76–85
    activities related to 123
    career advancement 83–84
        specific jobs 82
    certification and licensing 82
    Certified Quality Analyst 82
    Certified Software Project Manager 82
    Certified Software Tester 82
    computer skills and 80
    education 80–81
    entry point into industry, jobs as 81
    high school requirements 80–81
    hiring 82–83
    how to become 80–82
    internships and volunteerships 82
    job, described 77–78
    job outlook 85
    lingo of 78
    postsecondary training 81
    quality assurance analysts 77–78
    quality assurance engineers 82
    quality assurance supervisors 82
    related jobs 84
    salary ranges 84
    skills 79–80
    software engineers 82
    success, qualities necessary for 79
    what it is like to be a quality assurance tester 78–79
    word skills and 80

R

readings on computer science 161–170
    books 162–166
    periodicals 166–170
Red Hat 43
research and vocational opportunities in computing 9

researchers 10
Rise of Nations (video game) 20
Rochester Institute of Technology 32
Rose-Hulman Institute of Technology 32
Russell, Steve 21

S

Salary.com 84, 113
sales, careers in 12–13
sales representatives 63, 64
scholarships, requesting 178–189
    guidelines 178–180
    list of available 180–189
senior systems programmers/analysts 72
service careers 11–12
Sims, The (video game) 24
Smeglane, Stu 76, 78–80
Smithsonian Institution 12
software, structure of the industry and 9–10
software designers 10, 86–94
    activities related to 123
    applications programmers 88
    career advancement 92
    certification and licensing 91
    computer programmers 87
    education 90–91
    high school requirements 90–91
    hiring 92
    how to become 90–92
    internships and volunteerships 91–92
    job, described 87–88
    job outlook 93–94
    postsecondary training 91
    project team leaders 92
    related jobs 93
    salary ranges 93
    skills 90
    success, qualities necessary for 90
    web sites for aspiring software designers 87
    what it is like to be a software designer 88–90
software engineers. *See* computer engineers
software programmers 10
Space Invaders (video game) 21
Spacewar (video game) 21
Star Trek (video game) 21
Strand, Richard 57–60
structure of the industry 8–10
    hardware 8
    software 9–10
summer programs, participation in 120
support engineers. *See* technical support specialists
support supervisors 101, 103
Swift, Bivens 106
systems administrators. *See* computer network administrators
systems analysts. *See* computer systems programmer/analysts
systems programmers. *See* computer programmers
systems set up specialists 11
systems software engineers. *See* computer engineers

T

technical support specialists 11–12, **95–105**
    activities related to 123
    career advancement 103
    certification and licensing 101
    computer network engineers 101
    education 99–100
    engineering specialists 103
    high school requirements 99–100
    hiring 102–103
    how to become 99–102
    internships and volunteerships 101–102
    job, described 95–97
    job outlook 104–105
    lingo of 97
    microcomputer support specialists 97
    postsecondary training 100–101
    related jobs 104
    salary ranges 103–104
    skills 98–99
    software engineers 101, 103
    specific jobs 101
    success, qualities necessary for 98
    technical support supervisors 101, 103
    user support specialists 96
    web sites, best support 102
    what it is like to be a technical support specialist 97–98
technical support supervisors
    career advancement 101
    certified network engineers (CNEs) 103
Time (magazine) 12
2001: A Space Odyssey (film) 12

U

Ultima (video game) 21
Universal Automatic Computer (UNIVAC) 6
URL (Uniform Resource Locator) 107
U.S. Army 5
U.S. Department of Defense
    Internet, history of 108
    Internet development 6
U.S. Department of Labor
    computer engineers 34–35
    computer network administrators 45, 46
    computer programmers 51, 55
    computer service technicians 64, 65
    computer systems programmer/analysts 74, 75
    industry outlook, generally 14–15
    National Occupational Employment and Wage Estimates 34–35, 93
    quality assurance testers 84
    software designers 93
    technical support specialists 103–104
    webmasters 114

user support analysts. *See* technical support specialists
user support specialists 96

V

video game designers. *See* computer and video game designers
Visual Basic 48
VOIP (Voice-Over IP) 46

W

WAN support 30
Watson, Thomas 11
webmasters 13, **106–114**
    activities related to 123
    career advancement 113
    certification and licensing 111–112
    chief Web officer 113
    developers 108
    education 111
    high school requirements 111
    hiring 112–113
    how to become 111–112
    Internet, history of 108
    Internet content developers 114
    internships and volunteerships 112
    job, described 106–109
    job outlook 114
    postsecondary training 111
    programmers 108
    related jobs 113
    salary ranges 113–114
    skills 110–111
    success, qualities necessary for 110
    what it is like to be a webmaster 109–110
Web, surfing for information 171–177
West End Games 22
Wido, Michael 47, 49–51, 54, 55
wigglebits.com 123
Windows system 7
World Organization of Webmasters 111
    Native American Technical Education Initiative 109
World's Fair (1801) 4
World War II 40
World Wide Web 112, 113
    access to 8
    defined 7
    growth of 6, 14
    history of 108
Wozniak, Steve 6

Z

Zelda (video game) 24